MY PART OF THE SKY

MY PART OF THE SKY

A fighter pilot's firsthand experiences 1939–1945

By

Roland Beamont
CBE, DSO (and bar), DFC (and bar),
DFC (USA), DL

PATRICK STEPHENS LIMITED

First Published 1989

British Library Cataloguing in Publication Data
Beamont, Roland
My part of the sky : extracts from the
1939–45 war diaries of an RAF fighter
pilot,
1. Great Britain. Royal Air Force.
Beamont, Roland, 1920–
I. Title
358.4′1332′0924

ISBN 1–85260–079–9

Patrick Stephens Limited is part of the
Thorsons Publishing Group
Wellingborough, Northamptonshire NN8 2RQ, England

Printed and bound in Great Britain by
Mackays of Chatham PLC, Chatham, Kent

3 5 7 9 10 8 6 4 2

CONTENTS

Disclaimer

The opinions expressed in the following chapters are the author's own and do not necessarily reflect those of any other authority referred to in the text.

Acknowledgements

I would like to express my grateful thanks for their generous assistance in the preparation of this book to Joan Moores for coping so well with the manuscript; to Chrys Butcher of the Flight Operations Department of British Aerospace, Warton, and to Warton's Photographic Department; to Perry Adams and Reg Guppy for their invaluable help on 87 Squadron history; and particularly to 'Splinters' Smallwood, most distinguished airman and one-time CO of 87 Squadron, for his Foreword; to Conrad Voss Bark; and finally, as always, to my wife Pat — for her resolute proof reading and constructive and much valued criticism.

Dedication

To my friends in Nos 87, 79 and 609 (W.R.) Fighter Squadrons, and in Nos 150 and 122 Wings: and to the memory of those who did not return.

FOREWORD

By Air Chief Marshal Sir Denis Smallwood GBE, KCB, DSO, DFC, FRSA, FRAeS

I first met Roland Beamont in October 1939 at No 11 Fighter Group Pool, RAF St Athan when he was one of the hundreds of pilots who were to pass through that operational conversion unit to be taught to fly Hurricanes. I was an instructor on the staff at that time, and as the course only lasted barely one month, this encounter was brief. 'Bee' (as he became known to all of his friends) was posted to No 87 Fighter Squadron in France, and the first two chapters of this book describe with great clarity the appalling conditions on the French airfields during the Winter of 1939 and the sudden horror of the Blitzkrieg in early 1940.

My acquaintance with Bee was to be renewed a year later when I, too, was posted to No 87 Squadron, who by now were based at RAF Charmy Down, a small primitive airfield on a hill top near Bath, as Bee relates in this most readable and exciting book. The meeting at Charmy Down was one which I clearly remember as it formed the basis of what was to become a lasting friendship. Although I had been flying Hurricanes for well over a year, I felt very much of a novice on being posted to my first operational squadron. As I drove my car to the dilapidated dispersal hut, a Hurricane taxied in. It was painted black in the night fighter role and in the gathering dusk looked menacing, the more so with no less than twelve swastikas painted on the fuselage. As the young Flying Officer climbed out, I approached him respectfully and said, 'Terrific — have you shot down twelve?' 'No' replied Bee (for it was he) rather sourly, 'It's not my bloody aircraft!' His dour expression changed suddenly to a wide and rather embarrassed grin. I tell this anecdote because to my mind it sums up so much of the man's character: at once, impressive, tough and blunt and yet, modest, factual and to the point. Behind it all, one immediately detected an outstanding 'press on' spirit. Throughout this book Bee's character pervades, in particular his brilliance as a pilot. Some of the harrowing experiences he so vividly describes in flying the Hurricane in the Battle of Britain and later in appalling weather and by night from

7

Exeter and Charmy Down clearly illustrate this fact. Any lesser pilot would not have survived.

I could dwell upon these aspects at great length but I will highlight just two further points from the earlier part of the book. He describes several incidents where he escapes the possibility of being shot down by placing the Hurricane in a terminal velocity dive and pulling out with considerable 'G' and later a sortie in which he climbed to an altitude of 36,400 ft during a night flying test, merely to see what maximum altitude a Hurricane could reach. These incidents illustrate, firstly, the enormous versatility, strength and reliability of the Hurricane which, in my opinion, was never paralleled by any other fighter in World War 2, including the mighty Spitfire and even Bee's beloved Tempest Mk V (which he extols in the later chapters); and secondly, Bee's built-in inquisitive and exploratory nature which was to play such a big part in his outstanding success as a test pilot (described in fascinating detail in other books by the author such as *Testing Years* and *Fighter Test Pilot*).

The reader will be intrigued by the way Bee's narrative steadily, and at first almost imperceptibly, relates how the UK-based fighters started in 1941 to transfer from purely defensive operations to the offensive over enemy territory, and in Bee's case, with increasing emphasis on ground attack. These events begin with the spasmodic night intruder operations in Hurricanes over northern France and then later, after a spell of test flying with Hawkers at Langley, move on to Bee's experience on a Typhoon squadron for yet another operational tour. A second spell of test flying at Hawkers culminated with his last operational tour as Wing Leader of a Tempest Wing, first in South-east England combatting most successfully the dreaded V1 and finally in Holland with the Allied Tactical Air Forces when regretably he had the misfortune to force land in enemy territory and was taken PoW.

Roland Beamont's flying career is undoubtedly unique. I know of no other fighter pilot who flew almost continuously and so outstandingly on operations from the start of World War 2 almost to VE day. His two so called 'rest periods' on test flying were, in themselves, very unusual and as close to operational flying as one could get. The wartime experiences related with such fervour in this book are enough to set Beamont apart from the 'also ran'; but if one also takes into account his activity in the post war years as a chief test pilot with the British Aircraft Corporation, including the introduction of the Canberra, the Lightning, the early testing of the TSR2 and then the Jaguar and the Multi Role Combat Aircraft (now known as the Tornado) — his career is truly without parallel.

Even now, in so-called 'retirement', he won't give up, for he has become a prolific author, *My Part of the Sky* being his seventh publication.

A true fighting eagle who is second to none.

INTRODUCTION

During World War 2 I served with fighter squadrons continuously from October 1939 to October 1944 except for short rest period breaks in 1942 and 1943. I kept a form of 'narrative diary' at periods of particular interest and when time could be made available during five busy and demanding years.

Three 'tours' of fighter operations included Hurricane daytime air defence in France and in the Battle of Britain in 1940; night-fighting defence of Bristol, Cardiff and Plymouth in 1941; Typhoon ground attack operations over the Channel and Low Countries in 1942/3; Tempest operations throughout the 'D' Day period in 1944 and subsequently defence against V1 flying bomb attacks.

In September 1944 my Wing of Tempests was moved up to Volkel, the most advanced main base in Holland of the RAF's 2nd Tactical Air Force, for the final onslaught against the German homeland.

On 13 October 1944 I became a prisoner of war, and the last part of the diaries was written in Luckenwalde PoW Camp near Potsdam in March 1945 as the Allied forces made their final drive across Germany to victory.

The diaries were typed in 1945 and, with only minor editing and some explanatory linking passages, are now published as written.

It was a proud and inspiring privilege to serve with the pilots and ground personnel of Fighter Command throughout those critical years, and if the initial style of this account is that of a naïve twenty-year-old, hopefully the reader may find that this changes with the rapid increase in experience and responsibility that was an inevitable facet of wartime.

Chapter 1

THE FIRST PHASE

Four British Hurricane squadrons faced the might of Hitler's Luftwaffe as it was unleashed in the all-out attack by Germany on France and Belgium on 10 May 1940. They formed the fighter element of the Air Component of the British Expeditionary Force (the BEF) which was responsible for holding the line between the French-held 'Maginot Line' and the Belgian frontier.

With dramatic pace which has now become part of the history of war, the German Blitzkrieg swung across neutral Belgium and Luxembourg and completely by-passed the French in their Maginot 'strongholds'; and within ten days the 'Panzer' armoured spearheads threatened the French Channel ports.

The Commander-in-Chief of Fighter Command with brilliant foresight resisted extreme pressures to send the remaining main force home-based Hurricane and Spitfire squadrons to France to try and stem the tide in an already lost cause. Instead he retained all the Spitfires for home defence and moved forward only a few extra Hurricane squadrons to French airfields on daily reinforcements, returning them to the UK each night.

These and the four 'permanent' Hurricane squadrons saw intense action and detailed records could often not be kept so that it was not until they were permanently withdrawn to UK bases after 20 May, when it could be seen that the battle was already lost on the ground, that the cost could be counted.

87 Squadron returned to Church Fenton via Debden on 20 May with seven of its original sixteen aircraft, having lost nine pilots killed and five wounded in the ten days of fighting, but in that short time they had claimed more than eighty victories.

Formal assessments of the French campaign and the later Battle of Britain have shown that the actual enemy losses were seldom more than half those claimed and often much less, and that this tendency to over-claim in the excitement of battle existed on both sides. Nevertheless 87 Squadron's claims demonstrated that their Hurricanes' guns had been fired at at least eighty enemy targets during those fierce ten days — an intensity of air-fighting that had not been imagined in the early months of the 'phoney war'. It was a grim warning of the coming battles now seen to be inevitable over the Channel, and, if we could not hold the enemy there, over our own homeland.

With just one month at Church Fenton to re-equip with new Hurricanes and concentrate on the operational training of replacement pilots, 87 Squadron was again ready to face the Luftwaffe across the Channel in the south-west, and they had not long to wait. First a few small enemy formations came to attack convoys off Portland and Plymouth, and then, rapidly increasing in ferocity through July and early August, raids of '150+' became the norm against the major targets of Portland naval base, Southampton and Bristol.

The defence of these islands against the might of the German air force in 1940 is an established saga in the history of modern warfare, and the accounts of the Spitfire and Hurricane squadrons and their pilots have made enthralling reading. At the beginning of the main battle in August 1940, 650 Hurricanes and Spitfires in a ratio of 2 to 1 in 52 RAF squadrons, stood against 2,700 fighters and bombers of Hitler's skilled, determined and seemingly all-victorious Luftwaffe.

The pilots and ground crews stood firm and took on the invading enemy wherever he could be found, with a matter-of-fact approach which was a classic example of the character of this race in adversity. No-one who served in a fighter squadron at that time will ever forget how even the most desperate days were met with an almost casual 'this is what we are here for, so let's get on with it' attitude.

87, which was there at the beginning in France, lost two squadron commanders, five flight commanders and more than half its pilot complement before the Battle of Britain ended in victory. Its members believed that theirs was the finest of all fighter squadrons as did each member of all the other fighter squadrons, and that was, and is, RAF morale.

*   *   *

12 September 1940 — Exeter. No 87 Fighter Squadron
Johnny Dewar has gone today, perhaps the only one of all the boys

in whom one had complete confidence that he would never be caught napping. Yet it has happened so many times before.

At the outbreak of war, I was at No 13 FTS* at Drem in East Lothian and had not yet attained my wings. With the coming of the order 'uniform on and off duty'. I remember walking through the local town, North Berwick, in uniform for the first time with a naked feeling around my left breast pocket! This was not to last much longer however and within a few weeks, with wings on my jacket, I was feeling so inordinately proud of myself that my flying, such as it was, began to suffer from a bout of showing off! This ended (more or less) in my being confined to camp for the remainder of the term after 'beating up' a local country house in which, unknown to me, a court of inquiry was being held on a recent accident to one of our aircraft.

I had just had my first experience of losing a great friend in a crash. Alan Bishop, an Australian, had been perhaps my closest friend during my training. He was the most promising aerobatic pilot amongst us and at the same time level-headed and steady, and we always felt that he would most likely do very well in the coming war. Yet he was the first one of us to have bad luck, and one beautiful autumn evening he failed to return from a passenger ride with another student, and they were found a few miles from the camp in the burning wreck of their Hawker Audax. Thus Alan never had the crack at the Hun which he had longed for so much.

By then we were almost fully trained, and a fortnight at Armament Practice camp at Evanton in the far north of Scotland completed our course. It was a fortnight crammed with memories of flights at dawn to the ranges at Tain with the orange light of the rising sun spreading over the frost-covered mountains below, and turning to a deep purple on the distant snow-capped peaks in the west. Wonderful days when the curlews awakened us at daybreak, and wild geese clanged over at dusk.

Then came a thrilling day in October 1939 when we boarded the night train south, each of us with a posting to a squadron or other unit in his pocket. The time had come at last — we were going to war! It was a momentous occasion. We had been together for ten months, during which time we had learned to fly, right from the initial stages to being qualified pilots. Now we were separating, some to bomber squadrons, some to fighters and some to become instructors, and above all we (the lucky ones) were going to war.

By the next morning as the train slid into Kings Cross the

* Flying Training School

13

majority had got out in most cases never to meet again, and it was a very small remnant which split up with forced heartiness and self-conscious goodbyes on the platform.

I and two others were to go to No 11 Group Fighter Pool at St Athans in South Wales, and it was not until we actually arrived there that we knew what we were destined for. I shall not forget the morning in October 1939 when we walked through that vast camp on our way to report for duty, and found, outside the Flight offices, a row of formidable-looking Hurricane fighters which were to be ours! A month of learning to fly the Hurricane and training in the standard 'Fighter Command' fighter tactics followed, and then one wet afternoon in early November our postings arrived and we became, those two magic words, 'operational pilots' with action ahead of us.

Of the 24 hours between my posting to No 87 Squadron in the Air Component of the British Expeditionary Force in France, and my embarkation, I remember very little. There was just time for a rather break-neck drive in my old MG from South Wales to my home in Sussex; a hurried gathering together of kit and a few goodbyes, and then I found myself with my father, also joining his Army unit in France, looking through the steamy windows of the early train at the frost-covered meadows of my home county glistening in the sunlight, and wondering when we would see them next.

Within a few moments of arriving at RAF Hendon I was in a comfortable seat in the 10.00am 'Amiens Express' DH Rapide of No 24 communications squadron with my kit on board, and soon we were climbing over a haze-shrouded London with the balloon barrage reminding one of liver-spots after a party, only more so.

Landmarks began slipping astern; the Great West Road which I had driven up and down so many times somewhat lawlessly a year ago when flying Tiger Moths at No 13 Elementary and Reserve Flying Training school at White Waltham near Maidenhead; Windsor Castle, with its memories of early solo flights when one was always lost when out of sight of the aerodrome, and very often when in sight of it! Then Guildford by-pass passed beneath us with more memories of fearful driving in the antiquated MG. Before long we flew over the valley of the Arun and the South Downs rolling away west to the little town of Chichester with the beautiful spire which I had left so few hours before. And finally there was the sea and the coastline from Shoreham to Beachy Head, where we turned resolutely away from land leaving me musing on the coincidence which made Eastbourne my last glimpse of England,

14

the town in which I spent my school days and which I had not seen since I left, two years before.

It was an unusual situation in which to be 'going abroad' for the first time, but I was not very impressed with my introduction to the other side. We crossed the coast at Le Treport where the wireless operator wandered down and fired the 'colour of the day' out of the back door with a Very signal pistol. The dreariness of the next forty miles or so was a surprise: miles of muddy beet fields with an occasional poor-looking village consisting of a few barns and cottages and one or two stucco-fronted houses with the inevitable 'Chateau d'eu' all seen through the brown haze of late autumn. Then an airfield appeared and we landed at Glisy, the aerodrome of Amiens which I was to come to know very well within a few months, and so, on 16 November 1939 I smelt France for the first time.

After a meal consisting mostly of black sausage and chicory in the French Mess, which was at that time shared by the RAF transport squadron, I set about finding the whereabouts of my squadron. No-one seemed to know much, but eventually my kit and I were on another DH 89 bound for Lille, and after a short trip over beet fields even more desolate-looking in a rainstorm, we arrived at Seclin and taxied through a sea of mud up to the tarmac.

It was cheering to see a fine line of Hurricanes in front of the hangars, and near them I found two pilots, Boothby and Lee of No 85 Squadron, who explained that they were 'opportunity boys' — there on the off-chance that a Hun might come over. This all sounded very thrilling to me in my innocence!

Presently a batman came for my kit and we set off for the officers' Mess up a muddy road between the hangars. Eventually he stopped outside a rickety wooden shack with cinders around the entrance and a loose-fitting door with broken hinges and a latch which did not work, and, in reply to my natural query, he said: 'This is the Mess, Sir'!

I opened the door and found a long, bare hut with a concrete floor and two brick fireplaces whose chimneys poured forth volumes of smoke into the room and transformed the rafters into a mass of cobwebs. At first I thought the room was empty, the murk was so thick, but a voice said 'Come in and make yourself at home', and on further investigation I found two recumbent forms, heavily swathed in greatcoats and flying boots, lying on cushions and a broken couch inches deep in months-old periodicals, in front of two smouldering lumps of coal which formed the fire.

One of these figures stirred slightly and said: 'Have a drink', while the other offered me a chair after studying me for some moments from beneath a battered peaked cap. By this time I had discovered that I was speaking to Derek Allen of 85 squadron and 'Dimmy' Joyce of 87. I was also able to take a closer look at 'the Mess'. In all some five cane chairs, together with the broken-down couch, made up the seating accommodation, while in the corner near the door was a very reasonable bar (apparently from an *estaminet* in Merville) with an impressive background in the shape of a large black cross from a German aircraft hung on the wall over rows and rows of bottles. A very cheering sight.

But if I was expecting to fly now that I had joined a fighter squadron, I was a long way short of the mark. When I reported to the CO he immediately said: 'Ha, another "Ops B"'*, and in no time I was being instructed in the dark mysteries of the base Operations room which consisted of a map, two telephones and a chair for the controller!

Seclin was situated on the Douai-Lille road, ten miles from Lille, with the result that with a northerly wind the smoke from Lille blanketed the low, treeless landscape, while from the west and south, Douai and Lens poured forth their smuts. The result was that on those odd occasions when the junior pilots were allowed to carry out some practice flying, the weather conditions generally put an effective stop to it.

So the first few months in France consisted of endless dreary days and nights in the Operations room, or in our even more dreary concrete huts, the monotony occasionally releaved by a practice flight or an orgy of eating and drinking and other forms of entertainment in 'the big city'.

With the approach of Christmas, heavy and continuous rain grounded us for weeks on end and transformed the aerodrome and the area adjacent to the living huts into an unnegotiable morass. Driving, icy rain which froze where it touched, poured down every day, but in spite of the conditions and our primitive living quarters, several Ensa concert parties managed to reach us and to cheer us up with shows. Our attempts to entertain them afterwards in the bleak Mess hut where the temperature was if anything lower than that of the vast hangar in which they had performed, were inevitably somewhat inadequate.

Towards the middle of December, a flight was ordered on detachment to Le Touquet for Leave Boat security patrols, and in

---

* 'Ops B' — a daily roster of junior officers to assist the Duty Operations Officer and man the telephone links with Wing HQ.

the absence of a number of more senior pilots, who were either on leave or sick, I was included in those nominated to go. My first 'operational' flying, and it was very disappointing when the great morning arrived with weather even more impossible than before.

By midday the clouds had lifted, and after a few anxious moments of surging through the liquid mire of the airfield with our fixed-pitch wooden airscrew Hurricanes, we formed up and headed for the coast.

Following a low flypast over Le Touquet and the seafront, Voase Jeff, the Flight commander, waved us away and I circled round the seemingly impossibly small aerodrome by the Etaples canal and watched the first two aircraft go in to land, before approaching myself.

We had been warned that the surface would be very soft and rightly so, for as soon as I touched down the wheels dug in and the tail rose alarmingly. However all was well and I taxied up to the civil airport building where Voase Jeff and Chris Mackworth were already speaking to the French commandant.

Just then Joyce came in, and we watched anxiously in case he should touch a soft patch which we had missed. At one point his tail came up so sharply that we did think that he would nose over. But he finished his run safely and turning round, began to taxy in, when without warning his undercarriage collapsed and he subsided ignominiously on one wingtip. As he said afterwards: 'I must have selected "wheels up" instead of "flaps up"!'

Lunch with the French officers in their Mess followed, and then we set off into the pretty little town of Le Touquet to settle into our new billet, the White Star Hotel. That evening we found 'Alfred's Bar' which was to become our rendezvous for many occasions during the coming months; and it was a very cheerful company that strolled through the darkened streets and 'broke' into the Hotel that night.

With much cursing and groaning we dragged ourselves out of bed at 5.00 am and drove down through the silver birch woods to the aerodrome where, after a breakfast of omelettes and coffee, the first patrol order came through at 7.15 am.

It was a great moment as I took off and climbed away over the sand dunes towards Cap Gris Nez, just visible in the misty orange glow of dawn ahead. I was truly on 'operations' at last. The safety of the leave boat, now just departing from Boulogne with hundreds of men on board depended on me and my vigilance. That gun button under my thumb had a real significance at last. If anything with black crosses ventured into this area — and they had been doing so daily during the past weeks — it was up to me to deal with it.

At 20,000 ft over the Straits the coastline from Dover to the Isle of Wight, the Thames estuary and the shores of Suffolk, and the French and Belgian coast from Dieppe to Ostend, stretched out below in the clear wintry atmosphere like a gigantic relief map. While halfway across that wide river, below, the Straits of Dover, a streak of white against the deep blue of the sea showed the position of the leave boat.

In this way with patrols by day and exploration of Le Touquet's nightlife by night we passed an interesting and exciting weekend, and it was with great regret that we took off on Monday and leaving the sands, beech woods and sunshine behind, headed back to the mud and monotony of Seclin.

Monotony it certainly proved to be, for during the next two months conditions became so appalling after continued freezing rain and (eventually) weeks of heavy snow, that our lives became bounded by the four cold concrete walls of our huts and the bare boards and oilcloth of the Mess hut in which we huddled for meals dressed in greatcoats, leather jackets, flying suits, and anything but regulation dress provided that it could keep a little of the regular 30° of frost from our bodies. Whiling away the long hours was not easy, and the pilots soon began to find diversions suitable to the conditions.

Every morning at 11.30, the majority of 'B' Flight consisting of Chris Mackworth, Joyce, Edwards, Smith and myself, would foregather in Mitchell's room to consume quantities of strong cocoa brewed on the little stove which we could never keep alight long enough to warm the room. It was at these sessions that indignation meetings were held over the prevailing situation in the Squadron whereby only the experienced pilots flew regularly, and the less experienced a pilot was the less chance he seemed to have of increasing his experience.

But we need not have worried: in a few months we were to be flying more continuously than we could then conceive possible. In the meantime we could do nothing but peer through the grimy windows at the driving rain and snow outside.

As the days passed by the temperature dropped lower, until the huts becamed coated with sheets of glistening ice and the doors and windows were blocked with snow. Every morning before daybreak a deafening shuddering roar awoke us as the 'erks'* started up the

*RAF slang for their long-suffering and highly effective ground crews.

18

Hurricanes to warm them and, first covering our shivering forms with layers of sweaters and leather flying suits, we floundered through the snow to our respective aircraft to supervise their 'running up'.

Soon sickness became prevalent, and towards the end of January came a time when between the two squadrons not more than nine pilots could have been brought to Readiness, had such a state been required!

Of the next two months there is little to tell as conditions remained as bad as ever until eventually I too became bedridden with a high fever, and after a week of lying in my bed and watching the snow drifting down through cracks in the roof, while water froze solid in a glass by my bed as did even ink in a bottle by its side, I have a hazy recollection of bumping halfway across France in an ambulance; of lying in the open in falling snow for what seemed hours on a stretcher at a casualty clearing station; of unbelievable warmth and comfort in an extremely well-run army ambulance train; and eventually of arriving, feeling more dead than alive, at No 2 Base Hospital, the Casino at Dieppe.

In no time I was back on my feet and consuming lobsters and 'gin-fizz' with other convalescents in the town, mainly Army officers who were, like myself, awaiting their discharge. This eventually came but to my dismay I found that having been absent from the squadron for more than seven days, I was now 'off the strength' and was to be sent 125 miles south-west to the Le Mans 'Pool' to await re-posting. This did not appeal to me, so I embarked on an organization of my own calculated to sidetrack the authorities and create order out of chaos.

After much argument and persuasion I put through a telephone call to the AMPC at Douai, and within a few hours my father* was slithering in his staff car over the ice-bound roads to the coast to collect me. Eventually after a long and cold journey fraught with some rather tense moments on icy hills and bends, we arrived at Arras, only a few miles from our destination, and there indulged in one of the best and most appreciated meals I can ever remember having had, at a well-known but eventually sadly damaged cafe, the Univers.

Next day the situation at Seclin was much the same as when I had left. A handful of pilots appeared in the Mess huddling in greatcoats round the smoky fire while all outside was bitter,

_____
* A reserve Lieutenant Colonel who was stationed at Douai with the Army.

driving, frigid whiteness. However I was to have a very welcome break from this, for I was posted back on the strength of 87 Squadron and granted fourteen days' sick leave. The following day saw me breakfasting at 6.45 am in mid-Channel on the Dover leave boat which I had patrolled only a few weeks before from Le Touquet.

Returning to France in early March coincided with a Squadron posting back to Le Touquet, which was much to everyone's satisfaction. We settled into our quarters at the White Star again, and prepared to enjoy idyllic surroundings which we knew could not be our lot for long.

The duties were not strenuous, though sometimes as many as twelve leave boat patrols would be flown between dawn and dusk. At the same time our position on the coast brought us well into the area used by the German 'Met'* machine, which came down as far as Dieppe on most days, and after which we sent interception patrols without much success.

On one morning of low cloud and heavy rain we were sitting in the cottage opposite the airport buildings which served as our mess, drinking 'Champers' for, owing to the bad weather, a party was already brewing, when the telephone rang shrilly and Operations ordered two aircraft to patrol Bercq above cloud as they had a hostile plot in that vicinity.

Feverish excitement! John Cock and I ran for our aeroplanes and after mine refused to start I rushed over to another serviceable Hurricane. Starting up in a hurry, I climbed away down the coast into driving rain in the direction taken by Cock who was already out of sight.

The cloud tops were at about 9,000 ft, and breaking through into brilliant sunshine in the neighbourhood of the Somme estuary (as near as I could judge), I searched the sky for signs of the other machine. In the meantime the R/T was vibrating with information about the 'Bandit' which they said was now circling Abbeville at 10,000 ft.

I caught sight of a small speck ahead, and after chasing it for a few minutes it turned out to be Cock's Hurricane so I joined him, and then on the instructions of the R/T we turned and headed back towards the East, climbing hard.

The glare of the sun reflecting on the cloud-sheet below made searching a strain until everything began to take on a pinkish hue. Then, so suddenly that at first it had little effect on me, I saw the

* Regular weather reconnaissance flights by Heinkel III aircraft.

pale green under-surfaces of a twin-engined aeroplane immediately above us and flying on our course.

There could be no doubt of it, the swept-back elliptical wings with engine nacelles almost as far forward as the nose of the fuselage, positively identified it as a Heinkel III; and then as our eyes became accustomed to the glare, black crosses could be seen under the wing tips. A real live Hun at last! With throttles wide open we virtually stood on our tails in an effort to close the range, and at the same moment, seeing us, the Hun opened his throttles for quite the opposite reason, and we saw twin streams of black smoke pour from his exhausts as he did so.

By the time we had reached 17,000 ft the Heinkel was less than 600 yards ahead and above. He was almost in range and wild bursts of tracer came lancing down at us in long grey-white streaks from the obviously badly frightened rear-gunner, and I had great difficulty in restraining myself from opening fire.

The excitement experienced at that moment was difficult to describe. This was 'action' at last! The German ahead who was already shooting at me, would in a matter of minutes be within range of my eight machine guns.

I had outclimbed Cock's Hurricane and he was now well below and behind. It was going to be my Hun, and then — sheer tragedy! Suddenly I realized that my senses were becoming dulled: I could see nothing but the Heinkel in a small area of dark blue sky, and as I struggled to concentrate the dark blue turned to purple and an unbearable weight seemed to settle on me. Among a jumbled confusion of thoughts at that moment I can only remember two: the first, to wonder where on earth the Heinkel had disappeared to; and the second just as I passed out: 'My God, I'm going to spin!'

I had become unconscious at nearly 23,000 ft through lack of oxygen, and it was not until I came to at 11,000 ft in an inverted dive with the airspeed indicator 'off the clock', that I realized what had happened, recovered after some tense moments from the dive and started to search for the cause. I had not far to look, for in the confusion of my hasty take-off I had forgotten to lock in the tube which connected to my oxygen mask.

Cursing myself for a fool, I circled disconsolately over the clouds and called up Base to see if there was any chance of regaining the fight. I could get no answer as usual as I must have flown out of R/T range during the chase, and so I descended through the 9,000 ft of cloud to break out at 500 ft under a leaden sky and over an even more leaden sea, with no land in sight.

There was nothing to do but return home, and so I set a

southerly course expecting to strike the coast in the neighbourhood of Boulogne. But after fifteen minutes there was nothing but sea ahead and I began to wonder where on earth I had got to. Then I realized the horrible truth. I must have been at least 20 miles west of Boulogne above cloud, and so for the last fifteen minutes had been travelling parallel to, instead of towards, the French coast. This proved to be the correct answer, and after ten minutes of flying south-east the low cliffs of Le Treport appeared out of the rain, and twenty minutes later I was bumping over the wet grass of Le Touquet towards an excited group of pilots and 'erks'.

I told them all that I could while awaiting Cock's arrival, and received considerable and very well deserved ragging in the meantime. However on landing, Cock was able to give us the glad news that he had managed to fire all his ammunition at the Heinkel before it dived vertically into the clouds streaming black smoke.

It was nearly dark by now and in less than an hour the whole squadron was crammed into Alfred's bar, knocking back 'Hurricane' cocktails at John Cock's expense. At last we really had something to celebrate!

We enjoyed a further month of relaxed life at Le Touquet and enjoyed it to the full, because in some way we knew that before long there would be little chance of 'fun and games', and our time would be very fully occupied with other things.

At the end of March a code message came through at 2.00 am when I was spending a lonely night watch at the aerodrome as duty officer. After two hours of struggling with the code and cipher books, I gathered that we were on the move once again, and that afternoon we arrived over the aerodrome of Amiens, flying in tight squadron formation at less than 100 ft.

Our stay at Amiens lasted only three weeks during which I remember chiefly good food at the Godebert, parties at the Chanticleer, low level flights in brilliant sunshine back to Le Touquet between the poplars of the Somme at Abbeville in our 'Magister' trainer, standing by on cold, dewy dawns in our cockpits, waging huge warfare against hosts of maybugs which invaded our dispersal area, a visit to the Potez aircraft works at Albert with Chris Mackworth and Jimmy Dunn in our Hurricanes; and finally of getting up one morning to find that on the following day the squadron was to move down to the Maginot line to a sector known to be particularly populated with Messerschmitts.

The Squadron was to leave at 4.15 pm and so Taffy Edwards and I, who were taking the 'Magi', left soon after lunch just as the first

Messerschmitt 109 to be captured intact, arrived under Hurricane escort from Nancy, *en route* for England.

We landed at Rheims to refuel at the dispersal point of the Battle squadron which, though we did not know it then, was to lose 75 per cent of its flying personnel before the month was out.

Then on over the 1914–18 war shell-pitted and trench-scarred landscape of Verdun, until ahead appeared a lake on the edge of a forest and a field with Hurricanes and Potez 63 reconnaissance bombers dispersed round its edges. So we arrived at Senon on 28 April 1940, and though right up till the last moment we were not given the merest inkling of a warning, the storm was almost at breaking point.

In the few remaining moments of daylight we set about finding the tents and clearings allotted to the pilots in the woods, getting our kit into them and making up our camp beds. Finally supper in the Mess tent, and then a last talk over our chances of going over the lines on the following day before turning in and tying down the flaps of the tents for the night while nightingales sang all round in the woods.

The following morning Johnny Dewar, true to form, decided to take the whole squadron on a 'blackguard rush' over the front line towards Saarlauten, and there was much excitement as zero hour approached for I think every one of us imagined that an almighty battle was imminent.

At the sign from Johnny, engines crackled into life all down the line, and we were soon picking up squadron 'search' formation and climbing towards the frontier. We had been patrolling under the glaring sun for about 25 minutes, occasionally looking down at Germany which surprisingly enough looked quite inoffensive and peaceful, when suddenly 'A' Flight who were leading came peeling back past us, one after the other towards the tail of the formation.

We all thought 'Christ', and nearly ricked our necks in attempting to look both through and under our own tails. But the laugh was on 'A' Flight, as they had apparently decided that the formation of fighters climbing up under their tails were Messerschmitts and they had forgotten our existence entirely. The formation sorted itself out, albeit with much profanity over the R/T, and after a further twenty minutes patrolling, headed back over Nancy towards Senon, and landed uneventfully.

During the following week our main duties were the escort of Lysanders on photographic reconnaissance between the Maginot and Siegfried lines. The weather proved none too suitable for this work however and during the whole period rain and low cloud, and possibly lack of enthusiasm, seemed to keep the Messerschmitts on the ground for we saw nothing but odd and ineffective ack-ack bursts.

Time off-duty was very fully occupied with constructing our camp; repairing muddy tracks, building rustic seats and wash-stands, and doing all the hundreds of odd jobs to be found when living under canvas, and we achieved plenty of exercise by organizing armed reconnaissances and offensive patrols against the wild boar which lived in the forest, and which we heard and sometimes saw at night or in the early morning.

One day after a patrol in bad visibility, our formation became lost and after circling for some time and hoping that we were not in Germany, a town with an aerodrome appeared below and we went in to land. It was Nancy and therefore not far from home, so we decided to take off immediately and return. We did not take off in formation as the aerodrome was quite small and had the town of Nancy spread over a steep hill on its northern boundary, our direction of take-off owing to the wind.

Voase Jeff and Mitchell went off first and I followed. But at less than 100 ft and with the town and hills below, ahead and above, my engine cut out dead. It was a bad moment for I could see no possible way of avoiding a crash into the nasty hard houses ahead. Then I saw about one hundred yards of reasonably clear back gardens to starboard and made a quick turn towards them.

In the meantime I had, of course, been working the throttle furiously, and while actually in the process of holding off at about 80 mph with clothes props and sheds flashing by just below the engine caught with a roar and the crash was averted. But then it appeared to be a case of out of the frying pan into the fire for though still airborne, I was at 50 ft in a fixed pitch airscrew Hurricane with the wheels down, 85 mph on the airspeed indicator and the whole of Nancy with its church spires and shops climbing up to 900 ft ahead.

I just cleared everything, but it was the slowest and steepest climb I have ever carried out on a Hurricane without stalling and I returned to Senon to receive a 'strip' from the Flight commander for failing to keep up with the formation!

Chapter 2

BLITZKRIEG

On Thursday 9 May I squelched through rain and mud into our tent in the woods with very mixed feelings. I was to go on leave the following day, and at this inappropriate time I had suddenly begun to feel very ill.

I slept badly during the night and by daybreak I was just asleep when, as I thought, the usual morning ack-ack barrage began. Suddenly there was a terrific 'crump-crump-crump' which seemed to shake the tent. A muffled voice from Joyce said 'That ack-ack was close!'. At that moment Johnny Cock said: 'Ack-ack Hell!' and charged out of the tent as a further series of explosions sent the lamp swinging on the tent pole and a chatter of machine guns denoted that something was really going on. I got up and found a group of brilliant pyjama-clad pilots standing in the clearing, looking up at a formation of Huns through gaps in the green spring canopy which camouflaged the camp so perfectly.

There could be no doubt of it. On Friday 10 May the Blitz arrived and my leave was a thing of the past. In the meantime my stomach complaint had gained a firm hold, and while the pilots were all dashing out to the airfield, hauling flying gear over pyjamas, I had to just lie and swear and groan. The boys got four Huns before breakfast and Voase Jeff was attacked by an Me 109 while force-landing with a damaged radiator, but he got away with it.

The order soon came through to take up our planned position on the Belgian frontier, and I spent the remainder of the morning lying on some bundles of gear in our clearing while the batmen worked feverishly in the mud to collect all the kit and put it in the lorries.

The ambulance was to have been ready for me at midday, but after walking the half mile through the wood, an uncomfortable journey for my condition, I found that it had gone and left me with no transport at all. At that moment — '*Phee-ooo*' and the bombs began again.

The speed with which the Mess tent was evacuated (the boys were having a last drink at the time) has gone down in history. It is said that few troubled to go out by the proper exit but went straight through the sides. Every tree in the forest appeared to have a prostrate form behind it, and it was an interesting experience listening to the whistle of the bombs and having guessing competitions with one's next-door neighhbour as to where the next one would land, while a nightingale would absolutely on no account be diverted from his solo in an oak overhead.

Nature's reaction to the stirring events of the morning were rather wonderful: at the height of the strafing the nightingales and blackcaps in the forest seemed to be trying to out-sing themselves, while a cuckoo kept up a continual chorus to such an extent that one of the 'erks', with bombs and machine-gun bullets flying around like a 'Brock's Benefit', was heard to exclaim: 'Can't someone shoot that ruddy fowl, it's driving me crazy!'

At this point I found Captain Lasseud, our interpreter, taking his little Fiat along the bumpy road through the forest and discovered that he was off to Lille and had room for me. After breaking open some petrol tins to fill up and putting some full ones in the back, we set off on our journey.

We passed the pock-marked hillsides of Verdun, through Charleville to Le Cateau along the Luxembourg frontier with the defences being manned and troops moving everywhere. These defences seemed to consist of a few hundred yards depth of barbed-wire and gun emplacements (with 7.5 naval guns) at wide intervals, the whole manned by what appeared to be only one division of colonial troops.

We stayed for the night of 10 May in a village a few miles from the frontier in an inn whose sanitary arrangements were quite incredible. The excitement among the local people was at fever heat as troops billeted in the town moved out in a steady stream, and it reached a high pitch when four large saloon cars swept over the frontier, each bearing the coat of arms of the ruling house of Luxembourg.

We were heavily bombed during the night of Saturday 11 May and soon after leaving the following morning we passed an aerodrome on which there were a large number of Potez 63 reconnaissance machines. As we approached — *Crrr-umph* — the first bomb arrived! Altogether thirteen hit the field and one blew a house from one side of the road to the other (more or less!) behind us.

A few more miles of rather uninteresting country between

Le Cateau and Valenciennes, and we then drew near the France-Belgian border; the frontier which had been so resolutely closed to the BEF until Belgium itself was threatened was now wide open.

Above flew patrols of Morane and Loire fighters, and we entered Valenciennes to find the main square, veritably the southern gateway to Belgium, heavily damaged by the 500 kilo bombs of Ju 87s which had visited it some thirty minutes before. Our first experience of the accuracy of dive bombing, though the damage did not hold up traffic.

The road from Valenciennes was a heartening sight with streams of BEF going up into Belgium, well-equipped and looking as happy as sandboys. Finally we reached Seclin, only to find no sign of the Squadron there. We went down to the Mess and heard wonderful tales from the barmen of thirteen Huns shot down on Friday, and six already that morning.

Finding no officers of 85 Squadron in the Mess, we set off for the north end of the camp, and had barely gone 100 yards when there was a crescendo of falling Blitzkrieg and all hell opened up where we had been standing a few moments before as a stick of 250 pound bombs fell along the line of huts. At the North Camp we found the 'Wingco' and Steadman in 'battle bowlers'* looking at the pall of smoke over the other end of the airfield and cursing, while overhead the white puffs of our ack-ack showed the position of the Huns at something over 12,000 ft. Then a 'three-tonner' came lurching by with casualties.

Learning from the 'Wingco' that the Squadron were at Lille Marcq, I found 'Tommy' Sopwith, the 'stores basher' going into Lille for lunch and joined him. He had brought his convoy up from the Maginot through showers of bombs. At one village he had stopped his 'three-tonner' outside an *estaminet* and had gone with his party into the cellar as there was a raid on, when there was a heavier explosion than usual which blew in the cafe above them. Crawling out of the wreckage Sopwith looked for the lorry (containing officers kits and mess furniture) and found that it was no longer there; the last bomb had scored a direct hit. Meanwhile the Huns were now flying up and down the main street machine gunning the women and children as they crawled from their wrecked homes.

After a meal at the Rio we found Harry Tait and Watson having coffee with two 'jobs' of the usual type, and learnt the latest news from them. On the trip up from Senon the Squadron ran into some

* Steel helmets.

27

Huns and got three as far as I can remember, and later on the evening of Friday 10 May, Cock and Edwards got a Heinkel near Roubaix, while Voase Jeff had already had one that morning. This was making me feel very out of things and in my innocence I was anxious to make up for lost time, so as soon as possible I sought out the MO who seemed highly delighted to have established his sick quarters in the stables of an old French fort on the Roubaix road, but he immediately pronounced me unfit and sent me straight back to bed at the hotel in Lille.

The sirens, ack-ack and bombs kept me awake all night, so that the next day, Sunday 12 May, I slept heavily and the MO would not allow me back to the camp till Monday morning. When I got there I found an excited group standing outside the 'Ops room' farmhouse discussing the morning's show. They had run into a large bunch of Ju 87s near Maastricht — Johnny Dewar had one, Mitchell had one and Cock had one, but Jack Campbell and Sergeant Howell were both missing, the formation having been surprised by Me 109s on the way out.

Voase Jeff saw an Me close to within 100 yds of Jack and saw the cannon shells bursting on his fuselage before the machine nosed right over. One of them was believed to have baled out.

The MO still would not let me fly but after another day in Lille with Mitchell and Cock (both now down with dysentry) I went up to the camp on Tuesday morning 14 May and having avoided the MO, went across to the 'Flights' to stand by.

On Tuesday 14 May there were a few alarms and ack-ack fire during the afternoon, but no patrol orders till after tea when an order came through for two aircraft to patrol a village which was being bombed some ten miles west of Brussels. I ran to a 'kite' but just as I was getting in, up came Joyce saying 'Hi, my aeroplane!'. He and Chris Mackworth took off for the eighty-mile trip through air more infested with Messerschmitts than we realized at the time. Ten minutes later the rest of us went off on a 'panic', but made no contact with the enemy.

After Mackworth and Joyce had been away two hours we became anxious, but by dusk nothing had been heard of them. Would old Chris plague us any more with his practical jokes, or 'Dimmy' Joyce send us into hoots by sitting on a camp-bed and banging his head against the wall because, according to him, it was such a wonderful feeling when he stopped? We were afraid not.

So back to the new Mess, a lovely private villa in beautiful grounds, for supper and lots of beer and a chat with 'A' Flight about the day's work; and then sleep for a few bomb-shattered hours before 'readiness' at 3.30 am.

Wednesday 15 May found us shivering in the morning dew by our Hurricanes waiting for sunrise and wondering what the next few hours would bring, but nothing happened bar the arrival of 504 squadron from England — a cheering sight! Back to a huge breakfast and sleep till midday, our next duty period.

At about 2.15 pm the field telephone went *'Brr-ing Brr-ing'*, the sound that we were beginning to hate, and being nearest it I took the order: 'Blue and Green sections and a section of 504 to patrol Louvain-Brussels 10,000 ft, nine aircraft. Good luck old man.' My first show at last!

There followed the, by now, usual pandemonium of putting on parachute, helmet, goggles, oxygen and R/T gear, with the crackle and roar of the Merlins starting up, and then we were off with a roar and picking up formation over the field. Voase Jeff was leading Jimmy Dunn and myself, followed by David, Taffy Edwards and Culverwell with 504 Squadron as 'rear-end Charlies', as those unfortunates who protected the rear were called (or words to that effect).

It was a brilliant day as we climbed towards the battle area and there was no cloud cover, though we knew little about such things in those days. We had reached Brussels and were turning SE for Louvain when above and to the right we saw ack-ack bursts and small specks all over the place. Voase Jeff signalled 'line astern' and we climbed flat out towards them, switching on gunsights and turning gun buttons to 'Fire'.

Ahead the sky suddenly appeared full of twin-engined aircraft and as we approached they all began to form a defensive left hand circle, but we came in before they could complete it and I found myself firing my guns, for the first time in anger, at a Dornier.

Another Hurricane cut in front and at that moment the air in my immediate vicinity became thick with tracer. Just in time I caught sight of a twin-engined kite coming down on me like a load of bricks from ahead and above. Yanking everything back I fired a quick burst at him and as he went by I recognized him for an Me 110 'Destroyer'.

By now they were coming down on us right and left and I only just had time to half-roll out of the way of another which I sensed, rather than saw, coming down on my tail. Each time I attacked anything another was on my tail, so becoming tired of this I went into a tight turn till I couldn't stand it any longer, and coming out, found myself on the tail of a twin-engined machine. I fired nearly all my remaining rounds at this Dornier and saw first one motor

29

stop and then the other with much black smoke as it fell out of the sky.

My first Hun, but the atmosphere was unhealthy for anyone without ammunition, so without further ado I pushed the nose down for home. I worked out that I must be well on the wrong side of the front line so I hedge-hopped towards Brussels so as not to be caught napping, at least from below.

This was fine until tracer began to whistle past from behind and I thought: 'Don't look now but I think I'm being followed!'. A large Dornier 17 bomber was in fact sitting behind me firing away with his front gun for all he was worth. He seemed every bit as fast as the Hurricane at ground-level, and as I tried to get away he just used his extra height to gain on me. So we went round and round the tree tops for some time in this way; the Hun firing sometimes with his front gun, sometimes with the rear, while after firing a few shots I had no rounds left for such a sitting chance.

Eventually I 'pulled the tit'* for over-boost and then broke the circle from behind him, and from this difficult position he could not catch me up so he rocked his wings and made for home himself. In the meantime I appeared to be still over Hunland and fireworks of all sizes were bursting around the sky, so, still hedge-hopping, I set course for where I thought France might be.

After a few minutes I looked at the sun and found that I was heading WSW instead of NW (as the compass read). So steering by the sun I flew up to the Belgian coast and thence back to Lille by way of Gravelines, Calais and Armentieres. My landing was some 45 minutes after the others who had all for some unexplained reason experienced trouble with their compasses. The show hadn't been very successful as we could only claim two Huns destroyed, and Taffy Edwards was missing (I saw him go down with a 110 on his tail).

Back at the Mess we found that 'A' Flight had just had a show and Watson and Rayner had both got 110s, but Sanders had been shot down south of Lille. He had died in Lille Hospital, badly burned, asking that the bandages should be taken off his eyes as he couldn't see.

The next morning Thursday 16 May, broke cloudy but a Hun flew low over the field at about 5.30 am, and I went off after it. The EA got away in the cloud, and Tournai in Belgium was burning fiercely as I came over it. Then followed another day of tension listening for the ringing of the field telephone, until at 5.00 pm

* Emergency boost over-ride on the Merlin engine.

'All aircraft off the ground' came through and seeing ack-ack south of Seclin, we all went that way. Presently some specks could be seen ahead, and then suddenly a 'flamer' went tumbling down the sky ahead and took a very long time, as it seemed, to fall out of sight. A few moments later we passed two parachutes drifting gently down, and were about to attack the 87s which we could now see in a dense mass ahead, when down came Me 109s on our tails. I fired a long burst at one of them and then chased him into Belgium firing all my rounds at him but he was too fast to catch.

We were as usual awaiting patrol orders on Friday (17 May), when suddenly sounds of a dogfight came from the direction of Lille and a Hurricane with a trail of smoke behind it did a complete loop, at the top of which a puff of white showed that the pilot had baled out, and then it went straight in from some 12,000 ft at incredible speed.

The pilot was 'Woody' Woodscawen from 85 at Seclin, and there is a standing joke that on his way down he passed through a cloud and then went up into it on an upcurrent again. He was such a little man! Jarvis was missing after a show with Dick Glyde.

In the afternoon an order came through for eighteen aircraft to patrol Valenciennes-Le Cateau at 7,000 ft to cover some raids by Blenheims in that area. We were to take off at 5.15 pm but at five o'clock the 'Raid Approaching — All aircraft off the ground' came through! There were fifty-odd Hurricanes in Lille-Marcq and they were all off the deck in three minutes. How anyone got off without an accident was a mystery!

Once in the air we were ordered on patrol, and of the masses of machines milling around everywhere no-one knew who was which squadron! Jimmy Dunn and I found the CO Johnny Dewar, and two other sections joined us, and then the rest seeing a nucleus forming decided not to miss the fun! The result was that as soon as we set off for the battle area we had upwards of thirty Hurricanes behind us instead of the eighteen as ordered, which was very comforting!

Le Cateau was seen burning furiously, and turning south we ran into an ack-ack barrage so heavy and accurate that one of the machines disappeared in a direct hit and a number of others were damaged.

Shortly afterwards I caught sight of some fighters slipping behind the cloud under which we were patrolling. I called over the R/T: 'Look out — Messerschmitts!', and then they came through a hole in the clouds in line astern and were able to position themselves above the tail of our formation before Johnny Dewar realized that they were Huns. Too late we whipped round in a climbing turn, but the 109s dropped down before we could close the circle, and before we could do anything about it two Hurricanes were going down and two parachutes were drifting down gently, while the 109s were belting hell-for-leather home.

Continuing the patrol we once again passed over the ack-ack battery and again I watched the big black mushrooms sprouting around and in the formation, altogether too near at times. We had been patrolling for an hour and a half and it was becoming dusk when a solitary Me 109 passed in front of us, and David and Rayner dived down and finished it off.

Then we were heading for home with the fire in Le Cateau glowing ominously in the dusk. But we were not to land without one more scare, for south of Lille I looked into the setting sun and saw silhouetted there a large formation of fighters. But it turned out to be 85 Squadron returning to Seclin from patrol, and we were soon touching down at Marcq happy in the knowledge that the worst of one more day was over. Sergeants Tryce and Sanders, both ferry pilots, were missing from our morning show.

Huns dropped some bombs near the men's sleeping quarters during the night, but without damaging anything. Dog tired, we slept very heavily but it gave us rather an empty feeling to wake up on Saturday 18 May once more to the thud-thud of guns and the batman's 'Lovely morning Sir' at 3.30 am. Then the usual piling on of flying gear, followed by a bumping, crashing ride in the back of the 'C' Flight Commer truck over the cobbled streets, through the mule lines of the local Indian Labour Corps group, to 'B' Flight dispersal point.

Once there we lay down in the shallow ditch by the telephone which was our only cover from weather or bombs, or stamped around in the dewy grass trying to warm ourselves while little blue exhaust flames chased each other up and down the dark cowlings silhouetted against the pale light of the dawn, as the Merlin engines one by one thudded, crackled and roared into life to be 'run up'.

Presently all was quiet and as 5.00 am drew near, we, as was now the usual routine, fell to discussing the probable area of the next patrol. Opinion was divided between Le Cateau and Arras, but it didn't matter much as either were likely to be pretty bloody.

I was sitting in my cockpit fiddling with straps and oxygen mask, more for something to do than from necessity, when I suddenly heard shouts and saw everyone diving headlong for the ditch and, looking round, saw a twin-engined aircraft coming straight for us at ground level from the direction of Belgium.

Right *The author train-
ing on Hurricanes at St
Athan in October 1939*
(Author's Collection).

Below *87 Squadron
pilots at Lille in 1939.
The author is third from
the right* (IWM).

Above *Servicing a Hurricane I of 87 Squadron at Lille* (IWM).

Below *87's first victory: 'B' Flight's Heinkel in November 1939* (IWM).

Above *'Blondie' Walton with Voase Jeff's crew and Heinkel trophy* (IWM).

Below *87's Browning machine-gun 'SheepDippers', for aerodrome defence* (IWM).

Above *New Zealander Derek Ward, 'B' Flight commander, with his Hurricane in August 1940* (Watson Collection).

Left *'Watty' Watson of 'A' Flight in Exeter in June 1940* (Watson Collection).

By the time that I reached it the hollow ditch and 'B' Flight consisted of a row of upended backsides! In fact when I flung myself into the ditch I nearly bounced out, while the Potez 63 as it turned out to be, flew over at 100 ft. Whether a true Frenchman or not it was lucky not to get a dose from the 'sheep dippers', our home-made ground defence quadruple Browning machine-guns which had destroyed a Ju 88 so efficiently on the morning of 10 May at Senon.

The next hour or so was quiet until someone looked up and saw a smoke trail directly above us and apparently approaching for its second 'run'. Ack-ack guns opened fire and shell bursts appeared as little white puffs all round it. In the midst of all this excitement came the ominous '*swish-swish*' of a falling bomb. There was no case of bouncing off upturned backsides this time — the others bounced off mine!

Two heavy thuds followed and we thought: 'Delayed actions'. The 'Ops' telephone rang and we all jumped a foot. Someone crawled up the ditch and found that it was an order to stay under cover till further orders as delayed action bombs had been dropped. As if we didn't know it, and a fat lot of cover we had to get under anyway! That was the last we ever heard of those bombs however.

So the hours went by until the middle of the morning when, having had no breakfast, Flight Commander Voase Jeff sent me off for half an hour to the *estaminet* on the canal bank. As I walked down the lane by the canal I watched two Lysanders doing circuits and landings and wondered if they were new pilots from England, as the Army Co-op flight which lived in the south corner of the field were having a rough time doing 'shoots' over the lines every day in very unhealthy places. They were part of the Lysander squadron at Lille Rochaine, between the town and Seclin, who were practically all wiped out in that first week.

I had just entered the cafe and ordered my breakfast which the Madame had poured out and placed before me when I heard the sound of a dogfight and the stutter of machine guns. Outside the air was full of aircraft and at first I could hardly believe my eyes. Madame was bobbing up and down saying '*Ah, les braves aviateux anglais*' and it shook her considerably when I shouted '*mais non, les Allemands!*' and charged off up the road; for overhead at around 4,000 ft was a formation of Messerschmitt 109s. Over beyond the aerodrome one of the Lysanders was dropping earthwards with a 109 hammering away on its tail.

Suddenly wondering where the other Lysander was, I saw it just cruising overhead at a 1,000 ft and even as I looked at it another 109 broke away from the formation and dropped down in a diving turn on to the Lysander's tail. It opened fire at about 200 yards with a chatter of machine guns and a 'thud, thud, thud' of its cannon. It closed to about fifty yards and I could see the cannon shells bursting on the sides of the Lysander's fuselage, which nosed over sharply and dived into the ground in the wood behind 504 squadron's dispersal point.

The 109 broke away and fired a burst at the aerodrome before pulling out at about 500 ft and climbing away in the direction of Lille. At that moment the 'sheep dippers' went into action from 'B' Flight with a harsh chatter, and the Hun began to use such violent evasive action that a cheer went up from the boys, and eventually he was lost from sight behind the houses, losing height rapidly. He crashed south of Lille.

All this time (it was about two and a half minutes) I had been pounding along in the direction of 'B' Flight as fast as my flying boots and overalls would allow, and as I drew near puffing and blowing, one after another Merlin engines roared into life. Dick Glyde, Jimmy Dunn and Sgt Badger, the latter an experienced new arrival the day before, were soon streaking down the field, and Jefferies, another new man, was climbing in as I arrived. My kite was started already, but by the time I had sufficiently recovered my breath to take an interest in the proceedings there was no-one in sight. So I set off in the direction of Seclin.

Presently I found a small dogfight in progress which turned out to be Jimmy Dunn knocking hell out of a 109 which eventually crashed in flames without any assistance being required. After looking all over the sector for some time and finding nothing, I returned to base and taxying up to the dispersal found that the whole Hun formation had been caught by 85 at Seclin and that those left over had been mopped up by Dick Glyde, a 109, Jimmy Dunn another, and Badger one 109 and possibly another. Jimmy's Hurricane was a mass of bullet holes, and so was Dick's. The latter had apparently had a shot at Badger in the heat of the scrap, mistaking him for a 109! Badger's only comment on landing was with a broad grin on his face: 'You *are* a rotten shot Sir!'. New pilot Jefferies had not come back from this action.

The relief shift came at midday, and we were glad of a few hours respite in the shape of a run into the town to collect any remaining kit from the various hotels which had been our billets during the first part of the week. We had arranged to foregather at the Metropole bar before returning, and there I found an excited group in the centre of which was Sergeant Howell of 'A' Flight, back from the dead so to speak.

He had been missing since that show over Maastricht and we had thought that there was no more hope for him, but apparently he had baled out after suddenly finding his aeroplane falling to pieces around him and diving on its back out of control. He had been heavily shaken on landing and had spent the next four days travelling all over Belgium being passed from one unit to the other, until finally he travelled right through Lille on the Friday night and woke up to find himself at Armentieres, from whence he had returned that morning!

This all called for celebration and as the bar was crammed with Press representatives all eager for the latest news, the celebration was not an expensive one for us and we were all feeling considerably less fatigued when we returned to Marcq at 2 am. Our next shift was the evening from tea until dusk so most of us snatched some sleep until we were once more on our way down to the aerodrome.

On Sunday 19 May Voase Jeff and Mitchell, having seen more action than perhaps any of us, were sent home in a Douglas from Arras for 24 hours leave (Cock and I were to go on Monday if we lived that long) and so we hadn't enough pilots for all our aircraft, which meant that from now on there would be no shifts but just continual duty.

Soon after tea when we were once more in our 'B' Flight ditch, waiting for whatever the evening might bring, a raid interception or a patrol, a Vega Gull turned up, taxied over to us and out climbed the AOC of our Group. His first words to us were, 'Having a good time, chaps?', which sounded rather strange to pilots who had been fighting and standing by to fight from dawn till dusk for eight days with about three hours sleep a night and only spasmodic shifts for meals.

Yes, the first few days and one's first scraps were exciting, but after that it became just hard work. However AVM Ludlow Hewitt was pleasant and complimentary in saying that the squadron already had the highest score in the RAF, which pleased us considerably. He finally pottered off to the other side of the field to see the CO in the HQ farmhouse.

At about 5.30 pm the 'Air Raid Warning Red' came through, and all aircraft were ordered off the ground. The usual panic followed with aircraft roaring off in all directions and ack-ack and French air-raid sirens adding to the clamour.

Once off the ground I began to look round for the rest of the

Squadron when, through a gap in the very thin cloud layer, I caught sight of a large formation of bombers heading for Belgium. Breaking through the cloud I saw them again, now miles away to the East and high up. I chased them for some time but they must have been Ju 88s as I seemed to make no impression on the distance between us, and finally when nearing Brussels I gave it up as a bad job.

On the way back the light was failing and as there was a nice little bit of cloud over Roubaix I hopped under it and threw a roll or two. Pleasure flying for the first time, as it seemed, in years.

Presently the splash of green lined on one side by huge electric pylons, between the two town masses of Lille and Roubaix, which is Marcq showed up, and I dropped in to a landing in the long grass and buttercups just as the sun was setting amongst the factory chimneys in the west.

But the day was not finished as, while I was climbing out of the cockpit, everyone began running for the ditch for the third time that day. Just over the roof tops against the evening sky was a twin-engined machine travelling very fast straight for us. As it went over we could see the opened bomb doors from which we expected large and heavy objects to fall, and then that the machine was a 'long nose' Blenheim. It was learned afterwards that it had bombed Seclin just before visiting us!

So once more back to the Mess for supper, the first meal of the day, and the usual discussion of the events of the day over plenty of beer. The conversation at the long dining table was very single-tracked — from the group at my end including Johnny Dewar came: ' — and the Ju 88 went straight down — !' On the other side of the table — ' — he bally well blew up; I had oil all over my windscreen, couldn't see a thing coming home!'

Further down a group of pilots belonging to two squadrons which had come over that day were looking glum. They had lost a CO and two senior Flight commanders on their first trip over, and couldn't understand what was wrong. Well, if they must fly in 'Hendon' formation when there are Huns around, what else could they expect!

At the end of the table 'A' Flight had just come in: ' — afraid old Noels got it today; flamer near Seclin but he is OK in hospital' and ' — I just happened to look round and there were five of the baskets dropping on my tail like a ton of bricks! I streaked for the nearest cloud — the only one in the sky, and found the whole of 'B' Flight milling round inside it!' Immediate chaos of course — and so to bed for a few hours till the next 'dawn readiness'.

At about this time disturbing rumours were current everywhere; the French at Le Cateau had broken completely, Arras and Amiens were threatened; troops from the Belgian front were being brought down to reinforce the French on the Somme, our troops had fallen back to Tournai. Although these reports were unofficial, what we had seen from the air and the way the Messerschmitts patrolled Lille and our aerodrome all seemed to bear out the fact that the Hun was advancing unpleasantly fast. Still, we thought that was the army's affair and in the meantime we were tired, though the thought of parachute troops had our revolvers under our pillows.

Sunday 19th May dawned as usual brilliantly clear, but apart from an early raid warning patrol on which we did not make contact, I did not fly again that morning. Derek Ward, Badger and Cock caught a Heinkel 126 over Douai and literally blew it to pieces on an early patrol.

We had been warned to be ready to retreat that day, and at midday all telephone lines to Group were cut leaving us with no lines of communications bar despatch riders. Royal Engineers were mining the road as we left the Mess after lunch, and the scare of parachute troops and Fifth Columnists was gaining everywhere as parachutists were said to have landed in the area that night. At tea-time we had still done no patrols, all having been carried out by the other squadrons whom we had watched going up together all through the day and coming back in ones and twos.

A D/R* then arrived at the Flight looking for Johnny Dewar who was now Station CO, and being in charge I read the message. It was for immediate withdrawal to Merville, burning all stores we were unable to take with us. Apparently four D/Rs had been sent with the message, the first from HQ starting early in the morning, but this was the only one to get through.

The only way of finding the CO was by going with the D/R, so I bumped across the airfield on his back-mudguard and finally arrived at the Mess having stopped at the Transport section to give them the word to move.

By the time everything was in readiness and the road convoy sent off, the air party had gone and most of the transport, so I was wondering what I was going to use when I found 'Tommy' Sopwith, Sgt Howell and the adjutant outside sick quarters and about to leave in 'Doc' Curry's car. The Huns were fairly close by that time but still some hours away, though the adjutant seemed to think that they were liable to pop round the corner at any

* Despatch Rider.

moment! The latter was more possible than we realized however, judging by the remarkable speed with which the mobile columns were operating at that time.

We finally got everyone away and started ourselves, but that was all as the roads were so crowded with refugees that it began to look doubtful if we should reach Merville before dark.

On the way the subject of conversation turned to the results of the past week and for the first time I realized how incredible they had been. The squadron total of claimed victories was over fifty in the week for a loss of nine pilots. One didn't like thinking of those grand 'types' who made up the nine, never taking part in any more shows in the day or parties in the evening with us. There was little Taffy Evans, whose bracelet was brought to us by REs on their way back from Brussels, who had found his burnt-out kite after the 110s got him on Wednesday. Jack Campbell who was never heard of again. Chris Mackworth who, with Dimmy Joyce, apparently attacked a big formation of 110s who were strafing an ambulance train. Joyce, though still missing, later turned up in hospital with one leg amputated. A group of gunners who witnessed the fight and found the wrecks, wrote a completely spontaneous letter to Chris Mackworth's wife describing him as 'a very brave man'.

Little Jarvis, who only joined us on our arrival at Marcq, was perhaps the most unfortunate of all for on the Tuesday he, though far from completely trained, had to go on a patrol with Dick Glyde in which they met 109s. The result was almost inevitable, but I believe he 'got his Hun' first. Then Saunders of 'A' Flight, perhaps my closest friend in France. The day before (when I last saw him) I had asked him how many Huns he'd got. His reply was 'Oh, only one, but as long as old Saunders is walking along the streets enjoying the sunshine after this war, he doesn't mind!' Messerchmitts got him near Seclin; he was alive when they got him out but died in hospital later that day of the usual complaint these days — burns.

Of the others who had gone down, Tryce and Sanders were ferry pilots who brought new Hurricanes over to Abbeville on Thursday. The next day they brought them to us and stayed to fly them — they both disappeared on their first show, while Jefferies was shot down and injured.

The losses to the other squadrons on the field had also been terrific, and that morning a Flight of 111 Squadron came out from England to stand by during the day and returned in the evening, then to do the same thing again on the following day. It had been strange after six months 'exile' in France to be giving the 'gen' to pilots who had slept near London that night and would do so again that evening.

Eventually we threaded our way through the throngs of miserable, hopeless families stumbling westwards, on and on, past numberless abandoned cars (petrol was unobtainable), until Merville appeared and we turned down the road to the aerodrome which I used to beat up from Seclin when on 'Air to Ground' firing practice. Both 'A' and 'B' Flights were dispersed along the roadside, while opposite were 85 Squadron from Seclin and, further round, two squadrons whose numbers I never discovered. That small muddy field was covered with aircraft, and plumb in the centre on its nose was *LK-J* after Dennis David had tried to pull off one fast landing too many!

Dusk had arrived by this time and we all went up to the *estaminet* at the corner and celebrated the fact of the two Flights being together again after eight days of Blitz. By 7.00 pm most of the road convoy had arrived and so once more to work, billeting or attempting to billet the men. This proved to be no small job in darkness for there were over one hundred and fifty men to think of, and the next few hours were spent dashing in crazy fashion without lights all round the town in Tommy Sopwith's car looking for strayed lorry-loads of men. 11.30 pm found us helping Johnny Dewar unload his gear into a billet he was sharing with Dick Glyde, when suddenly hell broke loose over the aerodrome as a searchlight picked up a Heinkel 111 circling at 1,000 ft over the parked aircraft.

This looked like the beginning of the fireworks we and the civilian population had been expecting all night, for it was just asking for trouble to pack so many aircraft and troops into such a small area. The Bofors and Bren guns and heavier ack-ack put up a lively display, strings of orange and red tracer shells all converging on the Heinkel, but he passed out of range without dropping anything and all was quiet again until 'bang' and a Bofors shell came whistling across the road a few yards away as some blighter cleared his gun in the next field!

By this time I was practically out on my feet and I suddenly realized that I had nowhere to sleep myself yet. The only thing to do was to go back into Merville with Tommy Sopwith and see what was to be found there. The first house I tried was unlocked and seemingly untenanted so I walked straight upstairs, opened a door, found a soft bed with sheets and fell asleep almost while taking my boots off. I remember the incredible feeling of peace as I climbed between those sheets: I didn't care what happened tomorrow or if it rained bombs that night as the moon augured that it would, for I was going to sleep and I did.

Awakened by a dazzling light and the sound of feminine laughter, I thought that perhaps it had rained bombs after all! Peeping over the sheets however, I found the morning sun shining in through the open window and an apparition in the shape of a very pretty girl standing at the foot of the bed! She was no apparition however and when she had finished laughing, she asked, as far as I could make out, what I was doing in her bed! Replying 'Sleeping!' I turned over and proceeded to do so again. Some hours later I once more became conscious of the apparition who was this time rushing about the room pulling things from drawers and packing a bag with them; things thoroughly in keeping with the room, which I could see now was of a very feminine nature!

Seeing me awake, said apparition began a torrential and entirely one-sided conversation from which I gathered that I was lazy — and so I was, for it was past nine o'clock! Apparently the girl's family had evacuated the previous day, and she had come back that morning to collect as much as she could in her car — she was lucky to have any petrol.

It was Monday 20 May and the next problem was breakfast. The Officers' Club proved full to capacity, but at the Cafe Serafin I found Harry Tait and we set about coffee and omelettes which I had no great appetite for, after hearing the latest news. The enemy were on their way up the Somme, having captured Arras, Cambrai and finally Amiens (unbelievable to think of Heinkels at Glicy and Huns in the Chanticleer) and were spreading fan-wise towards us. Tait had that morning chased a Ju 88 into Belgium and eventually shot it down, and there had been various other scraps as well, so I hurried up to the airfield where I relieved Cock on Standby. On the way up a group of pilots were walking along the road and one of them I suddenly realized was Clift, one of my old friends at 11 Group Fighter Pool whom I had not seen since those days. We swapped hurried yarns — he thought he had shot down a secret twin tail-boom Focke Wulfe near Brussels (which sounded more like a Dutch Fokker GR1 to me).

Aircraft were going on patrol and returning all the time, but our only show before midday was a successful ground strafing raid on columns south of Arras. Lying on the grass by the kites I learnt all the 'gen' about 85 who had evacuated Seclin the night before. We had none of us expected it to come to this.

Dicky Lee had been shot down in German territory; captured

when hitch-hiking a tank: he had escaped and finally reached the Squadron, only to get shot down again and be wounded in the leg with which, as soon as it had been dressed, he was flying again and shooting down more Huns.

Sergeant Allard had shot down over a dozen Huns and had been shot down four times himself. Mawhood had asked permission to land one day, as he had lost an eye! Angus, 'Piney', Derek Allen and a number of new pilots including Crozier were all missing.

Bradshaw had been attacked by 109s while flying the 'Master' trainer back to Merville, but had avoided them. A Sergeant pilot had been attacked before he had reached 100 ft after taking off, and had piled straight in, and so on. There were so many incidents, each one an epic in itself, that they would fill volumes.

Meanwhile the sun rose higher and the atmosphere became more and more electric as the anticipation of the next patrol was always far worse than the show itself; and on that Monday 20 May, when so much seemed at stake and the maximum effort was being put out on both sides, we all knew what the next trip would most likely mean to each of us, yet that did not seem to matter, so great were the issues at stake.

The tension was added to later in the morning when a returning Hurricane was shot down and dived into the deck on the far side of the field with a great spout of smoke and flame; and even more so when heavy machine-gun fire began from the distance on the far side of the aerodrome and continued spasmodically for some time. As everyone wondered but at the time ridiculed, a local action was taking place with an advanced motorized column only a few miles from the aerodrome.

It was into this atmosphere that a thunderbolt broke. While I was wandering along the line of aircraft towards the 'A' Flight end, Johnny Dewar appeared with a Wing Commander from Group who was of all things complaining bitterly about the carelessness of pilots who broke aircraft on landing, referring of course to old 'J'. The fact that after so long a period of intense strain, pilots were almost too tired to walk, let alone fly, had apparently not occurred to him.

Seeing me Johnny said: 'Oh, feeling like a rest old Beamont?' and then went on — 'There's a Douglas going back at 12.30 and either you or "Coke" can go on it, you had better draw lots or something.' I hardly grasped the idea and asked what it was all about, and Johnny laughed and said 'Yes, England, you know, London!' The thought was so incredible that for a few moments I believe I gaped like a fish. The possibility of seeing England again and above all the chance of a break from this turmoil, all to be decided at the toss of a coin, the winner to be on his way in less than half an hour!

I won the toss. At that very moment the big Douglas DC-2 came taxying over to our corner of the field and I ran towards it in case it should not stop long enough for me to catch it! The crew opened the back door, climbed out in spotless KLM airline uniforms and said that they would be taking off in ten minutes. That left no time to collect any gear, or even my flying helmet from the dispersal point where also was Derek Ward's Scotty dog 'Whisky' which I had promised to take home with me. At this moment the passengers already on board got out or milled round inside choosing their seats, and a more battered bunch of warriors could not be imagined; almost without exception they showed signs of battle on their bodies and all, in spite of raucous good spirits, in their eyes.

Jefferies, whom we thought killed on Saturday, was there with an armful of splinters; a Sergeant pilot with terrible burns on his face and hands and legs was hobbling about cheerfully as if nothing were wrong. Woody Woodscawn whom we had seen bale out a few days ago, was there telling fearful stories as usual; Squadron Leader Oliver of 85 had just arrived looking grey and haggard — he had been shot down a number of times himself and had finally received a heavy dose of glycol fumes; finally Jimmy Dunn and Dennis David and a few others made up the complement of 23 passengers.

As we were all talking at once about our own particular shows during the past week, a familiar note was heard and there was a Heinkel and directly behind it puffs of ack-ack as the guns started up. The shooting was good but the Heinkel made two obvious photographic runs before disappearing, and a Canadian pilot voiced the opinion of everyone by saying 'Hey boys, time we got outa here!'

The motors broke into a roar and we scrambled into the, to us, incredibly luxurious interior of the Douglas and sank back into the cushions as the lines of parked Hurricanes, some with wings shot away, some crashed on their bellies and all battle-scarred, slid past the windows until she lifted gently and climbed away over Merville towards the coast.

Naturally the Douglas had no guns or protection and so we were far from out of the wood yet; excitement reached quite a peak in fact when a formation of Me 110s passed over us near Norrent Fontes airfield without attacking. This field was the only other left to us in the north-west corner of France and as we passed over it we could see large numbers of Hurricanes there as well. Two did rather vicious-looking quarter attacks at us from the sun, but recognized us before opening fire!

Soon we were nearing the coast between Berq and Abbeville and all the roads were crammed with refugees, on foot, with bicycles, cars, carts, wheelbarrows, in fact anything to carry their belongings in; all heading west but mostly at a standstill owing to the historic block at the Abbeville crossroads which we could see clearly as winding lines of dense, seething humanity stretching from ten miles east of the town on all roads, right through it, to as far as the eye could see in the west. It was a pitiful sight.

As we crossed the Somme estuary and flew low over the sandhills towards the sea, I thought of all those trips in March in the 'Magi' up the valley from Amiens between the Lombardy poplars of the Abbeville canal, now threatened by Hun columns. Then, as Le Treport appeared with its low dirty-white cliffs shining in the brilliant spring sunshine, I remembered my first glimpse of it nearly eight months before.

As we turned out to sea, now at only some 200 ft for safety, and the coastline fell behind, leaving only the brilliant sky and the almost as brilliant sea in sight, we sat back and savoured an extraordinary sensation — we were on our way home and in a few minutes the South Coast would appear — no more war for us, at least for two whole days!

The next few hours are but a hazy memory. The coastline of England and with it the sudden absence of danger. Yet even over the downs and meadows of the south I discovered that I was not the only one still casting anxious glances into the sun.

Then almost before we realized it the Douglas airliner was rumbling up the runway of sunlit Hendon to disgorge on the tarmac in front of the spick and span HQ administration block its motley cargo of humanity, so dirty and bandaged as to look totally out of place in this atmosphere of smart officialdom. But the station was ready to receive us, and after invading the Mess telephones for hurried messages to excited relatives, we received railway vouchers and instructions to report back to Hendon in 36 hours and then clambered on transport to our various railway stations.

As we rocked through the London streets crammed with shoppers, errand boys, tradesmen and people with no apparent concern about what was going on, one thought became more and more persistent; 'Did all these people know how serious things were? Did they indeed know that there was a total battle being fought?' It was soon to become obvious that most did not, and the two more weeks until Dunkirk were needed to show them that this was to be their war also.

Stopping at the RAF Club to disgorge Squadron Leader Oliver we suddenly realized the incongruity of the situation: a group of very dirty and unshaven pilots standing in the middle of the immaculate West End of unwarlike London.

Still in a dream as the lorry disgorged us at Victoria Station, I said goodbye to Jimmy Dunn and was soon rolling through Sussex towards my sleepy little home town, Chichester. The brilliant sunlight on the woods and fields began, after a time, to have more meaning than 'Messerschmitt weather', but it was still through a haze that an angry voice said 'Can't you read the notice!' Looking up I saw a middle-aged woman whose equilibrium was apparently completely upset by the fact that I had my pipe clenched unlit between my teeth and was in, as I now realized, a non-smoking compartment!

So home to the bosom of a somewhat shaken family for two blessed days. At least the first fourteen hours were spent in heavy, dreamless sleep, and then all too soon a telegram arrived saying 'Report to Church Fenton on expiration of leave'. It was the end of the first era, and I had not yet seen my 20th birthday!

Chapter 3

REFORMING

June 1940. Church Fenton
It took some time to become accustomed to life on a normal RAF station so soon after eight months abroad, and especially immediately after the recent period of intense action during which regulations as such had largely gone by the board.

The first week or so at Church Fenton was occupied entirely with trying to straighten up Squadron affairs, finding who was home and who still missing, and watching ferry pilots frequently bend our brand new Hurricanes as they arrived; in fact generally returning to normal. Inside a week we were once more 'operational' and had time to sit back and look around us.

The fine old town of York was no distance away, while if more riotous entertainment were required, Leeds more than filled the bill! In short we settled down to thoroughly enjoy being 'Home'.

Apart from sending a Section over to Leconfield for convoy duties, very little patrol work was done for the first few weeks of June, but Jimmy Dunn and I had fun pinpointing suitable 'invasion landing fields' from an Avro Tutor. This was one of the finest light biplanes of the 1930s and I put in many hours on those warm summer evenings giving the Squadron's lads local flights in it.

After about three weeks of this lazy existence we were ordered on night operations, and after one practice night flight each, we found ourselves patrolling Hull and Pickering in the difficult search for Huns in darkness. One night however the searchlights were behaving well and obtained a number of illuminations. One of these I recognized as a Heinkel 111, and I was almost in range until he dived out of the beams and left me in the middle of the Hull ack-ack fire!

Exciting nights these, one moment in pitch darkness, the next in the blinding glare of many searchlights; and doubly exciting that first sight of the little red flashing homing beacon when on the way home, for I never really knew where I was from the time I took off to the time I landed!

So the days went by, occupied pleasantly with practice flying and evenings at the Ship Inn at Ulleskelf, until the natural war-weariness which had come over most of us disappeared and the news of increasing activity in the South had all the pilots champing at the bit to be back in it again.

It was into this peaceful atmosphere that tragedy struck. Since returning from France, Jimmy Dunn and his sweet young wife had been living at the 'Ship', some two miles from the camp. We had many parties together and nearly every day I would run the MG down to Ulleskelf for a midday session with them in the sunshine by the river. Then on 1 June, Dunn flew his Hurricane over to Yeadon and never came back. Poor old Jimmy, one of the best and sanest of pilots, killed doing a 'beat-up' only two weeks after surviving the bloodiest air battle (to that date) of history.

His death brought home to us harder than ever the loss in France of Mackworth, Edwards, Saunders, Sanders, Thurgar, Joyce and Noels*, not forgetting those pilots who just came out as replacements and died almost before we knew their names.

We stayed at Church Fenton for a few more hot summer weeks, during which we spent our 'readiness' hours practicising aerobatics and formation flying, attempting the perimeter track record in our various battered old cars (still held, as far as I know, by my MG) or blistering in deck chairs at the 'Flights'. But one day I arrived at the Mess after 48 hours leave at Chichester and on asking 'Where are the boys?', found that they had all gone — the Squadron was posted to Exeter!

Exeter and the battle begins again.

July 1940

Watty Watson and I had a 300-mile road race from Church Fenton to Exeter on 7 July; a long journey considerably enlivened by a burst radiator hose and a choked petrol feed. Nevertheless we arrived in good time to find the Squadron dispersed in the farthest corner of a large uneven grass airfield, around two rather dingy bell tents. In the Mess, the peace-time aero club club-house complete
* Wounded.

with cocktail bar in full swing, we found members of 213 Squadron who turned out to be a grand crowd. Then we went off into the town to find that the CO had, inevitably, billeted us on the cheerfullest hotel to be found; The Rougemont.

Of the next few days there was little to record as they were occupied with the many hundreds of jobs that are always incurred by a squadron move, not excluding Sector reconnaissances for the best pubs.

By the time we became fully operational again the weather had closed in, and our days on Exeter aerodrome were spent crammed into leaking tents with the rain lashing down outside and making red torrents of liquid Devon clay of our dispersal area.

One afternoon in such conditions two aircraft went off, and when the pilots returned and burst in out of the rain, Maclure was giving a session on his guitar. Someone asked Mitchell how the weather was in a brief interval between 'She'll be comin' round the mountain' and 'A cowboy's farewell to the prairie', and his reply was: 'So bloody that the Ju 88 got away!' Very nearly first blood again, and no-one minded the long hours in the rain after that.

The Squadron's first days at Exeter were occupied with 'Readiness', which consisted either of grilling in the sunshine on deck-chairs or sleeping in the tent on wet days; and the Squadron developed its night-life comprehensively at the 'Rougers', as our hotel billet became known universally.

The Hun was quite active on cloudy days and sent over a number of reconnaissance machines, and they together with convoy patrols gave us plenty of flying; while every evening before dusk the whole Flight would go off for so-called 'Air Tests', which was nothing more than an excuse to 'beat-up' everywhere and everybody we could think of.

Working hours were quite strenuous: 05.00 hours to late in the evening, and so in addition to regular leave a '24 hours' roster was instituted. This caused a certain amount of argument as everyone was quite certain that he was not receiving his fair share of 'time off'. The arrangement proved very pleasant though, as it enabled one to have a complete change of scene once a week.

It was on one of my days off in July that the Blitz broke in our sector. Returning home from a run in the MG down to Plymouth on 16 July, I found nearly the whole Squadron in the bar rejoicing. Johnny Dewar, Trevor Jay and Badger had been on patrol over Portland when suddenly the sky appeared black with Huns. When asked over the R/T the numbers of the enemy, Johnny had said — 'I can see twelve, no twenty, fifty — Oh hundreds of the baskets!'

And so there were, with, as far as they could see, only three Hurricanes to attack them which they did — head on! All three got their Huns and Johnny had two. The war was on again for 87.

It was mid July then and there were two more weeks to go before the real Battle of Britain began: this was just an appetiser. However things began to brighten up generally. Reccos became more and more frequent and night patrols were added to our tour of duty.

On the morning of 20 July at about 7.30 am a twin-engined machine appeared from the south. It was clearly a Ju 88 and it flew in a leisurely circle round the aerodrome and Exeter at some 2,000 ft while everyone swore like navvies. Mitchell and I ran for our aircraft, haired off downwind in a terrific attempt to catch it and were rewarded with a nice view of it disappearing into the clouds over Exmouth. Hell!

Later that day the weather closed down to 200 ft with rain below that, but there was a Heinkel plotted off Plymouth so Derek Ward and I went off. Visibility was terrible and the rain was streaming over our hoods. It was all I could do to stay in formation, but still Derek kept on until finally we were confronted with cliffs covered in cloud a few hundred yards ahead and no way out other than the way we had come! In a split second we were in a tight turn at some 150 ft above the sea; Derek could just see it, but I was virtually in the cloud and sweating with exertion in the effort not to lose him. We got back to the aerodrome and landed after a 'split' circuit in 400 yds visibility — and went straight to the Mess for a drink.

We were just settling down to a few extra hours of sleep before breakfast on 24 July, after arriving for Readiness at 05.00 hours and kicking 'the dreaded Sam' (David's bull terrier) off the beds to the accompaniment of much growling and general bad humour, when the Operations phone rang and ordered a Section to patrol Lundy Island at 8,000 ft.

Climbing up through the grey dawn, it was almost better than sleeping to be amongst those rolling cumulus clouds, their summits already tinged with orange. Presently, through small gaps in the carpet below, the north Devon coast could be seen, and the R/T said 'Bandit right ahead of you now'. Lundy Island was just visible ahead and suddenly Mitchell waggled his wings violently and pointed down and to starboard, and there in a cleft between the clouds was the dark silhouette of a twin-engined aircraft.

Voase Jeff and Mitchell peeled off in the direction of the gap, but seeing the bearing of the Hun as he disappeared into the cloud I dived to the left in order to cut him off. Breaking through the cloud, I came out directly behind a Ju 88 with two Spitfires coming down from the right, while Voase Jeff and Mitchell, missing the boat completely, were to the left and well behind.

The leading Spitfire* was attacking as I arrived, but he broke away leaving me some 200 yds astern of the 88 exchanging burst for burst with the rear gunner. Presently he stopped firing and a thin stream of smoke began to pour from the fuselage as the Hun went down in a gentle dive towards Tiverton. We crossed the cliffs at a hundred feet, and just when it seemed certain that no-one would get out, a puff of white appeared from the top of his fuselage and I nearly ran into a parachute. The next moment the 88 hit the ground at some 150 mph, slid across a field, through a hedge, over a road into another field, slewed round, broke its back and caught fire. I shot over the top, throttled right back and circled round the burning wreck looking for signs of life. The rear gunner had baled out at too low an altitude and lay two fields away where he had swung down on the side of his opened parachute, which was stretched across the grass and heath beyond him.

On a third circuit I was amazed to see three men beside the burning crash, one standing, one sitting and the other either dead or unconscious. Presently an ancient Morris came swaying up the road and the local Home Guard came into action and successfully captured the half-dead Germans. We returned to breakfast with a considerably stimulated appetite.

Later that day (24 July) 'A' Flight having finished their week, we flew to Hullavington, a Gloucester training station, for night operations. No-one was very pleased with this as night flying was regarded as a 'bind' and the idea of operating from an FTS** did not appeal to us. The latter sentiment was reciprocated with interest by the staff of the FTS, as we discovered in due course.

However, when night fell the sky became aglow with searchlights and reverberated with the drone of Heinkels and Dorniers *en route* for Bristol or Gloucester. On that first night Cock and Voase Jeff were flying, and the former caught a Heinkel in the searchlights over Bristol. He fired all he had at it and was certain that it went down, and when he came back was full of excitement about it; so much so that when a tall dark figure in the blacked-out watch office started asking questions Cock said: 'For _____ sake, can't you _____ well see that I'm ____ _____ phoning!' The tall dark figure was AVM Sir Quentin Brand VC DSO AFC, Air Officer Commanding 10 Group! News soon came in confirming

* Squadron Leader Bob Stanford Tuck of 92 Squadron at Pembrey.
** Flying Training School.

that this Heinkel had come down in Somerset.

After that everyone was as keen as mustard and the following nights were full of practice or patrol flying. On 26 July at Hullavington as I stood in front of the watch office after dark watching some of our new pilots carry out 'circuits and bumps', a Hurricane roared off into the night on patrol and its tail-light immediately shot up like a towering pheasant. The inevitable happened and the light wavered, fell away to the left, checked as if the pilot was making frantic efforts to make sense of the instruments which should have helped him, and then it fell out of sight. A fearful flash followed by a dull thud and a lurid flickering glow, and we knew that we should not see Sergeant Culverwell again.

A few moments later I was ordered on patrol and it was with mixed feelings that I climbed away into the jet black night relieved only by a searchlight ahead and the flickering fire behind.

It soon became obvious that I was not going to be able to find the patrol line without wireless aid and when I called up there was no answer — the wireless was dead. By now I was well out of sight of any lights which could have helped, and after flying on a course which I thought was right for some time, I realized that I was quite lost.

It was one of the darkest nights I've known and a haze obscured all land-mark beacons unless one was right on top of one. In my dimly lit cockpit with its glowing instruments I felt almost as if I was in a little world of my own, but the silent R/T and the new complication of rapidly weakening cockpit lights brought home with startling clarity that the little world was liable to come to earth (which I couldn't see) rather suddenly if I did not do something appropriate quickly.

By this time all I could do was to carry out a form of square search in the hope of seeing a light. Suddenly I saw a beacon which seemed to be flashing the letter for Andover, yet could I be that far away? Switching on the navigation lights I headed for it and saw straight ahead a dim line of lights — a night flying aerodrome! Flying low over it the lights suddenly went out and I realized that, my own lights now having failed, the people on the ground thought I was a Hun! Thinking that I might find the aerodrome from low altitude I flew round and round as low as I dared till I caught a glimpse of a dim line of lights. Slamming wheels and flaps down I made an approach at the 'aerodrome', and just managed to ram the throttle open in time to avoid landing in a railway siding!

Climbing up again, perspiring a little, I made out the time on the luminous cockpit clock; I had been flying for two hours ten minutes and my petrol gauges had failed along with the remainder of the electrical gear and instruments. There was about twenty minutes petrol left I estimated, so I began to climb slowly to 5,000 ft at which height I would wait until the fuel was finished and then bale out.

Another fifteen minutes went by and I began to look at the parachute harness and the escape panel to see that everything was ready, when way down south of the red flashing beacon I could see a white light, then another and another. Andover was putting out its flare-path again!

I wasted no time but put the Hurricane down in semi-darkness before they had even put the fourth light on! Taxying up to the Watch Office in a filthy temper I tore into everyone on sight for not recognizing the sound of a Hurricane, but my rage somewhat gave way to thankfulness when I learnt that there was no more than five minutes' fuel left in my tanks.

It was 03.30 hours as I steered my way through the unknown camp towards the Mess, and I then relapsed into unconsciousness in an armchair as soon as I found one. At 06.30 I was wakened by a WAAF cleaning up like a young cyclone, and I was soon on my way back to Charmy Down, breakfast and sleep till the next, or rather the same night.

Chapter 4

THE BATTLE OF BRITAIN

August 1940 Exeter

With the first few days of August a period of hot and brilliant weather began. It was some weeks since the Portland fight, but news of heavy fighting over Kent kept the atmosphere full of excitement, especially the hours spent standing by at the Flights. There was not long to wait. For the second time in succession I came back from a day off to find that there had been a magnificent blitz over Portland.

'B' Flight had been in the thick of it and so far the score was at least nine destroyed, while Johnny Dewar, MacLure and Cock had all been shot down but were safe. The latter had been jumped on by six 109s and had baled out, landing in the sea. David had maintained patrol over him and returned home roaring with laughter at the sight of Cock swimming ashore minus his trousers, jettisoned for the purpose of freedom. The other two had both crash-landed at Warmwell aerodrome.

The 'Rougers' was in an even more animated state than usual that evening. Scruffy, war-scarred pilots shooting down Messerschmitts all over the bar as fast as they could knock back the pints so lavishly supplied by admiring civilians. Fearful 'line shooting', but after all they had something to celebrate!

A 'Panic' call came through at 06.30 on 13 August ordering all available aircraft to the Portsmouth area immediately. In keeping with my current run of ill-luck the ground crew could not get my aircraft to start, and when I finally climbed in the last of the squadron went roaring away down the field to join the others, now just specks in the sunrise of the East.

Taking off last and a long way behind I felt rather lonely as first Portland, then Bournemouth and Southampton, passed underneath, and especially when the R/T kept saying 'One hundred plus approaching Spithead from SW'! But when I arrived over Portsmouth the main battle seemed to be over, and taking the plunge and breaking through the cloud layer above at 7,000 ft, I only found a squadron of Hurricanes patrolling and no sign of Huns.

Descending over Hayling Island I came out right on the tail of nine bombers which turned out to be Blenheims from Thorney Island keeping out of the way of possible bombs! Then over Selsey a twin-engined aircraft broke out of the cloud ahead hotly pursued by three Hurricanes. Joining in the chase I saw it was a Dornier, but the boys ahead finished it off over Watling before I could catch up.

By this time fuel was getting low, and being too far from Exeter I decided to drop in at Tangmere to refuel. Taxying up to the duty pilots' hut, I found pilots from nearly every station in the South all trying to ring through to their respective units to report. A number of them had just been shot down and were wondering how to get home, while the luckier ones were all agitating to get refuelled and back into action against 'the Baskets'. So after an interesting half hour I took off for Exeter, returning by way of Fordingbridge where I looked down at the beautiful marshes of the valley of Avon, home of vast roach and vaster chub.

At Exeter I found that the show had gone badly. 'B' Flight had found a Ju 88 over the Solent and, Dick Glyde leading, had chased it fifty miles out to sea before finally 'ditching' it. The section then reformed with Johnny Dewar leading, and they noticed white smoke coming from Dick's machine. The next time they looked round Dick was not there, and nothing was heard of him again. He deserved a better end than that with his score of eight confirmed victories — only two days before, a bullet had smashed his hood only an inch or so from his head and everyone had made good-natured comments about his similarities to a cat. This was to be a black day however.

It was 11.30 when I landed, and feeling hungry I snatched a few moments to bounce across the field in the Flight 'V8' to the Mess for a late breakfast. There I heard the latest news from 213 squadron. Their scores had been considerable recently, but their losses very heavy. I had only just started my meal when a steward came in; 'Wanted at 'B' Flight immediately Sir!' Off across the field again and there on the north side ten or more spinning airscrews showed 213 about to go off. The next moment they were flashing by, one by one, and climbing away like a swarm of hornets in the direction of Portland.

The boys were already by the 'kites' at 'B' Flight, smoking last minute cigarettes and doing the other last minute things which generally became necessary on these occasions. 'Brace up, we're off in four minutes — a hundred plus approaching Portsmouth!' I braced up, but the fateful bell never rang and we were left chafing on the ground.

During lunch, first one, then three, then another two 213 Hurricanes began coming in. Another big scrap and another good score and so on.

That afternoon was our relief, so under the circumstances I was not surprised to hear at tea-time that the 'A' Flight boys had had another real blitz off Weymouth — again I had missed a big show, but this was not to last long!

Both Flights had been in this one and though the score had been astronomical it could nowhere nearly make up for the great loss we had suffered. Jeff, our Flight commander, had gone down in flames twenty miles out to sea with a score of over ten victories. He missed his wedding by ten days.

Some days before, Johnny Dewar had received promotion to Wing Commander and had taken over command of the station, to our great loss. His place as CO was taken by Squadron Leader Lovell-Grieg, a very 'keen type' whose name was in no time corrupted to 'Shovel!' He had come from Training Command and was so keen to get into action that he hardly ever left the Flights. He had not long to wait.

With the absence of both Flight commanders and the second in command, Derek Ward took over the Flight to everyone's great satisfaction, and another day of tension began on 15 August but nothing happened for the first part.

At 3.50 in the afternoon there was a hasty donning of shirts and Mae Wests by some near naked pilots who had been attempting to change their alcoholic flush to a healthy tan, when the news 'Aircraft massing over Cherbourg' came through.

'A' Flight were away, 213 were already on some other job, and we only had five serviceable aircraft so it looked as if there was going to be work done very soon. At 4.15 pm the 'Ops' bell rang and we all 'took off' about ten feet. 'One hundred and twenty plus approaching Warmwell from the South — Good luck chaps!' said the nice kindly voice from 'Ops', and immediately there followed the usual stampede out to the aircraft of begoggled pilots and half-naked ground crews encouraged by the inevitable 'Sam', Dennis David's bull terrier.

Last minute remarks such as 'OK boys, this is it', and 'See you in the "Rougers"!' then the roar of Merlin engines drowned the rest. A blackguard rush down the field and then, taking up formation, 'B' Flight climbed away eastwards under the glaring August sun.

At Lyme Regis at some 12,000 ft we began to 'weave' and search the sky above and behind and then, way out to starboard, there appeared what could be best described as a gigantic swarm of bees all revolving round each other in a fantastic spiral from about 8,000 ft up to 14,000 ft. Swinging round towards them the CO opened his throttle wide and we all packed in closely behind him; Trevor to the left, myself level with him on the right and Mitchell and David close behind.

As the distance closed, the swarm ahead developed into a great formation of Ju 87s some fifty to sixty strong flying a defensive circle in sections astern, with a close escort of a large number of Me 110s. Above there appeared to be another large formation of Me 109s. 'Shovel' called 'Tally-ho' over the R/T, and I looked across at Mitchell, gave a 'thumbs up' and the next moment 'Shovel' waggled his wings and we were diving 'into the brown!'*

At about 500 ft above the leading enemy formation we peeled off to the left and right into the midst of the swarm, which looked for all the world like some immense spiral staircase. Half rolling inverted, I found a section of Ju 87s coming into my gunsight, when the owner of all the tracers that were suddenly flashing round my cockpit appeared blazing away from right under my nose.

I was diving vertically while the Me 110 was climbing up at the same angle. Just at the crucial moment he stalled right across my bows and I squirted a good burst into his belly from such point-blank range that the bullets could be seen striking and buckling the plating of his wings and fuselage. A flash of flame and a puff of smoke, and I jammed the stick forward just in time to avoid colliding with him.

This had taken some five seconds from start to finish and I was still in the top of the 'vicious circle', and going down fast. I did not have to look for another target as straight below, or rather ahead, came another 110 firing as he came. His shooting was much better than the first and feathery gray lines came slanting past the cockpit on both sides; so close in fact that I remember noting with considerable interest a line of tracer bullets between myself and the roundel on the port wing!

I had more time to aim than on the previous attack and had the

* Shooting term — 'browning the covey'.

satisfaction of seeing my tracers intersecting in the bead of the reflector sight which I held dead on the oncoming Hun. He did not hit me but as, holding it to the last minute we flashed past each other less than about 50 ft apart at a combined speed of over 500 mph, I caught a glimpse of a puff of white. Aileron turning I looked up and there was the Me on its back with a parachute just opened behind it. Number 2!

The air was thick with aircraft: — dark grey Ju 87s, dark green Me 110s with sky blue bellies, pale green and silver 109s; a black Swastika'd horde!

Our attack had apparently upset the whole organization, for no more was it a well-ordered armada filling the sky tier upon tier, but a confused 'dogfight' stretching from Portland to Dorchester, Warmwell to Lyme Regis; while everywhere one looked long black vertical oily streaks in the sky showed where friend and foe alike were on their way down.

By now I was nearing the bottom of the scrap, when suddenly a single Ju 87 appeared in the windscreen. Hauling everything back I fired my last rounds at him and then levelled off at around 400 mph nearly blacking out in the process, and looked round. Apart from the smoke left by 'flamers' on all sides, a 110 flashed past on its back with no tail, while another appeared some distance away violently endeavouring to avoid the attention of two Hurricanes who were busy sealing its fate.

Into these observations a familiar criss-cross of grey pencil lines in my immediate vicinity brought home the fact that Me 109s appeared to be dropping from the heavens again and I was in the way — with no ammunition! Deciding that it would be far better to depart in peace rather than in pieces, I rolled the already ill-used Hurricane into another 400 mph diving aileron turn, and shot into a billowing cumulus cloud upside down just ahead of the Me's.

The cloud base was 4,000 ft as I came out at the bottom, and apparently the battle had taken place right over Portland for Weymouth appeared directly below with both the Bay and the sea off Chessil Bank dotted with yellow circles where aircraft or bombs had gone in.

The tension over I suddenly felt very hot and looking down saw that my uniform jacket was dark with sweat. Sliding back the cockpit hood, I headed back down the coast for Exeter and glanced at my watch; we had been in the air for only 35 minutes! Ten minutes later the aerodrome appeared and I gave vent to my supercharged feelings by beating up 'B' Flight dispersal thoroughly, where all the 'erks' were crowded round one aircraft which was back already.

Dropping in to a landing on the grass by the Mess, I taxied up to the Flight and switched off as all the lads crowded round. Titch Turner, Pond, Guppy, Hazel and all the old-timers were well to the fore. 'How many Sir? Where are they? Good show, that's four so far!' When the hubbub died down I found that Mitchell was back with two destroyed, but no sign of the others. As I walked to the hut talking to some twenty people all as excited as myself, to report to Intelligence, a Hurricane appeared low over the field. It was one of 213, then another as the squadron eventually arrived one by one. They had evidently had a scrap too, but there was still no sign of ours. Then after a quarter of an hour 'R' arrived in a beautiful roll and Dennis David came in claiming two and a half.

Still no sign of Trevor Jay or the CO, but at that moment the telephone rang and on picking up the receiver Trevor's voice came over: 'Hallo Bee, how did it go?' He was speaking from Weymouth police station where he had been taken after crashing on the beach and being mistaken for a short time for an Italian! He was quite unharmed and had two more definitely destroyed. But of the CO there was no news nor was there after a further two hours, and then came a message that he had died trying to force-land near Warmwell.

All these stirring events gave just cause and vast thirst for, as the boys put it, a 'gi-normous' party at the 'Rougers' that evening of which the least said now the better!

The following weeks were a seemingly endless period of blistering days spent at the dispersal awaiting the inevitable 'stand-by — aircraft massing over Cherbourg'; of 'panic' take-offs on further interceptions, and of evenings after days of tension, spent in the style of formation aerobatic and beat-up practice that soon began to give 'B' Flight fame in the neighbourhood. It was not until the end of the month however that we took part in another large scale battle. 'A' Flight had collected all the glory while we were in Gloucestershire at Bibury on night operations.

On the morning of 25 August I was at home in Corsham on the last morning of a 48 hours leave, and after lunch I jammed myself into the MG and set off back through Bath on the Exeter road. After little more than an hour and a quarter I bumped slowly round the perimeter road towards 'B' Flight, just to see how things were going before I went on in to Exeter to change.

Almost as I entered the hut a 'panic' began — 'One hundred and fifty plus approaching St Albans Head,' and before I had time to collect my thoughts I was in good old *LK-L* hastily cramming Mae

West and harness over my spotless 'Branders' (brand-new 'No. 1' uniform); and then we were off.

This time the Squadron was all together, and a brave sight it made climbing away into the usual grilling sun. 'B' Flight with eight aircraft, Johnny Dewar now Station Commander leading, and 'A' Flight above and behind led by 'Widge' Gleed and including the new CO. 15,000 ft was reached as we neared Portland and over to starboard ack-ack bursts revealed twelve fighters circling in line astern. We turned in towards them only to find that they appeared to be Spitfires.

Meantime the R/T was bellowing for all aircraft to proceed to Warmwell, so we headed that way and straight ahead appeared eight little dots which developed into twin-engined bombers as the distance closed. Then five more appeared behind them, then six more and another five until finally as our straining eyes grew accustomed to the glare we were heading for not one formation, but upwards of a hundred German bombers. In the next few seconds as the CO gradually heeled over towards the leading formation of Ju 88s, we scanned the sky above for the fighters which were obviously there. The Huns had seen us by now and a shower of red signal lights shot out and down from them. They were too late for, when we compared notes afterwards we had all fired at least one bomber in the first attack. My particular pigeon was a Dornier 17 which rolled over after one burst.

For a moment I thought of using the speed of my dive to execute a split turn back into the fray again, but lines of tracer bullets caused me to glance over my shoulder, and there directly behind came the Me 109s! Having already seen quite enough of them, *LK-L* went downstairs faster than it was ever designed to and I blacked-out momentarily during the subsequent pull-out.

At 5,000 ft over Dorchester I took stock of the situation. I had evaded the 109s and high above the confused battle was still in progress. As I watched, a ball of orange fire appeared above and flashed by, a sheet of livid flame, and I saw that it was a Hurricane. Then a smaller object fell past at a less rapid pace; it was the wheel and oleo strut of some bomber's undercarriage.

I was now climbing up again when from about dead ahead an aircraft appeared diving from a cloud. Here was a chance — it was a Messerschmitt 109 all by itself and obviously making for home in a hurry. The next moment I was on his tail and as he broke left we slammed round into a dogfight.

In no time the Hurricane got the better of it and as I fired a burst across the circle, the lines of tracer cut into his fuselage. He didn't like that and half-rolling, dived on his back. Following I managed another burst as he rolled out of the dive and that finished him. He slowed considerably and tried one more turn in which I closed right up, then seeing the Hurricane positioned for a *coup-de-grace* he rolled beautifully and followed with a stalled-turn which took my sights off him. The next moment he was side-slipping down towards a large field near Abbotsbury, with a thick trail of smoke behind. Slipping over the hedge he put down neatly on his belly and slewed round in a scurry of dust and smoke or steam. Coming down low to possibly prevent him setting fire to the aircraft, I saw the pilot already standing on the wing doing something in the cockpit. I could not fire at this man who had just put up such a fine exhibition of flying, and the next time round he was standing back as a tongue of flame appeared from the cockpit. Finally the flames took hold of the sky-blue and scarlet Messerschmitt, the tall German lifted his hand in salute as I flew low past him and waved, and he walked slowly across the field to captivity.

Flying round the now-raging fire, I waved at Dennis David who had seen our scrap and come down to have a closer look. Though in my shirt-sleeves this time I was soaked in perspiration, and the silk scarf round my neck was saturated; so I took it off and opening the hood, allowed the slipstream to cool me down as I headed for home at low-level along the coast, waving to groups of soldiers who were everywhere gazing up at the sky.

After the mandatory 'beat-up' I landed and taxied in to find most of the boys already back and gathered round in the usual group, all talking at once. It had been a good scrap and the score seemed to be eleven definitely destroyed among the seven of us. The 'A' Flight phone tinkled and Roddy Rayner's voice came over asking how we had fared, and giving their score as six with two not yet back.

Presently news came through of Sergeant Cowley who had been shot down and was in Weymouth, injured. Then a Hurricane was sighted approaching from the east, but before reaching the aerodrome it nosed over and dived into the ground some miles away. So Peter Comely died. There were many bullet holes in the wreck and his left hand was practically shot away, so he probably fainted through loss of blood.

Back at the Mess for tea to tell everyone the news and hear how 213 had done. The station score for the day was over thirty destroyed of which total 87 Squadron contributed more than half. The next day a message came from HQ, No 10 Group saying 'Congratulations. A great part in a great day, keep up the good work.'

'B' Flight's next week on night operations began on 3 September and we set off in high spirits to Bibury knowing, that we should have ahead a week of real work but under virtually holiday conditions.

Leaving Exeter in a tight 'Vee' of five aircraft with Trevor Jay in 'the Box', we arrived over Bibury in the same drill but much closer and at near ground level. Great fun and always appreciated by the lads on the ground who, once their pilots have put up a good show, can more than hold their own with rival or other units on the camp.

As soon as we had straightened out the mess in which, we considered, 'A' Flight had left our two bell tents, we piled into the Squadron Humber and, driven by Derek Ward in his usual style (either stopped or flat out) we sailed into the pretty village of North Leach to our billet. Here we found Mrs Rigby, our billet host, who really seemed to like having six rather scruffy and noisy 'P/O Prunes' in her lovely old house for weeks on end.

The next move was of course to the Lamb at Burford, and we were soon washing down new bread, cheese and pickled onions with 'Malt 'n 'ops', the delicious ale brewed on the premises.

It had been a cloudy evening and we had not expected night flying, but later looking out we were surprised to find a clear dusk with promise of plenty of starlight. Under the circumstances it was a cheerful if not very efficient group of pilots which emerged from the Humber on Bibury aerodrome as the last rays of sun shone on the balloons on the distant horizon, and dashed into the mobile wireless tender to get 'the gen' from Operations. We should not be wanted for an hour or so yet, so we had time to go to the Mess tent where 'Mitch' was preparing supper.

The meals during our periods of duty at Bibury were unforgettable. The rations were good; the cooking, and on a mobile cooker at that, better; and the red steaks with chips and onions, chops and sprouts, and excellently cooked fish, which we used to eat by the light of a swinging hurricane lamp on the tent poles, are at the moment but painful memories of an all too distant past. Neither will the orderly's 'Bacon and beans Sir!' at five o'clock in the morning ever be forgotten by any of us, but I digress.

The low throb of the unsynchronized enemy engines which we were soon to become accustomed to, now filled the night air until, with a shattering roar, the first Hurricane took off on patrol. A few more moments of sitting round the Primus in the bell tent and drinking tea between intervals of going out to look at the weather, then the next patrol orders came through.

Stampeding feet followed the Flight Sergeant's shout of 'Start

Up "*L*" and "*Y*"!' Little blue flames chased each other in the dark along the cowlings until the exhaust stubs, becoming hot, glowed red.

Then we were away down the flare path and climbing in a gentle circle round the home flashing beacon while gaining height and testing R/T. Setting course for the Bristol area it was not long before the weaving searchlight beams, which everywhere pierced the darkness, began to pick me up for a few dazzling moments until they recognized my identification signal. Presently, after casting about for some landmark to check on and failing to see anything I called up for a position and got no response, but at that moment I sighted the dim outline of the Severn and began my patrol.

There was no visual horizon owing to the thick atmosphere, and in my very inexperienced state where night flying was concerned I was continually 'crossing the controls' and finding myself at all sorts of odd angles. This necessitated constant reference to instruments and therefore relaxed vigilance. Soon however, Operations warned of five EA approaching my patrol line, and almost immediately an intersection of searchlights appeared to the south, clearly heading my way. Passing a thousand yards or so to port and turning sharply towards it, I closed up to roughly five hundred yards behind and a few hundred feet below the apex of this brilliant intersection of more than twelve searchlights. As I followed almost in the lights, the guns of Bristol opened fire and though the shell bursts around were somewhat disturbing, I felt sure that I must soon see the Hun who was so obviously just ahead somewhere; but nothing was visible in the glare.

We eventually passed out of the searchlight zone and as the beams swung off after fresh targets one by one. I was forced to return to the patrol line. This was not difficult as there were now at least six searchlight intersections, some containing up to twenty lights, illuminating the Bristol area. I was climbing up towards the apex of the nearest group with the intention of trying again, when right over the heart of the city intersected in so many lights that the glare reflected faintly on the ground itself, was a Hun; a glittering fly in the centre of a gigantic irridescent web.

At full throttle and shouting 'Tally-ho' down the wireless, I dived all out in an attempt to close the range, for I knew that if I did not reach him before he got to the edge of the searchlight zone I should lose him. At an indicated speed of 290 mph the distance began to close, slowly; too slowly in fact as the Ju 88, as I now recognized it, was also diving and already south of Bristol. A glance at the altimeter showed 6,000 ft and I knew that the balloons must be uncomfortably close, and the more northern searchlight posts in this particular group were switching out one by one already.

The range was at least 400 yards still, but the Hun was making good shooting and his bright red tracers were sailing by quite close. At the same time his speed had increased so much that it was obvious that I should be unable to close any more and so I fired a short burst to see the effect. One of the AA shells which had been much in evidence during the past moments chose to go off very close at that moment, and after bouncing round the sky in the concussion I managed to get the gunsight back on to the target and let fly a number of bursts at him.

It is difficult to put into words the picture I shall always retain of that moment: the dark outline of the hood frame, the glimmer of the instruments and the glowing red bead of the gunsight in the centre of the windscreen, and outside nothing but a confused jumble of brilliant beams of light. In the centre an aeroplane, light grey in the glare with little white flashes appearing all over it and apparently connected to my aircraft by slightly curving lines of red and white tracer bullets looking like tramlines on a wet night. The whole, seen through the glare of flame from the gun muzzles in the wings at each burst, gave the mounting impression that there was no earth and sky. Certainly there were no material indications of these facts, everything else being obliterated by the glare, and the Ju 88, the searchlights and tracer bullets were it seemed the only things in existence.

Four searchlights only held us now, and a stream of the red short-range Bofors shells floating by were a sudden reminder that we were both probably about to dive into the ground. We were in fact still over 3,000 ft, but the 88 dived even more steeply and my ammunition ran out in the middle of a burst at some 200 yards range: one engine at least must have been hit. At this point the Hun half-rolled slowly on to his back, and not wishing to go downstairs inverted at night at that altitude myself, I saw him fall away vertically out of the last of the searchlights, and then avoiding them myself I looked over the side hoping to see an explosion. Nothing happened, so I tried to find my position and was somewhat shaken when I did so. Returning roughly the way I had come I suddenly realized that I was approaching Avonmouth from the sea and at 3,000 ft. Our chase had taken us right through the balloon barrage without doubt!

Back at the camp excitement reigned as Trevor Jay had also 'squirted', and hopes ran high. It was a cheerful huddle of pilots round the Primus as we told our tales, but we could get no definite confirmation, though the 'guns' had reported my scrap and had last seen the 88 diving out to sea beyond Avonmouth, at which point all other reports of it ended also.

The following night there was greater keenness than ever to get into the air. Again Trevor Jay and I had the luck to sight Heinkel 111s and fire all our rounds at them, though in my case from indecisive range unfortunately.

The weather closed down on the following few days and nights, and some pleasant parties were indulged in. On 12 September however came terrible, incredible news: Johnny Dewar was dead. While on a visit to Tangmere he had joined in a battle over Southampton and was never seen alive again. It was difficult to believe that this man who was almost worshipped by the airmen and universally admired and backed by the pilots for his love of action and intense devotion to duty at all times, was now out of the running.

A cloud settled on us and, aided by continuous wet weather which turned our encampment into a morass and our tents into canvas covered waterholes, depressed us to such an extent that we were looking forward to returning to Exeter once again.

The day for our return came on 14 September and we squelched over to our four remaining serviceable aeroplanes laden with pyjamas and gear to tuck away in any odd available places. We flew down to Exeter in open 'Box' formation, with Johnny Cock leading, Mitchell and Trevor Jay on the left and behind respectively and myself on the right, and in the neighbourhood of Bath climbed through the clouds and set course above them.

Cock was somewhat out in his calculations and when we broke cloud again we had overshot Exeter and were way down towards Plymouth. After caustic R/T remarks from Operations about our navigation and suitable replies from nearly every member of the formation, we headed back towards Exeter, and when passing Dartmouth closed in to the tight formation which we had perfected during the past months.

Suddenly, without any warning, Cock's Hurricane fell back. His motor had cut and so sharply that Mitchell and I were only just able to pull out and away on each side to allow his wings to pass back underneath. I throttled right back, turned left gently and there, a few hundred feet below I saw Trevor Jay gliding with the stumps of his shattered airscrew spinning slowly. Cock, who had smashed straight on to Trevor in his position in the 'Box', was nowhere to be seen. Mitchell and I closed in towards Trevor, and glancing at my altimeter I sighed with relief when I saw 1,800 ft on it.

At that moment Trevor knocked away his escape panel, waved and then climbed over the side and slipped back past the aircraft, turning over and over. I was counting seconds unconsciously until I realized that I had counted over twenty and Trevor was already very low. There was to be no puff of white silk, and Trevor dropped into a steep hillside and rolled down it into a gully on the other side of which lay his blazing Hurricane. I did not know where Johnny had got to, but he managed to recover and he crashlanded at Exeter with very little remaining elevator and rudder surfaces.

Cock and Mitchell were posted away from the Squadron, and I went on leave. When I returned the other two had both gone to Training Command, and 'B' Flight was looking very thin and depressed. But under Derek Ward's energetic leadership we carried on with occasional blitzes in the South and weeks of night flying at Bibury for the next month, and soon the old high standard showed signs of returning.

Mud and rain began to render Bibury almost useless towards the middle of November, and disturbing rumours began to circulate. They were substantiated when the Squadron was moved from its happy home base at Exeter and the 'Rougers', and Bibury operations were cancelled.

The Battle of Britain was now seen to be over and so bidding a sad and alcoholic farewell to hundreds of friends, we departed to our new base in the Bristol area to become, as the boys put it, full time 'Night Hawks!'

'Johnny' Dewer, CO of 87 Squadron and the first DSO, DFC in the Battle of Britain. Exeter August 1940 (Watson Collection).

'Roddy' Rayner of 'A' Flight, 87 Squadron, at Exeter (Watson Collection).

Rolls-Royce representative 'Matter' Martin flies in 87's Tiger Moth at Bibury. (L to R) Tait, Gleed, Comeley (Watson Collection).

Above *The author's Hurricane LK-L on a wet day at Bibury* (Author's Collection).

Left *The author at Exeter in August 1940* (Author's Collection).

Above right *Johnny Cock's Hurricane after colliding with Trevor Jay's propeller in September 1940* (Perry Adams Collection)

Right *Cowley, Thoroughgood, Rayner at Bibury* (Watson Collection).

Above *'Rubber' Thoroughgood's blind 'landing' on a dark night near Yatesbury* (Penny Adams Collection).

Left *'Mac' MacClure of 'B' Flight, 87 Squadron 1940* (Watson Collection).

Chapter 5

NIGHT FIGHTER

By January 1941 87 Squadron, with its replacement pilots following the end of the Battle of Britain had acquired a high standard of day and night training, and practice was indulged in whenever possible from our new 'mountain' retreat, Charmy Down in Somerset.

One day we went down to Blandford for 'air-to-ground' firing on the range. On arrival both signal discs were removed denoting the 'cease-fire', and a smoke candle lit to tell us to go back. Therefore Derek Ward, displaying his propensity for overcoming obstacles, dived to the attack followed by the rest of the Flight.

After beating merry hell out of all available targets we set course for home, beating up a Curtis 'Mohawk' (from Boscombe Down) on the way to show that there was no ill-feeling. We landed to discover that it was not our day for air-firing and that the Whirlwinds, whose allotted day it was, were ever so cross!

January and February passed slowly, the days spent in visiting other aerodromes, practising formation aerobatics and dogfighting. The nights were spent crouching round the dispersal hut fire trying to keep at least one's front half warm, between patrols in the darkness, sometimes in snow or rain and nearly always in severe icing conditions, hoping against hope to find something to shoot at. Typical of this period is the following diary entry.

Feb 21st 1941
After section aerobatics by Badger, Ward and Beamont, in the evening cloud increased to 8/10 after sunset and a squadron patrol was ordered over Swansea. Naturally as it was outside our Sector we had never received the Swansea patrol lines, or knew where they were.

Under these circumstances therefore, together with very doubtful weather conditions, we were not in any way surprised when the order came through at 20.00 hours for ten aircraft to proceed halfway across England without wireless assistance.

It was a moving sight to see the airfield lit up with slowly moving red and green lights as the Hurricanes taxied out. From my position as 'last off' there seemed to be a practically endless procession of them as they swung one after the other onto the runway, and then roared off into the night leaving a flurry of snow dancing in the flickering light of the paraffin flare path.

Then my turn came and I was away down the narrow channel of lights suspended apparently in nothingness, until that too was gone and all outside was blackness.

A brief circuit to gain height, set course, and then in the climb even greater blackness than before as the clouds closed round until an age later, with a sensation akin to waking from a very deep sleep all became grey light as the last filmy wisps of cloud raced past and I headed west under the moon and stars with an endless carpet of grey-white cloud beneath.

Keeping a careful check on time, height and airspeed, I flew on until ahead and a little to the north a dull glow lit the cloud sheet below. Obviously the Hun had not wasted his time, but at the end of an hour of searching over the target area I had not sighted anything to shoot at, or any landmarks, and it was time to return home.

The clouds had thickened considerably by this time and after entering the tops at 7,000 ft I did not see a thing for some ten minutes: then I broke cloud at 1,500 ft right over a flashing beacon. A quick glance at my 'gen' card for the letter it was flashing gave my position, and within five minutes the home beacon appeared winking cheerfully out of the night ahead: time 22.30 hours.

Finally the landing: there's the green signal light. Wheels down, flaps down, turn in at 800 ft, airscrew fine pitch, throttle back to 100 mph, 95 mph at 150 ft, here's the end of the flare path, throttle right back and hold off, damn those exhaust sparks! Rumble-rumble. Not bad, only two bounces. Now for a cup of tea and sausage and mash.

For a week after this snow fell heavily and it was almost impossible to navigate our way to 'B' Flight through the snow drifts. The main road became littered with ditched, bent and over-turned cars.

These conditions failed to deter 10 Group however, who gave us to understand that on no account must snow be regarded as a non-operational condition. So every morning two runways 1,000 × 50 yards had to be swept clean. It needed at least 200 men with shovels working eight hours to do this, and everyone turned to: working contractors, technical personnel, pilots, Flight commanders, in fact anyone who could wield a shovel.

After one particularly heavy night's snow-storm, 150 extra men were fetched from the Labour Exchange in Bath and dumped on the frozen aerodrome with shovels. They were to be paid 'time and a half' for this job of really immediate national importance. In fifteen minutes they had all departed, saying it was much too cold there anyway, and left the job to the pilots and groundcrew who had been on duty all through the previous night and would be again that night.

From time to time mention has been made of the work of the ground crews in the squadrons, but not enough. The work of 87's ground crews, servicing aircraft by the light of hand torches from five o'clock in the winter evenings until five the following morning, often in driving snow, bitter winds and, worst of all, the driving rain that freezes where it touches, was incredible. It was work which necessitated hours on end in the open, under conditions which completely numbed the pilots during the three minutes taken from the Dispersal Hut to the cockpit and often caused cases of frostbite among the airmen. This work called for the highest endurance and devotion to duty and has not, to my mind, been widely acknowledged, especially as the people concerned were those same lads who a year before had endured the mud of Merville, the ice of Seclin and eventually the putrid water and bombs of Senon, throughout the Winter and Spring of 1939–40.

On the night of 8/9 March Derek Ward decided to carry out a practice night cross-country exercise to Exeter in formation. At nine o'clock we went off into a moonlit but hazy sky, and for the next thirty minutes I saw nothing but the flaring exhausts and navigation lights of the other two aircraft, relying entirely in the usual way on the leader's navigation. Eventually Derek Ward turned the formation steeply to port, and looking down through a grey void there was the Exeter airport building vaguely outlined in the hazy moonlight beyond the dark silhouette of Ward's Hurricane.

After diving low over the field in tight 'Vic' with all our lights on, always a pretty sight in a night sky, we broke away and 'beat up' the area individually before landing.

The station was in a state of considerable excitement. 'Night formation cross-countries for practice! Never heard of such a thing in fighters!' was the general atmosphere, and a car was waiting to convey us to the Mess where the bar had been kept open.

Here, around a blazing fire, we swopped yarns with Micky and Tony Rooke and some 504 pilots over cans of ale, until it became obvious that the latter practice had better cease! Later, on the way back to Dispersal, the atmosphere appeared to be considerably more hazy, though no-one ventured to suggest that this pheno-menon might be more alcoholic than meteorological.

Once in the air my suspicions proved correct and I had difficulty in locating the small white tail-light of Derek's aircraft, more especially as every time Badger and I attempted to close in to formation with him, Ward dived back down on the moonlit camp and rolled up into the night sky again!

Eventually we sorted things out and set off in formation into the haze in the rough direction of Charmy Down. When our estimated time of flight had been exceeded by about five minutes I began to take an active interest in things once again, and taking a good look round I was somewhat concerned to note that we were apparently flying into a blank wall of mist on all sides with no lights or other ground features in sight.

Presently Badger's voice piped up over the R/T saying to Derek: 'Hey, where the Hell are you off to? We passed the beacon some minutes ago!' Back we went and presently our beacon reappeared dimly to port but was lost again as Derek began a turn onto the heading for the aerodrome circuit. Very sticky this. We changed formation into line astern and I followed Derek's tail-light in the mist somewhat grimly until I realized that we were turning gently to port and again passing directly over the beacon which, though normally visible at our height for 25 miles, was now only dimly in sight from a few hundred yards.

Realizing that Derek was beginning a near-blind approach, I swung out and throttled back to a position about 800 yards behind him, but just keeping in sight the little white tail-light ahead which was still my only guide to the aerodrome. Ward had seen a rocket from the airfield while over the beacon and was thus able to gauge the rough direction of the down-wind end of the flare-path.

At this point I caught sight of a rocket and then a succession of 'Very' lights. 'B' Flight was obviously enjoying its nightly 'Brocks Benefit'. The tail-light of Derek's machine then suddenly disap-peared into the ground mist ahead. A quick check of undercarriage, pressures, temperatures, revs and harness showed that I could go in now, so rather than try to find the place again and make another approach with the weather becoming even worse, and knowing that Badger was behind also trying to follow me down, I went straight on hoping that Derek would be off the runway when I arrived!

The mist layer closed round at 400 ft and at 200 ft I became apprehensive; at 150 ft on the altimeter and still in cloud at 100 mph, my left hand was itching to open up the throttle. But it was now or never, and then as the altimeter went 'off the clock' lights appeared miraculously almost dead ahead. Arriving over the flood-light in a steep turn half in and half out of cloud on a long burst of throttle, we hit hard ground solidly and every bounce brought a feeling of relief until we rolled off the flare-path and I saw Derek's navigation lights as he waited for us before taxying back to dispersal. Together we watched Badger suddenly appear out of the glaring white mist bank which seemed to touch the top of the 'Chance' floodlight.

It had been an exciting evening with a dramatic ending and we were more than ready to go to bed 'early' at 2.45 am when 'Released' because of the weather!

For the remainder of the moon period the nights continued to be fine and clear and when the Hun was active, 15–20 flying hours per Flight each night was quite a normal occurrence. They were mostly 'Politician Patrols' as we called the ordinary 1½ hour patrols between specified points, and not the more interesting style of controlled interceptions with which the Beaufighters were beginning to steal our thunder. On one night, however, MacLure did one of the GCI* patrols and was definitely under the impression that he had flown for some time in a Hun slipstream without being able to sight the machine in the thick hazy darkness.

On some nights after sitting round the fire singing to the accompaniment of MacLure's guitar, eating supper cooked on the stove, brewing tea or cocoa and yarning until midnight with no patrol orders having come through, rather than waste clear flying conditions we would, with 10 Group's permission, all take-off for an hour's practice. This took various forms such as night navigation, practice attacks, but chiefly formation. Often on these 'quiet' nights the neighbourhood would be treated to the throb of five, sometimes six Hurricanes and to the sight of six pairs of navigation lights and six tail-lights wheeling as one against the night sky. It was good fun and good training, especially when we extended this to night formation aerobatics.

Sometimes I was able to go up and enjoy myself in the

* Ground controlled interception.

moonlight, a thing which I could always do happily for hours, trying loops and rolls off loops and eventually inverted flying, although I did not accomplish the latter with confidence until the following summer at Fairwood.

On 25 February 1941, a night of wonderful visibility, I decided to see what high altitude was like in darkness. After about 45 minutes of climbing I found that I could just hold 34,600 ft indicated. I was now very cold and using full oxygen, and looking down to check my position I was surprised to see two red beacons winking almost side by side and was puzzled at the problem which this presented. Where on earth in this sector were there two beacons so close together? Then I realized that the southern light was flashing the letter for our base and that I was looking down at two lights, not one mile, but 35 miles apart, the other being our old base, Bibury.

I could see the Bristol channel stretching mistily away into the west. In the south the moon shone clearly on the sea in the neighbourhood of Weymouth and again in the direction of Bournemouth. Fierce gun flashes illuminated the east and I imagined that London was being raided; while dotted here and there throughout the whole dark area little winking lights gave the positions of nearly a dozen different aerodromes.

A night fighter's dream but it was getting even colder and I was in no mood for further soliloquy, so putting the nose down I began the long and tedious process of losing all this height as quickly as possible without damaging my eardrums. Then, when I landed and walked into the hut and started a cup of tea before turning in, 'Ops' came through with 'two aircraft patrol line B at 15,000 ft: two others line E at 10,000 ft'. No sleep for us before dawn now, but perhaps there was a chance of getting a Hun.

On 14 March 1941 a cloudless but hazy day, we were having tea in the Mess when Roddy Rayner and I were summoned to the CO's office urgently. Group had just ordered a moonlight raid on Caen Carpiquet, an enemy aerodrome in Normandy, and we were to leave for Warmwell in Dorset in thirty minutes.

Chaos! The office floor was soon covered with maps and aerial photographs of the target aerodrome. Tracks were worked out and plans of attack discussed with reference to targets and gun-posts. Then with our pockets crammed with revolvers, electric flotation torches, 100 franc notes and other essentials, we took off into the evening mist heading south.

Landing at Warmwell at dusk we set about checking the wind and weather to calculate the courses, and make final arrangements before going over to the Mess for a meal. Then for seven and a half hours we sat in the empty Mess occasionally eating bread and dripping and drinking coffee, there being no other provisions for us in this day-only fighter station, while odd Huns droned overhead on their way to Bristol or the Midlands.

A few times we drove down to the airfield in the cold moonlight to warm up the engines, but it was a very long wait before the order to take off came at 2.00 am. Then while starting up Roddy found that none of his electrical gear would work: so amid much vituperation from Roddy who seemed to think that I had something to do with it, in my capacity as spare pilot I started off after the CO myself. I had hardly become airborne however when a Hurricane came by at full throttle with all navigation lights blazing and wings rocking violently. Roddy had found that his generator switch had been in the OFF position!

Now it was my turn to swear, for the order was that definitely only two aircraft were to go over, so there was nothing for it but to return and, after much arguing with the controller who did not seem to know what was going on, I obtained permission to return to Charmy Down after a patrol out to in-sight of Cherbourg on the off chance of an interception.

I reached base in poor visibility at 3.30 am and was depressed when I heard of the excitement the chaps had had; but I need not have been as I was soon to have plenty of that sort of activity myself.

On arrival at the camp one evening for the usual night flying tests, we noticed a pile of firewood in the middle of the aerodrome and after a microscopic examination of the various pieces decided that it had once been a Miles Magister. In the Dispersal hut we found a rather jaded pilot who had apparently come over to collect a Whirlwind which had gone already in any case, and he said he had 'swung a bit on landing'. It was quite a masterly understatement.

Soon after dark a huge fire in the direction of Bristol augured hard work for us, and continuous patrols were flown till after midnight.

During the evening, billows of acrid smoke and a livid glare from the Dispersal kitchen caused considerable apprehension among the pilots either just in from or going out to patrol. Excitement reached fever point when a platefull of blazing sandwiches came hurtling out of the conflagration, to the accompaniment of a roar of flames and an undercurrent of language as lurid as the fire itself. There was no need for alarm however, as it proved to be only the Flight commander attempting to make some supper.

1 April 1941 found me hurtling dangerously through a wild snow storm *en route* for the Balkans! A taciturn message which had reached my billet from the Mess at Batheaston to the effect that we were off overseas immediately, did not appear to me in the treacherous light in which it should have on such a date, and I lost no time in driving to the Mess, only to be greeted with roars of merriment and assurances that all the others had been caught in the same trap!

Three days later, came an order for a section to operate from Exeter which had been receiving much attention from the enemy at dusk recently. Arriving there at teatime, Derek Ward and I were strolling across the grass talking of the 'old days' in 1940, and wishing that we were back in Devon for good, when round came MacLure with our spare aircraft from Charmy Down and landed with his wheels up on the runway, just, apparently, as if he didn't need them.

By last-light the weather had closed down and a fine rain was falling under cloud at 200 ft, making flying unlikely we thought and so we went into Operations for a conference with the senior controller, an old friend from our previous spells at Exeter, who gloried in the unusual though magnificent nickname of 'Gdumphy!'

The day squadrons were 'released' by 10 Group owing to the bad weather, a most unusual proceeding, and the night was therefore expected to be quiet. So for some minutes in the 'Ops Room' we watched with surprise a plot of three suspected hostile aircraft which was a hundred miles out to sea and heading WNW down Channel. Suddenly it turned NW and the next three plots showed it heading for Start Point. There was a convoy putting out of Dartmouth and it was becoming irksome watching the enemy approaching: after all if they could fly in that weather, surely we could.

For once Gdumphy, who was always enthusiastic for any type of difficult operation, seemed rather dubious; but seeing the glint in his eye at the chance of an interception, Derek and I lost no further time in bumping over the field in our Ford van, which back-fired all the way. In two and a half minutes from reaching the aircraft (which had been stood down) we had started up without groundcrew and were off the ground and heading down the Exe at 150 ft. I was rather regretting all this and had lost Ward at take-off as visibility in the last grey light of dusk under thick cloud and in very heavy rain, was little more than 1,200 yards.

On reaching Dartmouth, clouds on the cliffs forced me out to sea until I saw the harbour entrance just dimly visible to starboard, and then I began a sweep due south hoping as I did so that I would be able to find land again without hitting it first.

Gdumphy came over the air at this point with 'Bandits two miles south of you'. This was getting exciting and suddenly a shout of 'Tally-ho' came from Derek over the R/T, apparently very close. At the same moment green and white tracer fire came out of the rain in all directions and a Hurricane curved over above me into the cloud; I disappeared into cloud at about 300 ft and thought 'now for it' as I pushed the nose down to find the sea again. The next moment tracer fire seemed to come out of the sea itself and there ahead was a twin-engined aircraft only about 200 yards away. With thumb jammed down on the gun button I fired at it until it disappeared into cloud again, and as I followed I continued firing into the cloud ahead for a second.

With a certain amount of relief I emerged clear of the cloud-base just in time to become reoriented by the sight of a dim shadow of land to port, and so avoided diving into the sea. The land turned out to be Torquay, 'the Huns must be heading east now — God! Exeter!' were the thoughts that flashed across my mind. The wireless was vibrating with vituperation from both Derek and I, for we had each lost sight of the Huns. Derek was even worse off than I for he could see neither Huns, sea nor land.

Creeping down the coast, which I could still just see from 200 ft by peering hard through the rain-swept hood, I flew on. Gdumphy was giving positions of the Huns at intervals of only a few minutes and I appeared to be within a few hundred yards of them continually. At the mouth of the Exe tracers again came out of the rainy darkness to port, and turning quickly I got in a short burst at the Hun which was flying on a parallel course to mine before. I then lost him again in the darkness, and the next coherent remark of the controller was: 'Bandits five miles south of and heading for Base. Brace up chaps!'

What could one do but carry on at full throttle in the rough direction of Base which almost immediately erupted ahead into a glare of explosions, tracer shells and bullets and incendiary bombs against the storm-swept night ahead.

A Hun then made the mistake of machine-gunning the ground on his way over. Seeing the lines of tracer going down instead of up just below me and to starboard, I turned on him, firing as I came and continued firing as he climbed steeply until disappearing into the very low cloud-base. Cursing I circled disconsolately round the fires and wondered what to do about landing, while the one-sided conversation which Derek was carrying on over the R/T with the now obviously defunct ground station would undoubtedly have set fire to the Operations room had it not been burning already.

The cloud base was becoming even lower and the now torrential rain rendered the blackness almost opaque, and if it had not been for a burning Wellington on the tarmac I should certainly have never found the aerodrome again. As it was I had to keep spinning round in tight turns almost 'on the deck' to keep what was actually a very big fire in sight. It was also an interesting point that Derek's Hurricane was probably doing the same thing unseen in the same area.

The main trouble was that all the ground personnel were so busy putting out fires and incendiaries that they had forgotten (or did not intend to in the circumstances) to turn on the runway 'glim lamps', and there was no hope of getting them to do so as the R/T was out of action. There remained two alternatives: a crash landing with wheels up somewhere near the bonfire, or an attempt at finding and landing on the narrow and possibly obstructed runway, while the whole time one's windshield was opaque with rain.

The last course was the best, naturally, and after a very low circuit, keeping the fire just in sight, I glimpsed the vague line of the runway which was into wind. Wasting no time I lowered wheels and flaps and turned to where I imagined the end of the runway should be, keeping direction from the fire. Luckily I caught a fleeting sight of the main Honiton-Exeter road as it flashed by 100 ft below and realized just in time that I was some 50 yards to the left of the runway centre-line and flying parallel to it! A frantic and very 'ham' S-turn manoeuvre and then I was bouncing along in the darkness at 80 mph with nothing to steer on except the short-range aircraft landing-light, and the fact of having to aim well to the left of the flickering fire. On the deck at last and rolling to a stop, and there came Derek's navigation lights following me in.

Descending from the cockpit shakily, for the last half hour or so had not been very easy, I found a shambles. Seemingly dozens of heavy bombs had landed between the administration block and the main hangar, and that area seemed to consist of piles of wreckage and heaps of earth and rubble, eerie in the glare of the fire which was defying all attempts to extinguish it.

Damage was quite heavy but not as bad as it looked. The Operations block had received a very near miss; about four 500 kilos all within 25 yards and one, which did most of the damage, at about ten feet. The Ops staff were crawling rather shakily from under the plotting tables, and the Intelligence Office was wrecked, while the other end of the block was no longer in existence.

During our groping tour of inspection we encountered a swaying figure dolefully surveying a dent in his 'Battle Bowler' which he, our spare pilot Badger, affirmed as being the result of blast hurling him head first into the nearest brick wall. In fact on the following day he had definite shellshock and was quite shaky.

The only serious casualties other than the one man killed, were two of our most valuable men: Corporal Gilby and 'Blondie' Walton who had severe bullet or splinter wounds through shoulder, arm and chest. After seeing them in the sick bay, by which time they were barely conscious, we went to the Mess before turning in. Here we heard that only two aircraft had bombed the camp, and as Derek had seen three in formation off Dartmouth, there was a chance that we had got one of them or at any rate winged it and prevented it from reaching the target.

So finally to bed, but there was another shock to come yet. The next morning we wandered round the camp, viewing craters, wrecked aeroplanes and the courageous demolition squad headed by the station armament officer, cheerfully hammering away with cold chisels at 500 kilo bombs, four or five of which had met the ground at such a shallow angle that they had just skimmed along the surface and failed to explode.

Then came the blow. I saw Derek staring rather fixedly at something over my shoulder and looking slightly pale, and there right in the middle of the runway down which we had effected landings in pitch darkness and rain without runway flares or lights of any kind, was a crater fully thirty feet wide and ten feet deep which must have been caused by another 500 kilo (1,000 lb) bomb. If either of us had been straight during our landing runs on that runway we should probably have suffered broken necks at least. Oh well!

This raid made us more than ever keen to get into the air after the Huns which came over every night, though perhaps the scandalous accusations put out by our day fighter friends in 504 that we only flew to keep out of the way of the bombs had something to do with it! The work, though hard, was interesting as there was no dearth of enemy activity; weather from the point of view of interception conditions was often good, and above all the wireless control was becoming really excellent.

Derek went off from Exeter at dusk on 6 April over 10/10ths cloud, and from then on we maintained patrols throughout the night. I went on my second patrol at 03.00 hours on the 7th, and as soon as I became airborne realized that the weather was deteriorating. However the R/T was working well, so I set off and entering cloud at 1,500 ft, broke through into hazy moonlight at 3,500 ft.

Once above the dead flat cloud sheet I climbed to 10,000 ft in wide circles waiting for R/T instructions. These soon came and an hour went by following various vectors and searching the moonlit sky with concentration, for on some occasions I came, according to Control, very close to enemy bombers. Presently I asked for my position as it is always comforting to know roughly while above cloud, and the reply was '120 miles due south of Start Point'. I wished that I had not been so inquisitive and began to check the fuel gauges and my Mae West.

Another EA plot appeared just then and I was vectored after him and did not give up the chase for about thirty minutes, by which time the next position given to me was 'overhead Minehead', there being a strong southerly wind blowing us along at that altitude. The fuel gauge showed that it was time to go home now and Control gave a course to fly on which would, by descending all the way, hopefully bring us out of cloud over the coast, always a good landmark on a dark night. (Although there was a moon, it would be dark below the thick cloud sheet).

Setting speed and a comfortable rate of descent I soon found that the cloud was considerably thicker than before, and at 7,000 ft entered the tops and settled down to some intensive instrument work. Cloud flying at night is a unique experience in a fighter. It can be best compared with an underground train. You are in a small, quite brightly lit box with a continuous noise and vibration which reminds you that you are travelling fast, but there is nothing outside to confirm that fact. Occasionally wisps of exceptionally thick moisture will be visible racing by faintly illuminated by the glow of the exhaust ports, but the instruments a few inches in front of you are the only true indications that things are still happening fast outside your little world.

The ASI showing 240 mph, the revolution counter steady and the artificial horizon and giro showing a straight course and a wings-level, gentle descent, all flatly deny the sensation inevitably growing that you are doing a sharp climbing turn and will soon be stalled or inverted.

After fifteen minutes Control said: 'You are now crossing the coast, descend to 2,000 ft and return on a reciprocal bearing until you sight the coast'. The next order was 'Descend to cloud base', then 'Are you out of cloud yet?' At 800 ft and still in cloud I began to perspire and describing the situation rather pointedly over the

R/T, I climbed back to 2,000 ft on my original course.

Control then said: 'You are now 20 miles south of Exmouth, turn 180° and fly on reciprocal. Try to get below cloud'. This turn having been gingerly carried out, the instrument panel was beginning to play tricks with my eyes by this time as I watched the altitude dropping, 800 ft, 600, 200 and still complete blankness outside; so up we went again to 1,500 ft to ensure clear radio contact.

Control sounded almost as worried as I felt by now, and said 'OK, we'll bring you over Base. You are now over Exmouth'. Then they gave a correction of course and said 'You are two miles south of Base, come as low as you can and you should see the flare-path'. So once again the altimeter swung down and when passing 400 ft, almost immediately below I saw a red light and then a white one. I had broken out of the cloud after half an hour of cloud flying right over the floodlight at the end of the flare-path. There could be no better praise for the ground station control than this episode, which speaks for itself.*

So with the first light of daybreak tinging the eastern darkness, we rolled into bed feeling that nothing less than twelve hours' sleep could possibly put us on our feet again. Almost after touching the pillow it seemed, but in reality four hours later, we were up again and off back to Charmy Down to collect new aircraft and spares needed in time for more operations that night.

From dusk onwards work began at pressure as high as the previous night, and we had to shake off fatigue with benzedrine supplied by the MO. The following day we returned to Charmy Down feeling very drowsy indeed, but this was soon forgotten when we heard that at last Derek Ward and I were to go over to France that night, 9 April.

---

* This was in the earliest days of radar recovery by the original surveillance/defence radars and before the development of the precision 'Ground Controlled Approach' systems with special radar which began to be introduced late in 1941.

Chapter 6

RAIDS AND THE END OF THE FIRST PHASE

At Charmy Down on 9 April there followed the usual feverish collecting of revolvers. Port Fires*, maps, French francs and odds and ends, and the emptying of pockets of security items; and then with 'Good luck' from the ground crews in our ears we took off for Warmwell in Dorset. After overcoming the disorganization and lack of co-operation which seemed characteristic of that station at that period, we settled down to six hours of suspense in the Mess.

By the time the order to take off came at 01.00 hours I had begun to feel quite nervous and I think Derek felt much the same, but once the crackle of Merlins broke the calm of the moon I felt an exultant thrill. 140 miles away were the enemy and we were going off together to beat them up. It was a good feeling.

We had no need for the flare-path as we took off under a bright moon down the misty grass airfield, and in a few moments the white cliffs of Dorset fell behind as we climbed towards broken clouds silver-edged with moonlight over a sea pock-marked with cloud shadows. There was then some energetic formation work through a rough cloud layer before we settled down to fifty minutes' flying over nothing but cold sea, throttled back and in very weak mixture, for our fuel endurance was at the most two and a half hours, and this raid would take a minimum of two hours with no mishaps.

Descending through cloud we found no horizon at all at 2,000 ft, but we could see the sea and presently Cap de la Hague loomed up briefly as a comforting shadow to starboard before disappearing as we headed into the Seine Bay.

At 45 minutes no land was in sight but another five minutes saw the low French coastline passing underneath with the clouds

* Flares.

breaking above. That peaceful-looking countryside below was Hunland, and home was 130 miles away across the sea. Now for it. Gun buttons on 'Fire', gunsight on; straps tightened and with everything set I swung away from the dark silhouette of Derek's Hurricane and began to weave in search of the target, but there was no need as it found us! A few moments after we had left the coastline behind and split up, and were searching for the canal which would lead us to the aerodrome, four searchlights snapped on and two of them illuminated Derek immediately.

In accordance with pre-arranged plans I dived towards the brightest light which was holding on to Derek tenaciously as he weaved. I opened fire from behind the beam at about 400 ft, continuing until I flashed over the emplacement as it snapped out. At that moment I could clearly see men lying on the ground in the open where they may have been hit by some of those hundreds of tracer bullets.

That post never came to life again, but now the sky was weaving with streams of red, green and orange shells from a number of ack-ack posts. It was a wonderful sight until two guns opened fire almost under my nose, I was flying at 500 ft still, and as twin lines of tracer shells flashed close by my cockpit I ducked instinctively. The blighters were becoming offensive, and I remembered that the aerodrome had still to be found.

To starboard the night was a storm of weaving interlacing lines of tracer fire from many guns and Derek was obviously having a warm reception, so feeling that I had better go in that direction, I opened the throttle wide and, just skimming the faintly outlined tree tops, headed towards the nearest active gun position.

My lines of tracer slashed down into the post and the gun stopped firing, but then all the other guns realized that another attack was on the way and swung in my direction. Instantly the air became an intricate pattern of balls of fire, but except for when I flew directly over a gun at point-blank range, most of the fire went overhead as I was at very low level and presented a difficult target.

Straight ahead I saw a line of hangars, and flying across runways and grass at an altitude for which I should have been court martialled at home, I was able to pour a long burst into the dim shape of a bomber parked on the field. Continuing the burst into one of the hangars and then down a long line of barrack huts, I had to pull the stick back hard to clear a wood which suddenly loomed up ahead. Immediately two searchlights held me and all Hell was let loose again. Adding to the blinding glare at that altitude, tracer shells flashing by made it impossible to see either ground or instruments, and for a few moments things were very uncomfortable.

Eventually the guns were left behind and I looked round to take stock of the situation. A railway line appeared glinting in front and a red signal light and the glow of an engine furnace showed the presence of a train. A closer inspection showed it to consist of a line of box cars and then machine gun tracer fire came up from it, so sweeping round I came down to the level of the fields, and approaching the embankment raked the train from guards van to engine down to such close range that I had to pull up sharply to clear it. This last burst had used up my remaining ammunition and so I throttled back, wiped the perspiration from my face and turned towards the coast.

The 'time of flight' clock showed 1.10 hours and crossing the enemy coastline at 1,000 ft with two searchlights still weaving hopefully behind, I began to climb steadily on course for Middle Wallop and settled down to the 45 minutes' crossing ahead in clear moonlight over a flat white cloud sheet at 7,000 ft.

I got no answer from Derek over the R/T and began to wonder whether he was safe, but before long I heard him carrying on a long-winded conversation with the home station which I contacted myself to ask for a bearing.

Still keeping strictly to my time schedule I descended through the clouds hoping to see Bournemouth and there indeed was friendly coastline below once again — it was good to see it. The clouds above became broken and then almost directly overhead I caught sight of something that was darker than the surrounding sky and which appeared to be moving rapidly. 'My God, a Hun and I've no ammunition left!' Then another thought flashed into my head and stayed there.

There was no need to turn and investigate that first dark shadow for there ahead was another and above to the left another and everywhere I looked there were more. Balloons! I had descended unwittingly into the middle of the Southampton barrage through a slight error of navigation!

Now I had to get up through it, and the following moments of standing the Hurricane on its tail at full throttle and violently avoiding more balloons as they appeared, knowing that I had no hope at all of seeing the cables, were as exciting as anything which had happened during the past two hours.

In a few minutes we were clear and soon the friendly lights of Middle Wallop came into sight. After a tight circuit, *LK-L*'s wheels were rumbling over home turf again on the Wiltshire fighter station. While the Station Flight groundcrew set about refuelling the aircraft I stretched luxuriously, and one of them, seeing the open gun ports said, 'Been having some fun, Sir? Do you come from Charmy Down?' I said 'Yes, via France' — an answer which seemed to surprise him.

Finally after reporting to Operations and hearing that Derek Ward had landed at Warmwell, I took off again and map-read easily in the moonlight back to Bath, and so on to bed at 5.00 am with the comfortable feeling of having been on the offensive for the first time for nearly twelve months.

The week which followed was full of incident. Heavy Hun activity and brilliant nights combined to keep us very busy. Rayner of 'A' Flight damaged a Heinkel near Gloucester one morning, and it was later 'confirmed'. Not to be outdone, Peter Roscoe shot at one a few nights later, and the following night 'Junior' Musgrove intercepted a Heinkel over Bath and firing at it all the way to the South coast until his ammunition ran out, finally left it barely maintaining flying speed and sinking rapidly over the sea.

This period of intensive night operations reached a peak on 22 April when, only one hour before dusk, Group surprised us with an order to send six aircraft immediately to Exeter, to be at readiness by nightfall. A tall order and there was obviously a 'Buzz' on.

We accomplished this and having settled in to 504 squadron's dispersal point from which we were to operate, we visited the Mess in search of a meal, which would probably be our last for twelve hours. Here we found that Group had thoughtfully informed Exeter that we had had a meal before leaving Charmy Down, and therefore there was no food available of any description and the Mess staff had all dispersed to their billets off the camp at nightfall. So we sadly returned to the airfield to face a cold night's work on empty stomachs, with no means of even making tea.

In a few minutes a dull glow and continuous flashes to the west heralded the beginning of a heavy attack on Plymouth. Just as the first three aircraft were ordered off a Havoc came in and crashed on the runway, breaking the new runway lighting. This resulted in a complete lack of illumination or flare-path of any description and made our take offs in darkness rather a menace, but there were no mishaps and we were promised a flare-path to return to!

The night was pitch dark with thick haze up to 7,000 ft, and cloud layers above that made flying anything but pleasant. Finding Plymouth was simple however, as great fires led the way more effectively than any beacon, glaring through the layered clouds.

During my first patrol, cloud layers, mist and a rolling smoke cloud reaching 8,000 ft made effective searching impossible, and I could only fly back and forth over the dreadful fires raging below which were at times clearly illuminating the Devonport dockland, cursing at each new stick of bomb-bursts. Searchlights were not penetrating the smoke and showed only as circles of light on the cloud layers, and the only indications of the position of bombers were the ack-ack shell bursts, and we often flew through these in fruitless search. Lack of effective R/T eventually made returning to Exeter difficult, and it could only be done by flying on an easterly course for a calculated time and then descending very low in the hope of finding the sea. That everyone effected this without mishap was nothing more than Providence, for even the Flight commander had some trouble at the end of his last patrol, but there was indeed a flare-path to land on!

At dawn we found our way to the Mess, tired and depressed after such an abortive attempt to help the hapless people of Plymouth, and we breakfasted with the crew of a Wellington just in from Brest on stale bread, fish paste and beer! Refreshments for visiting night fighter or bomber crews were not easy to come by at day fighter stations in that period!

Early in May I returned from a week of leave to find the Squadron eagerly awaiting the new moon, for apparently our offensive operations during the last moon period had been regarded with distinct favour by 10 Group, and the order had come for raids to be continued under suitable conditions and on a larger scale. Accordingly on 6 May, the first fine evening, Peter Roscoe and I, together with three of 'A' Flight led by the CO, set off for Warmwell and landed there under conditions of thick haze. After the now-usual long wait we obtained a weather report for northern France. This was bad and a few minutes later the 'Operations cancelled' came from Group. So, having comfortable beds in view we took off into the foggy moonlight and headed back for Charmy Down.

Arriving there safely we beat the dark aerodrome up quite effectively, and then landed to discover that the AOC had been on the aerodrome during the 'beat up', and also that patrols had started! So at 03.00 hours after flying to Warmwell and back and spending half the night trying to go over to France, we now began patrol flying and it was not until well past daybreak that we said 'Good night' and, after an oatmeal stout in the Batheaston Mess, went to bed.

That evening, (7 May 1941) we were off again to Warmwell, and our hopes of being offensive became certainties as the moon rose.

The thick cloud which had closed in during the afternoon began to break and by 23.00 hours conditions were perfect as the order 'First two aircraft take-off and attack "N" as ordered', came through.

The CO ('Widge' Gleed) and 'Rubber' Thoroughgood raced out and were soon two small white lights climbing away among the stars towards France. Roscoe and I returned to the Watch Office to await their return, but in less than twenty minutes a Hurricane arrived overhead and landed, followed by another. It was the CO back already and his answer to our natural query was 'Bloody Hell, I didn't get there. I almost collided with a ruddy Dornier on the way out, and managed to turn on to its tail and shot it down in flames!'

A good start to the evening, and with a last minute check of course cards, maps and revolvers, I started my Hurricane up, and followed by Peter taxied across the field to take-off. With a final heart-thump as I opened the throttle, we took off and crossed the Dorset cliffs climbing on course into the moonlit mist. At 10,000 ft I levelled off with Peter a comforting shadow on my right and a little behind.

Below, the top of the haze was thickening into white patches of cloud: then, very small and lonely in the dark void below, a red distress signal curved up, hung for a moment and faded back into the black expanse of sea. Poor blighters – probably survivors from the CO's Dornier.

A further quarter of an hour with eyes in ceaseless search for possible Huns coming out, and then Cap de la Hague appeared. Enemy territory and therefore worse for us than the sea. I often wondered whether those pillars of staunchness and dauntless courage, the 'Bomber Boys', feel the same exhilaration when sighting Hunland as I have on my trips over. Most probably the sight bores them entirely.

Glancing at the map for a last check I found the bay and the wood which were my chief 'pin points', and there ahead of them and 10,000 ft below was the target, Maupertus aerodrome on the Cherbourg peninsula harbouring, according to Intelligence, at least two squadrons of Me 109s. A hand wave from me and a quick wing-waggle and then Peter slid away to the left as we dived to begin our attacks individually.

Arriving over the aerodrome at about 350 mph after a spiral dive, I flew low across it and tried to pick out targets, but this was too fast so I throttled back, turned steeply and crossed the field again this time quite slowly, and from about 200 ft I could see aeroplanes scattered all round the southern perimeter and runway, and also on the north-east side.

So far there had been a surprising lack of opposition and I began to wonder if our party was going to be carried out unchallenged. I was now to the west of the aerodrome, and gaining height once more in a climbing turn I headed back to the south dispersal point where I had seen the main concentration of 109s, nose down and throttle wide open. The perimeter road came into sight shining in the moon against the dull grass, and with thumb hard on the gun button I aimed the streams of tracer at the first of the line, only raising the sight on to the aircraft further on in order to avoid diving into the ground.

With this first burst the Huns opened up with everything they had in the vicinity, and the sky became a crazy curtain of weaving criss-cross patterns of ack-ack tracer shells, dull red chains of machine gun tracer bullets, brilliant blue searchlights and, luckily above us and out of range, the flashes of exploding heavy ack-ack shells.

I was very low now and most of the flak went overhead, and as I reached the far side of the airfield I realized that at least half the concentration of fire was swinging over to the northern end. Peter had miraculously timed his attack from the opposite direction on the other target area to coincide with mine, which must have been confusing to the Boche gunners.

As I sped away over the dim tree tops and fields, jinking* hard to avoid the now really unpleasant fire, a series of flashes giving birth to a stream of balls of fire which seeemed to bounce off my hood, appeared directly ahead under the nose. Thumb down on the guns again and the tracers lanced down into the gun post which I could see lit up by its own gun flashes. There was no more fire from it as I went over less than 100 ft above it.

Back up to 3,000 ft and then down again in a full throttle dive into the centre of the flak, firing from 500 ft again down to 100 ft at aircraft on the north of the field; then hard back on the stick and up over the hill and straight into the beams of two more searchlights at the best range for the ground gunners, a situation of which they took immediate advantage!

Now dazzled by the glare of shells and searchlights, I could not see the ground or my instruments, and at that dangerously low altitude there was only one thing to do. So screwing up my eyes I turned down the beam of the nearest light holding fire until the range closed, and let fly a long burst straight into the heart of the

* 'Jinking' — sharp turns from side to side to evade ack-ack.

84

glare. With frightening suddenness the light snapped out, and though the other still held on from behind and a brilliant moon overlooked the whole scene, I seemed to be in a sudden darkness even more intense than the glare had been a second before.

A brief vague vision of the searchlight post in the corner of a field; then a huge dark shape looming up and flashing by almost overhead which was probably a group of tall trees, and at last I could see again and was able to climb away towards the coast after firing a last burst towards a gun post situated on the hill overlooking the aerodrome. On a number of occasions I had noticed streams of tracer shells, fired at almost horizontal elevation in order to reach us, bursting on this hillside, which must have been quite unpleasant for those gun posts positioned on it.

So, after a careful check of instruments and fuel gauges to make sure that nothing had been hit, I flew back down the coast and turned out to sea at Cap Levy heading north with one searchlight and a single chain of bright tracer shells groping up after me.

Thirty minutes later we broke cloud once again and there, only visible immediately below in the thick haze, was the friendly outline of Lulworth Cove, and I was soon rumbling across the rough grass of Warmwell airfield and watching Peter's navigation lights appear overhead as he too arrived safely.

The others had been awaiting our return and they crowded round as we climbed stiffly out of our cockpits. It had been a good show, and apart from the gun posts and searchlights attacked, we felt certain of having damaged if not destroyed a number of Messerschmitts; and that together with the CO's Dornier was a satisfactory result to a very interesting evening.

Then the Hurricanes began to take-off one by one to return to Charmy Down, and waiting for my guns to be re-armed I was last off. As if to cap the evening's entertainment my port wing gun panel tore off as I was just clearing the aerodrome boundary and it caused the aircraft to all but stall. I had barely recovered control when the starboard panel tore off, and in this condition the aircraft was obviously dangerous at low speeds, so after a noisy and buffeting flight to Charmy Down I prepared to land much faster than usual, and approaching with at least 20 mph excess speed, managed to arrive on the flare-path with very few more bumps than usual.

The story, of course, had to be told again to the pilots in the dispersal hut who were still at Readiness, and then away to our Batheaston Mess to bed. The time was 4.15 am and I thought of the hearty welcome we had been receiving two hours before, as in the security of my little MG I patted its steering wheel affectionately as we sped down the hill under a sky already greying with dawn.

Until the middle of the next month the Hun was less active in our area, and much useful time was spent in practice flying both day and night. Every fine evening before dusk found Derek Ward leading Badger and myself through highly vigorous formation aerobatic beat-ups, until we became quite accustomed to them and could roll and loop in this way on into full darkness without a second thought — until afterwards!

As usual night-time would find us grouped round the hut fire, singing songs, sometimes bawdy and sometimes not, to MacLure's guitar; while 'Mitch' the ops clerk busied himself making 'a nice cupper-tea' in the background.

Among the more popular ditties were two Squadron songs written by various pilots in bits and pieces and at odd times. The most popular one, sung to the tune of 'Scatterbrain', was this:-

In the morning, in the evening
Whether fog or cloud or rain
87 Squadron are at Readiness again
★AOC and Group Controller binding solid on the 'phone
Never mind the weather, there are roads and railways home

CHORUS

We've no comfort, food or clothing
We've no Hurricanes or spares
We've no Chance light, beacons, wireless sets or flares
Though it's cold and bleak and dreary and it's pouring down with rain
87 Squadron are at Readiness again

Christmas Eve or Easter Sunday
Fly at 'Angels' twenty-nine
On Patrols 'Ack' and 'Beer' or 'C' for Charlie line
Don't forget that dear old Quentin doesn't really care a hoot
Whether you return by aeroplane or parachute!

The other, entitled fittingly enough 'Bloody Woe', was of a less publishable nature, and in an abridged and expurgated form began thus:

* AVM Sir Quentin Brand, AOC No 10 Group.

All bloody day, all bloody nights
We bloody haunt the bloody Flights
We almost look like bloody kites
  Oh bloody, bloody woe

No bloody sleep, no bloody rest,
No bloody time to get undressed
Fly bloody East or bloody West
  Oh bloody, bloody woe

No bloody 'jobs'*, no bloody booze
No bloody food, all bloody queues
We might be Hitler's bloody Jews
  Oh bloody, bloody woe

No bloody tools, no bloody spares
No bloody beds, no bloody chairs
No bloody clothes, who bloody cares
  Oh bloody, bloody woe

The bloody phone bell never stops
It's bloody Group, or bloody 'Ops'
They bind us till we bloody drops
  Oh bloody, bloody woe.

It was into one of these 'musical' evenings that Group broke, 'binding on the phone' with an even more surprising piece of information than usual. The hour was 1.30 am on 11 May and most of us had rolled up in blankets in the hope of some sleep though MacLure was still strumming quietly by the fire, when the Group phone rang.

Picking up the receiver I heard the apologetic voice of the Controller saying 'Group orders 87 Squadron, twelve aircraft, to proceed to London immediately via Middle Wallop'. I mumbled sleepily 'OK — twelve aircraft — London. What!'

Then a drowsy voice came over the phone from Roddy Rayner of 'A' Flight saying ' — a bit much, isn't it!' Thereupon we decided that while we were prepared to go anywhere in our Sector at any time (well, more or less) we took a poor view of the ordering off of twelve pilots, few really experienced, to some unknown Sector for which we had no maps; and without the aid of wireless as naturally the other Sector was not on 'our' frequency and we could not re-tune to theirs; and all this in the dead of night!

Within fifteen minutes of the order however all twelve were

* 'Jobs' — a rather unchivalrous name for casual girlfriends.

airborne, and of these eleven successfully found and landed on the advanced aerodrome Middle Wallop, which the majority of us had never even seen in day time.

A few moments spent in the Pilots' room with Beaufighter crews of John Cunningham's squadron, who had already had a long night and who told us of the tremendous raid that London was receiving, and then the order to take-off came sent us all running across the grass past the great Beaufighters running-up engines in the moonlight, to our shadowy line of black-painted Hurricanes.

Thuds and flashes erupted along the line as one by one the Merlins surged into life, and then as I began to roll forward, navigation lights snapped on all down the line and the aerodrome became a sea of moving red and green lights. I climbed away on a north easterly course into the cloudy night sky, and looking back over my shoulder saw an array of lights following close behind. It was a great moment, and then one by one the lights snapped out as the pilots settled down on their courses for London.

Soon there was no doubt as to destination, for in spite of patches of cloud a great red glow appeared in the sky ahead. From 12,000 ft the Thames appeared below and the reservoir at Staines, while ahead London burned. The clouds through which we had climbed up, now transpired to be a huge, unbroken smoke sheet from London's fires rolling up to 8,000 ft over Kingston and stretching clearly down a north east wind to Southampton Water which gleamed dully on the moonlit horizon.

It was by now nearly 4.00 am and only the stragglers remained over London, their positions given away by spasmodic ack-ack from the direction of Woolwich and Tilbury.

We were too late. Had we arrived an hour earlier we might have been able to add to the good score of Huns shot down that night. But now all we could do was to complete our patrols during which six of us had interceptions in the brilliant moonlight — of other Hurricanes, and we looked down with bitterness and pity on the horror below, with a sneaking feeling of shame that we had been unable to do anything to avert it. Not one Hurricane left London until well beyond the end of our allotted patrol time, and not until well after the eastern sky had tinged with the rising sun. Then only we headed west for Base.

We mostly made the same mistake of descending low too soon to check our positions and in doing so became well lost in the thick smoke haze which now covered the area south west from London to the coast at Southampton. However only two pilots landed at other aerodromes and the remaining nine eventually came swinging in to land at Charmy Down in the mysteriously metallic half-light of dawn as a blood red sun peeped over the edge of the world in the east.

After a further week of patrol flying in the paths of northbound Huns, the weather again deteriorated and low cloud closed in after dark nearly every night. It was on one of these occasions that Group ordered not just two or more patrols, but all our aircraft to take-off and proceed to Exeter immediately. Casting dubious glances at the flickering glare of the flare-path reflecting on the clouds only a few hundred feet overhead, we ran out and started up.

After take-off, no sooner had I bent down in the cockpit to retract the undercarriage than swirling cloud closed round, glowing wierdly past the wing-tip lights.

Breaking through this layer at 1,500 ft and setting a south westerly course, it became obvious that the patrol was going to be every bit as difficult as we had expected for the low cloud sheet seemed unbroken while above at some 6,000 ft was another layer. Luckily, after some thirty minutes dark holes appeared in the sheet below and through one of these I caught sight of the outline of an estuary.

It was the Exe, and from this pinpoint I began to patrol over the aerodrome. A number of EA had already attacked the city that night, but now there was little chance of further activity as the weather was too difficult. Descending to the top of the cloud sheet in the approximate neighbourhood of Exeter I checked that the altimeter showed 800 ft.

The cloud-base must have been on the ground but the patrol had to be completed, and during the following forty minutes of circling, searching and keeping position by occasional glimpses of the outline of the river through breaks in the low cloud, the only excitement was the sudden appearance of another Hurricane close below and silhouetted against the low stratus!

Eventually it was time to set course for home and I began to wonder how I could find Charmy Down with layered cloud everywhere. I was already checking my fuel when suddenly a mile or so to starboard a ball of orange fire appeared dropping, seemingly slowly, down the sky. Thinking 'Good show, someone has got a Hun', I went on and eventually after some difficult moments in cloud almost on the ground, with pitch black conditions below, I went in to land on the Charmy Down flare-path.

Stumbling stiffly into the Pilots' hut, I found that the 'flamer' had not been a Hun but one of our 'A' Flight Sergeant pilots shot down by a Beaufighter and badly burned while returning from this patrol. We were distinctly cross about this, for this work was tricky enough by its very nature without the added menace of pilots who could not apparently distinguish between a twin-engined bomber and a single-engined 'friendly' fighter. So cross were we in fact that another verse was added to our song of woe as follows:-

Fly bloody high, fly bloody low
Fly bloody fast, fly bloody slow
Get shot down by a bloody Beau!
  Oh bloody, bloody woe

After such a lengthy period of night operations it was not surprising that towards the end of spring all the pilots began to feel the need for a change. We wanted to get back on 'Day operations'. At first 10 Group would not hear of it. Through our own efforts and endurance we had become a night squadron and a night squadron we would remain, we were told.

To those of us who remembered the squadron in the previous summer, and to the few who remembered the winter and spring of 1940, the thought of remaining permanently 'Night Operational only' was a hard one. Memories of little formations of Hurricanes each containing a close friend, diving under the glaring summer sun to meet and drive back the hordes of would-be invaders, were memories we held dear; and above all we felt that while the night bombers had to be defeated, there were now others more fitted by the nature of their special equipment to deal with them: and that we single seat fighters should be playing our part more effectively in offensive, rather than defensive operations.

Accordingly in April we set about organizing things in our own way. The CO and Derek Ward became furtive in manner and would often disappear for days at a time, while at most other times they could be seen poring over maps and muttering together in Headquarters. Then the 'gen' began to leak out. A scheme was afoot to persuade the Powers to allow us a trial week on anti shipping-raider operations at a certain very strategic point in the West which had hitherto been overlooked owing to its lack of a suitable airfield from which to operate fighters.

Derek visited the only airfield remotely possible and decided that though its longest run was only 450 yards, experienced pilots would be able to operate Hurricanes there reasonably safely. Eventually Group became interested, and finally the order came for four aircraft to proceed to St Mary's on the Scillies to operate there as an isolated unit under local command of our CO. At the same time we felt sure that this was only done with a view to giving us a holiday by the sea and getting rid of Derek Ward and the CO (who were being troublesome!), if only for a few days, rather than a serious attempt at a new operation!

On the day we were to begin the operation a signal came from Fighter Command that the C-in-C, Air Marshal Leigh Mallory, would visit us at 3.00 pm that afternoon! By 3.30 pm he had only just arrived, and by the time he left we had precisely three hours of daylight in which to carry out a two-hour flight including an intermediate landing at Portreath, and come to Readiness at the end of it at a strange base before dusk. One could always expect red tape to crop up in the middle of the best laid organization.

Once in the air however, we made good time and were soon circling the tiny field overlooking St Mary's harbour which was to be our new temporary base. It was nothing but a clear area of turf on the cliff edge, humped in the middle and bounded on one side by rocky outcroppings and the cliff edge; on the other side by a steep hillside falling away to the village and harbour below, and on a third side by a thick plantation of young firs.

There appeared to be only one landing run, either to or from the cliff edge according to the wind; and this run appeared to my eyes to be the shortest possible strip to land a Hurricane in! Circling low I watched the CO come in over the cliff edge, bounce on the hump and roll down the slope towards the plantation from which the ground crews ran to catch his wing tips and prevent him over-running.

He stopped with twenty yards to spare however, and so lowering flaps and undercarriage I approached the cliffs from low over the sea to attempt a landing myself. Reducing speed as the cliff edge rushed up and by underneath, I throttled back with piles of rock flashing past below and the next moment rolled and bounced over the hump and down the slope with brakes full on, to pull up within some fifteen yards of the boundary and the other aircraft.

Watching Roddy Rayner and Badger coming in was exciting too, as the Hurricanes would disappear below the cliff end of the field and reappear an age later bouncing down the slope towards us at about 65 mph, and little more than 200 yards away. When we were all in safely, we gathered round the CO for briefing on the ways in which we were to operate. Then realizing that there was still an hour till dusk, Badger and I were detailed to remain at Readiness while the others, including the CO, went off in an antiquated commandeered Austin to reserve the best bedrooms for themselves in the billet!

I walked over to *LK-L*, but the crew still had the engine covers off and were attempting to trace the cause of the harsh running which had developed on the way down. They discovered that at least two valve springs had broken and so I could not fly it. At that moment a morse signal by Aldis lamp was seen from the Coastguards some five miles away on an island indicating 'Aircraft south'. This meant that something believed hostile was approaching from that direction. I shouted to Badger who was already in the cockpit of *LK-A*, the CO's machine, there being no others available at that moment, and instantly his warm engine coughed into life and he was away up the slope and sinking down out of sight behind the cliff. There were sounds of gunfire and then in little more than five minutes he came diving in from the sea. He did a climbing roll over the aerodrome and I noticed that he still had some flap down after his take-off! Then he came in and hit the ground a resounding thump on landing. He was obviously excited, and then we saw that his gunports were blackened and open.

Leaping up behind him before he stopped his engine I yelled questions at him in the slipstream, and he shouted 'I've just shot down a Hun seaplane'. That within twenty minutes of our arrival!

No sooner had he passed over the cliffs than he saw two aeroplanes flying low over the sea roughly a mile offshore. Overtaking them quickly he saw black crosses on them, and then, recognizing them as obsolescent Dornier 22 float planes, he dived on the leader. The second Dornier broke away to starboard and disappeared, but the first dived to the level of the waves and turned violently to avoid Badger's fire after first jettisoning the mines which it had been carrying. After one short burst Badger closed right in and corrected his aim as he fired. Bullets poured into the Dornier, and it nosed over and struck the sea, sinking immediately.

How many times the tale was told that evening I could not guess, but our little group were not the only excited people in our billet, the only hotel open in the town: after all it was a great occasion. Our first Hun in daylight for nine months, and the first enemy aircraft ever shot down from the Scillies. Badger had to deal with so many admiring females that even his equilibrium seemed temporarily shattered!

In such an atmosphere of success our first evening in the neighbourhood was one of great excitement. But comprehensive as the celebrations were, there were five pilots on the airfield at dawn next day, though only two were required for Readiness.

Keenness to stand by in the chance of getting more Huns was a feature of our first week on this operation. In fact, idyllic though the surroundings were it became almost impossible to make anyone take a morning or afternoon off duty. When we settled down to a normal routine, life was very easy. Readiness hours were spent lazing on the cliff edge of the aerodrome or in carrying out occasional searches for possible enemy aircraft reported by the Coastguards, with an interesting landing in prospect after every sortie. For off-duty hours an endless variety of amusements presented themselves for our choice: Sailing, bathing, walking, and for those who preferred to exercise their elbows rather than their legs, the never-failing hospitality of the Navy in the Ward Rooms of the two MLs moored in the Harbour.

A few days of this pleasant existence and then one morning the weather closed round us like a wet blanket and we could do nothing but sit indoors and read or, if at readiness, remain wedged into our cockpits listening to the rain beating on the closed hoods and watching it drive in slashing parallel lines across the cliff tops and St Mary's below. The next morning we awoke to gunfire at about 8.30 and to hear the news that the CO had just shot down another Hun.

The weather was dreadful. Clouds racing low over the cliffs and heavy rain made flying conditions nearly impossible. However soon after dawn the Coastguards had signalled a warning and the CO and 'Rubber' Thoroughgood, already in their closed cockpits out of the rain, had taken off. After an unproductive search under the existing difficult conditions the CO returned and prepared to land, but as he lowered his wheels and flaps and approached the airfield still in heavy rain, a Dornier 18 flying-boat loomed out of the mists dead ahead, the front gunner firing as it came.

Raising his wheels the CO turned steeply and, still with flap down, closed in on the slow-moving German, firing burst after burst into it. 'Rubber' soon joined him and almost immediately the great boat heeled over into a left-land turn well on fire. It struck the water with a wing tip just off St Mary's and broke up, sinking immediately and leaving a patch of blazing fuel on the surface of the water which could be seen from the aerodrome.

Later in the morning of 24 May I flew home on leave, and so for me ended the first era, though I did not know it at the time. After a few days at home Roddy Rayner rang up from the Squadron to tell me that I had been 'gonged', and a few hours later came my posting to another squadron on promotion.

After nearly two years in one squadron during which it had seen no less than five commanding officers and seven Flight commanders, it was not easy to contemplate leaving. But the first of my private ambitions had been achieved and in a matter of hours I should take over command of my own Flight in 79, a fighter squadron whose record of service was almost as great as ours, though not quite I felt sure! Of the future three things only were certain: there would be plenty of fun, plenty of friends and above all, plenty of flying.

Chapter 7

TYPHOONS AT DIEPPE

Following two years' continuous service in fighter squadrons 87 and 79, I was posted on 'Rest Period' to the Hawker Aircraft Company at Langley to join the team of pilots testing new Hurricanes off the production line, and this experience soon led to test flying the latest Hawker fighters, the massive Tornado and Typhoon which were in development testing prior to entry into RAF service.

By July 1942 this six months' 'tour' at Langley had come to an end, and I applied for a posting to one of the newly-formed Typhoon squadrons and soon afterwards was given command of 'B' Flight in 609 West Riding Auxiliary Squadron at Duxford.

*   *   *

On the morning of 18 August 1942 at Duxford following the Defiant show* it was decided that as we were not required for operations during the day, I could have a day off. So after an hour of flight formation led by Paul Richey which turned out surprisingly well, I climbed into another Typhoon and set course for Cornwall.

Despite the 300-mile journey, within the hour I was tearing long white condensation trails off the wing tips as I turned steeply over Predannack and reduced speed before approaching to land.

An hour later it seemed almost incredible to be strolling along the cliff tops at Mullion Cove. The sky was unusually clear for Land's End and the sun shining down on to a white-capped deep blue sea reminded one of peace-time and white sails on Chichester Harbour.

Gradually as the evening drew on the land, sea and sky became

---

* Typhoon Wing cover for an operation with Defiants off the Belgian coast, which was uneventful.

flooded with an orange glow. The wind dropped and the only sound was the restful lapping of the sea against the rocks below.

Then over the brow of the hill came a running figure. It was an orderly from the Mess and coming straight to us he said: 'An urgent call from Duxford Sir, you are to return to your unit immediately.'

Shirley* and I looked at each other. It was no good, we could not escape the war even for a day.

Thank goodness I had a fast aeroplane anyway, because I should be able to reach Duxford by dark, and so after a subdued goodbye I was soon heading the thundering Typhoon back over the coastline towards Plymouth, with the ASI showing a steady 310 mph.

The sun had set as we passed over Warminster, and as I looked north to where Bath lay in the gathering dusk and then south to the dim outline of Portland and the Dorset coast, a flood of memories came back of two years before.

Formation flights in our faithful Hurricanes on just such evenings as this down to Warmwell in Dorset in preparation for those offensive night patrols into northern France. Formation aerobatics with our navigation lights on over Charmy Down, and then a long night sitting round the stove waiting for the enemy. We seldom had long to wait.

As the earth grew dark below and the horizon behind became a sharp line of orange and yellow, I could almost see those Hurricanes close alongside. There was 'Junior' Musgrove over on the left; Peter Roscoe below 'in the box', and Derek Ward in *LK-P* leading. They were all dead now. I was still around and doing the same job except that the aeroplane I now flew could attain 400 mph as against the 300 mph of our old Hurricanes.

What did it all mean? I had lived through one phase and the others had not, but would I live to see a third? Hell this is a damned stupid line of thought, but I would have liked to see old Derek up here in a Typhoon with *LK-P* on the side.

It was now full darkness, and soon the Duxford flashing beacon was in sight and then the flare-path. At Duxford no-one knew what was on except that there was to be a big show on the following day, and that briefing would be at 10.30 that evening. It appeared reasonably certain that we should be supporting a ground

* Shirley Adams, serving at that time in the WAAF as a cypher officer; later my wife and mother of daughter Carol.

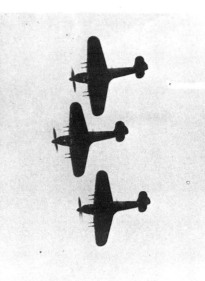

Above *Hurricane IIcs with 20mm cannon and one with .303 machine guns in the very tight formation practised by 87 at Charmy Down (IWM).*

Below *A 'B' Flight Hurricane coming in carefully over the cliffs at St Mary's, Scillys in the spring of 1941 (Perry Adams Collection).*

87 Squadron CO's Hurricane IIc at Charmy Down in 1941. Squadron Leader 'Splinters' Smallwood later gained a DSO leading 87 in the Dieppe raid (RAF Museum, Charles Brown Collection).

Evolution of the Typhoon's cockpit vision: The second prototype at Hawker's Langley factory (RAF Museum, Charles Brown Collection).

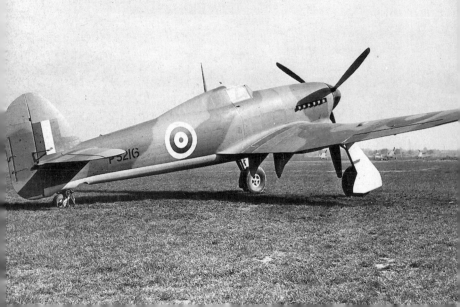

A series IB Typhoon on production test from Glosters at Hucclecote (RAF Museum, Charles Brown Collection).

A Series 2 aircraft with the fully transparent canopy (British Aerospace).

The author's PR-G, *serial R7752, at Manston in 1943* (Ziegler Collection).

Close-up of PR-G *showing the directly reflected gunsight, the Squadron Leader's flag, score panel and the Squadron badge: January 1943 at Manston* (Ziegler Collection).

operation, and there was much talk over the inevitable cans of beer of a 'Second Front'.

Presently the Sector Commander, Group Captain John Grandy, came in with the news that we should not be required before 10.00 after all and the briefing would be at 8.00 am.

He had some news of a considerably less pleasant nature however. The fatal accident which had recently occurred in an aircraft of 'Cocky' Dundas' No 56 Sqdn had now been proved to have resulted from the same structural failure which had caused the deaths of three other pilots including Ken Seth Smith★, during the past ten days. He was considering the grounding of all our Typhoons until a ruling had been obtained from the 'Air House'★★ as to whether we should continue to fly or not.

However tomorrow was to be a great day for the RAF, and it was likely that we would operate first and decide on this difficult problem afterwards. Accordingly I gathered the boys together and told them the situation. After all it was not exactly a pleasant prospect to know that they were going into a real battle, many of them for the first time, in an aeroplane which might quite possibly disintegrate if dived fast!

Then, after a few more beers, we went off to bed and soon, as I lay half asleep, my thoughts drifted back to the early days of the war. The Battle of France, the Battle of Britain, God how frightened I had been! I could remember so clearly lying in bed at our billet, the Rougemont Hotel at Exeter, thinking 'Christ, what will happen tomorrow. Hope there'll be some cloud'. Then that horrible feeling at the pit of the stomach when dawn broke in the clearest of clear skies! — 'Standby: aircraft massing over Cherbourg; how many can you raise? What, only seven! Well good luck, you're off in two minutes!' I could feel again the striving not to show the tension which was to last right up to the point, generally over Portland with '100 plus' already in sight, where one became too busy to worry about mere feelings.

Yet here we were awaiting the biggest 'show' of the year, and my reactions seemed to be typified by the thought which was constantly recurring: 'I hope the weather keeps clear'. Oh well I suppose one can become acclimatized to anything! It was going to be fun though to be able to wade into the enemy for a change for there would certainly be plenty for everyone on an operation of this description. I could see them coming out in droves below us — a

★ Hawker's No 2 experimental test pilot.
★★ Air Ministry.

perfect 'bounce'. Brrr-rrm; — there go my cannons.

'Good morning Sir; wake up Sir, it's a lovely morning!' as the batman pulled the curtains letting in golden sunlight.

On 19 August 1942 the weather was indeed perfect, and that dream seemed a good omen as I told the boys of it over breakfast. A perfect 'bounce' was just what we wanted — and the radio was announcing that Dieppe was being attacked! As we cycled down to the briefing, 56 Squadron arrived with a shattering roar from Snailwell, broke formation and came in to land in sections.

The Intelligence Room sounded like a mothers' meeting until one caught snatches of individual conversation! The great question was — was this the long-awaited invasion of the Continent? At briefing the Duxford Wing, consisting of 266 (Rhodesian), 56 and 609 (WR Auxiliary) squadrons, was first addressed by the Sector Commander, John Grandy*. He had been my CFI at No 13 FTS, Drem, and he now told us in his usual blunt and cheerful style that a major operation had begun which would take our forces back to France for the first time since our hurried withdrawal in May 1940. For some of us who had taken part in that battle and the subsequent Battle of Britain this was a tremendous moment, but he went on to say that in view of the prevailing engine problems and tail failures with our new Typhoons, all he would do on this occasion was to tell us that we could go on this operation if we wanted to, but if we thought the Typhoon wasn't ready he would go along with that.

The Wing Leader, Dennis Gillam, then outlined the operations plan for the Duxford Wing to reinforce West Malling and from there 'sweep' behind Dieppe at 10,000 ft to provide fighter cover over a sea-borne attack on the harbour and coastal defences.

There was no hesitation at all — the Duxford Wing would go to Dieppe! Grandy was clearly delighted, and the next hour was a whirl of preparation and repolishing of windscreens, running engines, checking guns and going over the briefing.

The Wing was in fact at the end of a drawn-out and frustrating introductory period with its new Typhoons and was more than ready to have a go; and so on the morning of the 19 August the Typhoon Wing took off from Duxford to sweep down the enemy coast from Dunkirk to Calais, but without result, before landing at West Malling, 609 led by Paul Richey taking the opportunity for some close formation practice on the way back.

Malling was hot and dusty in the August sunshine and it

* Later Chief of the Air Staff and Governor of Gibraltar.

appeared to be almost submerged in fighters as we taxied in past squadrons of Spitfires, Hurricane bombers and Beaufighters. Then, after a quick refuelling we were back in the cockpits awaiting the green Very light which would signal 'start up'.

This, when it came, resulted in an eruption of starter cartridge explosions, smoke, exhaust flame and dust as thirty-six 2,000 hp Napier Sabre engines fired. Taxying out over the dry grass airfield caused problems as the big three-bladed propellers churned dust and debris into the eyes of pilots straining to see through their cockpit side-windows, opened until take-off to try to avoid excessive heat.

Then the CO's section was away in a rising cloud of dust, and I was leading 'B' Flight in hot pursuit. With no preliminary circuit to join up the formation we set course at low level across the Weald of Sussex for Beachy Head closing to 'search formation', and then crossed out over the chalk cliffs with climb power, ignoring the enemy radar on this occasion and going directly up to 10,000 ft.

Immediately the VHF became noisy with the menacing sound of enemy radio interference, and with spasmodic instructions and excited observations from other squadrons already in action. Levelling over mid-Channel at 10,000 ft Dennis Gillam, leading the Wing with 56 Squadron, maintained high power until we were indicating 300 mph for fast target penetration, and then the enemy coast came into sight through a layer of broken cumulus cloud at about 2,000-4,000 ft. Turning west from the Somme estuary the three Typhoon squadrons made an impressive sight with their blunt nose radiators and aggressive overall shape, and then the action began.

Confused radio chatter suggested enemy aircraft inland some- where, and almost simultaneously I saw unidentified aircraft momentarily through gaps in the cloud below, and also the harbour and sea front of Dieppe which I had last seen when hospitalized there in February 1940. It was now ringed in smoke and fires, with white tracks off-shore of weaving naval vessels and assault craft and the unmistakeable white splashes of sticks of bombs.

We could see no immediate target although at some point a section of 266 broke away and dived after some Dorniers claiming 'prob- ables', and then Gillam led the Wing in a long diving sweep at 400 mph round behind Dieppe and down through the broken cloud layer to look for activity. I again had a fleeting glimpse of some 190s or 109s (or possibly Spitfires) before they disappeared into cloud, and our rear section (of 609 Squadron) saw some 190s in and out of cloud for long enough to attack them and claimed three damaged.

Then we were crossing out and on our way back to West Malling for a welcome cool drink while refuelling, before setting off to do it again, but this time with no enemy sightings.

At the end of the day when we landed back on the undulating Duxford grass in the quiet, warm dusk of the Cambridgeshire countryside, we had lost one Typhoon with engine failure and another shot down by a Spitfire; we had claimed two 'probable' EA victories and three damaged, and had taken a very small part in a great and heroic raid. But I had not even fired my guns. The enemy may possibly have been as apprehensive of the Typhoon as we were at the time, though I doubt it — but the day of the Typhoon was still to come.

Chapter 8

THE MANSTON TYPHOONS

At Manston in November 1942 with the enemy coast in sight from 1,000 ft and a mere ten minutes away, I felt, as 609's new Squadron commander that our chance had come to prove our new Typhoons both defensively against the coast-raiding FW 190s and offensively against anything that the enemy might provide on land, sea, or in the air.

Consequently, after discussions at 11 Group HQ, a programme of standing patrols was arranged which would keep the squadron extremely busy and which would rest with us practically the entire responsibility for detecting in the SE the low-level tip-and-run raiders which habitually came in below the radar defences. That was after all the major issue. Ramsgate, Deal, Folkestone and all the small towns along the coast from North Foreland to the Isle of Wight were being raided almost daily, and civilian casualties were becoming serious. Defeat the Hun in this phase and we could take our Typhoons on any type of offensive operations that I thought suitable was the promise of the AOC, subject of course to formal approval of each operation.

When I gathered the squadron together in the dispersal hut and told them the situation, they brightened up perceptibly. Then, as I walked back to the office the stillness of the autumn morning was rudely shattered by the roar of engines and cannon fire as four 190's swept low over the western side of the field, strafing the powerhouse as they went. They did no serious damage and two of the Squadron on patrol off Deal intercepted as they left the coast and destroyed two of them. The battle was joined.

From that moment the spirit of 609, dormant for many months, rose steadily again until it reached a peak in 1943 which gained it lasting fame.

The pilots flew in pairs from dawn to dusk, two, three,

sometimes four patrols a day, and always wanted more flying. They would not take days off and often asked to defer their leave.

They flew out over the icy North Sea and Channel, always lower than 100 ft, generally in sight of the enemy coast and seldom in sight of ours.

On some days the cliffs of Calais and the sand dunes of Gravelines reflected the white glare of the winter sun on a white-capped blue sea, but more often icy nor'easterly gales drove the rain in horizontal streams between lowering cloud and spume-whipped leaden sea, and the Typhoons maintained a blockade of the coast.

The enemy came most days, using every ruse in the book to avoid battle. In rainstorms, mist, dawn light and dusk and always at more than 300 mph, they came sweeping in in formations of two to eight to drop their bombs on the first group of dwellings on the coast and then wheel out to sea again at 50 ft or less. The attack could last less than two minutes from first sighting to last. Chances of interception seemed very low, but within a week of the first success a 609 patrol met two FW's heading for Dover at mid-Channel. The Germans, thinking that they had the advantage of speed turned for home, and within sixty seconds were at the bottom of the Channel. The Typhoon was living up to my hopes. Thus we were able, little by little, to improve our tactics.

In anxiety to prove my theories about the Typhoon, I flew every day and often twice a day and more. Patrols seemed endless as we flew out over that cold, icy water which was a greater enemy if anything than the Hun himself, for engine failure at that altitude meant almost certain death. A Typhoon would not 'ditch'*, and engine failure was an all-too-common occurrence at that time. Three Typhoons were lost on patrol with their pilots in that first month. One of them tried to land in the sea in half a gale and his aircraft disappeared almost without a splash amid the flying spray.

From the moment one left the runway, tucked the wheels up over Walmer and roared out low over Pegwell Bay, constantly scanning the engine instruments, one strained to hear the slightest change in engine note. Out to the broken water over the Goodwins, south for five minutes then south-west on the long mid-Channel leg until Dungeness lighthouse appeared low down on the starboard horizon. Then backwards and forwards on the patrol line until those two welcome specks, the relieving section, appeared in the distance, always to be carefully identified before leaving patrol

* land on water.

— they could just as easily be FWs.

On days of bad visibility, and there were many of them, we often only saw land at the end of the patrol having maintained position by flying accurate courses and pin-pointing on the various shipping lane buoys and the Goodwins.

They seemed long patrols, sometimes with a glassy sea merging into fog which necessitated constant reference to the instrument panel, but more often with biting rain slashing at the windshield and tearing the paint from the wings; and never has steaming cocoa tasted as good as it did round the red-hot stove in the dispersal hut after landing. An ex-Commanding Officer of the Squadron, by now a very senior officer, had presented the Squadron with two large thermos urns and these were kept full all day: a comforting arrangement.

In the meantime the Squadron was becoming comfortably settled into the Mess at Westgate. We had taken over a large house known as the Nook, with the unaccustomed luxury of central heating and hot water in all the bedrooms. The 'Old Charles', where we bought the beer by the jug and played fanfares on post-horns normally hung from the ceiling, and the 'Cherry Brandy House' where we consumed quantities of piping hot sausages under the low beams, were both less than twenty minutes away by my staff car or the Belgian 'Barouche'. The Mess itself had a cosy little bar with a cheerful fire burning and murals of air fighting, and the Squadron prepared to enjoy the winter under ideal conditions. Canadian 'Moose' Evans took one look at the footprints in soot on the bar ceiling (of many squadron pilots stationed there before), and said: 'Jees, I'll have my cheek prints up there soon', and he did!

The end of the month was approaching rapidly, and with it the full moon. This gave me an idea which I proceeded to expound to AVM Saunders, the AOC of 11 Group. It was this: I believed that the Typhoon was an easy and safe aeroplane for night flying. At the same time it was evident that the enemy was resorting more and more to the cover of darkness for moving his rail and road trans-port. Moreover, while our fighters were continually sweeping at high-level over France and the Low Countries in daylight, the enemy's lines of communication received little attention in either daylight or at night. I suggested that this was where we came in.

The AOC was slightly sceptical at first. True, the Hurricanes of 'one-armed MacLachlan's' squadron had ground-strafed by moonlight during the previous summer; but that had ceased as their aircraft became obsolete, and after all the Typhoons were extremely high-performance day fighters. Surely the pilots would experience difficulty in even flying them at night, let alone attempting the difficult and even hazardous business of attacking ground targets at night. I felt that it was merely a matter of training, and suggested that I might be allowed to carry out two or three trial sorties during the current moon period, the final outcome to be based on the results.

This was agreed to, and I thought that I could see a twinkle in the great man's eye as he said: 'Right, try it out Beamont and let me know how you get on.'

Back at Manston I worked out courses, studied maps and flak diagrams, and finally decided to make a first sortie to Amiens via Le Touquet and the Somme estuary as I knew the landmarks well and as there was practically certain to be traffic on the Calais-Amiens-Paris line.

On checking the cockpit of my Typhoon, *PR-G*, I found that the night-flying equipment had been dealt with by the makers in their, at that time usual, rather carefree fashion. The panel lights were dazzling white and illuminated one's face and the interior of the hood so effectively that it was quite impossible to see out of the aircraft at all — but they did not illuminate the instrument panel! The compass light cast a lurid glare on the floor of the cockpit, but did not shine on the compass. My crew got to work with a will and the lamps were dimmed to a pleasantly low shade with the application of many coats of red dope.

The gunsight brackets were repositioned and a special slide was made for the reflector which blanked out all unnecessary light from the windshield. The tracer ammunition was taken out of the cannon belts (these would be too bright and cause glare at night), and everything was ready except the weather. It was essential that I should have a night of good visibility and little or no cloud to cut out the light of the moon. The greatest difficulty which I was likely to encounter was that of judging the range of and angle of approach to an indistinct target, and the better the vision from the cockpit the better the chances of success.

For three consecutive days the weather cleared perfectly in the late afternoon, but as the sun set, heavy low cloud swept in. Finally, on 17 November the moon appeared from behind scattered thin cloud in a hazy sky. Conditions were not perfect, but I decided to try it out at least. Seeing my helmet, black flying overalls and Mae West as I went out after dinner in the Mess, Joe Atkinson said: 'Going flying Sir?' Then as he noticed my personal papers emptied out on to the table he said: 'You're not going "Intruding" are you?' Replying somewhat facetiously I went out to *PR-G*, smiling as I thought of the remarks I had heard through the open door.

'Where the Hell's the CO off to now! He'll want us up there next. We're day pilots, not bloody owls!'

Strapped in with the door shut, the windows wound tight and the cockpit lights spreading a warm red glow, I soon lost the tension which always accompanied the period of waiting for a 'show'. Aircraft on either side, hitherto shadowy shapes in the moonlight, sprang into lurid relief in the momentary flickering glare of long exhaust flames as the Sabre engine, slightly overprimed, broke into harsh life. A final check of engine and fuel gauges; cockpit lights dimmed; the green signal from Flying Control; then that brief impression of uncontrollable speed as the lights of the rough grass flare-path flash by at an ever-increasing rate until, just when a crash seems imminent the aircraft reaches flying speed, the controls become firm, the jolting ceases, and the flare-path gives way to darkness.

Once clear of the runway with wheels retracted and rpm and throttle set, I steadied into a climb at 200 mph and looked around at the weather.

Visibility was poor and I could only see the ground vaguely, directly below. But as I looked over my shoulder I could see the flashing beacon and beyond it the moon path on the sea cut short abruptly by the dark outline of the coast at Deal.

Climbing steadily south the light cloud dispersed and the sharp outline of Dungeness appeared jutting out in the moonlit Channel, and then looking back through the flat top of the haze I could see aerodrome beacons flashing as far away as London itself.

The last faint view of the friendly Kent coastline gave a feeling of acute loneliness and a keen appreciation of the possibilities which the next hour or two might produce before I saw it again, if in fact I did. The feeling was to become familiar during the coming winter months.

By now *PR-G* had reached 10,000 ft and, levelling off, began to increase speed. It was magnificent to be heading for Hunland again and to be on the offensive after so long on the defensive. Ahead appeared a whole bank of cloud and I wondered if it was obscuring the ground. The moon path stretching out into the distance below gave a quite erroneous impression of mirror-like calm to the water.

I had always hated flying over the sea, and the cold loneliness of the night did nothing to help in this respect. So that it was with an odd sense of relief that I saw the first sign of the enemy coast, a beacon on Cap Gris Nez, appear out of the haze to port.

The cloud bank was over the coast and as I crossed it in a slight dive, turning a few degrees every few seconds to discourage possible flak, the vague outlines of Le Touquet and Etaples were visible briefly through gaps in the cloud.

The last occasion that I had seen those towns had been two years previously, and they had been friendly. Le Touquet had been a very friendly place in 1939–40! Now we were over enemy territory. The suspense was ended and now for a target.

The cloud dispersed again a few miles inland and there was France spread out mistily below. There were no lights and as yet no searchlights or flak. It seemed incredible that somewhere on the grey and indistinct but peaceful-looking countryside slipping by below were enemies whose duty it was to kill me; enemies whom it was my duty to find and destroy.

The dunes of Berck showed clearly to starboard as I began to lose height in order to search the ground more carefully.

The 'V'-shaped mirror of the Somme Bay, shining in the moonlight ahead, was a reminder of the reported flak position at St Valery. I turned left towards the Abbeville canal, thinking as I did so of the times Tom Mitchell and I had flown down it between the trees in 87 Squadron's Magister in 1940, and then I caught sight of a patch of light smoke (or was it steam?) where I knew the railway to be.

At this point the clear path of weather ended abruptly. The sky grew very dark as we flew under cloud at 3,000 ft, and as I banked left vertically in order to keep the possible target in view I found that there was no horizon and the ground itself was only vaguely in sight directly below. Completing the turn by instruments and diving back towards St Valery I broke into hazy moonlight again with a suddenness that was almost dazzling, and searched ahead with straining eyes.

There it was! A long trail of white smoke and ahead of it the moon flashing and glinting on railway lines. A diving turn at 320 mph round it confirmed that it was a train travelling fast towards Abbeville.

As I prepared to attack, turning on gunsight, setting guns to 'FIRE' and keeping the trail of smoke in sight over my left shoulder, I realized that that preliminary dive had been a mistake.

I had given myself away and even as I looked the steam began to dwindle, until it was touch and go whether I would reach it before the steam was quite shut off and the target lost.

But I was coming in now, throttle well back, height dropping steadily, 1,000, 800, 600 ft, speed about 280 mph. Through the windscreen I could just see a thin stream of white against the greys and blacks of the countryside.

Now. I ruddered the gunsight on to the source of the steam, a high sighting line to allow for inevitable nose drop, and fired.

The darkness was split on either side by the flash of the cannon muzzles projecting from each wing, and a second later by a pattern of exploding shells ahead.

In their light I had a momentary impression in sharp relief of permanent-way, hedgerows, a long line of coaches, and a large engine with shells bursting all round and on it, apparently rushing up at me and then we were clear and climbing round over the Somme Bay.

I had come within an ace of misjudging the range and crashing straight into the train.

That the train was hit soundly was demonstrated by a patch of white escaping steam against the darkness behind. I thought of whether the driver had escaped and whether I had killed any enemy troops — flashes from small arms fire had given away their presence on the train.

Then with scalp-prickling suddenness the night became brighter than day and apparently unlimited quantities of fiery projectiles sped past the cockpit and then sailed away in chains of six or eight into the distance. Cursing myself for a fool for I was blundering along quite slowly at less than 2,000 ft over St Valery, the home of two known searchlights and an unknown number of light guns, I threw the Typhoon down towards the ground at full throttle, twisting and turning violently until I was so low that in order to hold me the searchlights were lighting the trees and ground below.

The guns were still pounding out tracer shells which roared away over my shoulder well behind. But the searchlights were a different proposition and I was sweating by the time I had outdistanced them and could regain a safe altitude. Even so, there were a difficult few moments until my eyes re-adapted to darkness.

By this time we were well away from the target area and once again under dark cloud. Checking the compass showed that we were heading south, so I turned back towards the north again until the Somme re-appeared.

Avoiding St Valery rather carefully I searched for the target again. There was no difficulty this time as a pall of escaping steam gave the train's position away clearly and I made another attack, opening fire at 500 ft and firing all the way in to about 100 yards and 150 ft. The shells bursting all along the train lit it up as before, making aiming relatively easy, and by the time I dived in for a last attack there was a cloud of escaping steam enveloping the engine.

After the final burst which finished the ammunition I circled once to watch the scene and then climbed away north towards Berck, and the St Valery searchlights flicked on, wavered towards *PR-G* and then flicked out again. As I gained height the pressures relaxed and I realized that I was quite wet with sweat. With fuel and temperatures checked I sat back and looked at the cockpit clock; only five minutes had elapsed since the first sighting of the train yet it seemed that quite three times as many had passed.

Climbing through the clouds near Etaples, I set course for home in the clear night sky.

It was a beautiful scene that unfolded itself as the tension eased away.

In the grey haze below, the vague coastline of France spread north in monochrome to the headland of Cap Gris Nez without giving any impression of distance. Above, the stars in the north gave way to the cool light of the moon almost overhead which cast a silhouette of the cockpit hood and my helmetted head on to the smooth curve of the port wing.

The flat top of the haze formed a clear cut star-edged line round the whole horizon, broken only by the white cloud tops stretching inland behind into France.

Turning up the cockpit lights seemed to have the effect of shutting out this pale, unreal world.

This confined box containing my legs and body and boots stretched out on the rudder pedals, gloved hands on throttle and stick, and a maze of glowing and flickering dials bathed in the soft red glow, seemed, for a moment, my whole sphere of existence. The roar of the engine had dulled in my ears long since and as I studied temperatures, pressures and revolutions, I found myself half thinking that there was no world outside.

Into these fantasies broke a more sober thought. I had been out of sight of land for some time. There was insufficient fuel to allow for bad navigation, yet where was the land? Could I have headed too far east and missed the Foreland completely?

The sea looked bleak in the narrow moon-path behind. The compass showed the correct heading.

I stared ahead and then glanced at the clock; a mere eighteen minutes had elapsed since leaving the enemy coast and there were two more minutes to go before I could expect to see land!

It seemed unbelievable, but it was another illusion which night-flying over the sea was always to give.

Presently I could see a vague white line in the mist ahead. It had no distance or altitude, but as I drew near rapidly at 300 mph the thin line developed into the sheer chalk cliffs of South Foreland, bright in the moonlight.

Ahead the Manston beacon now winked redly. Already the vague circle of lights which surrounded the airfield could be seen extending almost across the North Foreland. Home!

'Hallo Control, Crooner leader approaching base. Yes, I am OK. May I pancake?'

'OK Crooner leader, switching off to you'.

I switched on all lights and dived off the remaining altitude until, at over 400 mph I pulled out low over the flare-path and up, up to the vertical and beyond until the moon swung back into view over my head and I rolled off the top of the loop for the sheer joy of the thing!

A green light winked from the flare-path controller as the undercarriage dropped into position with a series of thuds. The engine note rose with a whine as I increased the propeller pitch, and then to a blustering roar as I opened the left window for better vision.

Speed down to 150 mph, winding the elevator trim wheel back as the flaps forced the nose down.

The twin lines of lights stretching out ahead, then disappearing under the nose only to reappear flashing past on either side.

Throttle right back and stick further and further back until pressed against the parachute release buckle. Bump, bump, rumble, rumble — hard rudder and brake to prevent a swing at high speed.

There was the marshalling torch waved by my groundcrew to lead us into the Dispersal, crowded with shadowy shapes which momentarily showed up in the red and green lights at my wing-tips.

A final roar of the engine and then, switches OFF. Silence.

A sensation akin to depression crept over me as I fumbled stiffly with the harness, and stretching hugely, climbed out to the wing. It was gone in a moment as I sat with the cold night air beating through my hair, released from the hot, tight helmet, and answered the questions of an excited circle of airmen.

'How did it go Sir? A train! Blew up! Good show Sir! Any flak? Guns go all right Sir?' (this from the armourers).

'Yes, wizard thanks.'

'Good show Sir.'

I walked over to Intelligence to give my report, blinking as I entered the glare of lights shining on wall maps and aircraft models.

'Anything doing Sir? Oh wizard! Group would like you to ring.'

'OK. Hallo, Intruder Controller please. Hallo old boy; yes it went off quite well. Pranged a train near St Valery. Yes, I think this thing could be worked up. Yes, you see the target quite well enough to make decent attacks, but there must be good moonlight. I'll have another couple of cracks myself during this moon period, and in the meantime get the boys off on some practice. Oh, they'll like it all right! OK, old boy, cheerio.'

As I drove down the road to the Mess in the Hillman I felt that I had begun something which would develop, and it did. In the Mess over bacon and eggs and a jug of beer I gave the inklings of the plan to the Flight commanders Joe Atkinson and Johnny Wells. Van Lierde was his usual exuberant self, and by the time I went off to bed after a pint or two by the fire in the bar he had wangled from me the promise of a flight the following night.

Later as I lay in bed pleasantly tired and relaxed, I went over every moment of the flight and then switched my thoughts to plans for the next night.

I was in the act of strafing my tenth train in the face of intense flak and a particularly dazzling searchlight when the batman said: 'Lovely morning Sir', and I found the sunlight streaming through the late autumn leaves into the room.

The trees and grass sparkled with hoar frost as I entered the Mess for breakfast.

At brief intervals between the consumption of bacon and eggs and concentration upon the exploits of 'Jane' in the *Daily Mirror* there were endless questions: Had I been over the other side that night?

'Yes.'

'Any luck?'

'Yes.'

'What ...? A train!'

'Flying at night must be wonderful!' (This from a WAAF Officer.)

'It is.'

One was never at one's best at the breakfast table. At the office an 'IN' tray piled to overflowing and almost hiding the reproachful countenance of Hal, the adjutant (Halliday Tidswell) indicated that a considerable part of the day would have to be devoted to administration. However there were more important things to attend to first. I picked up the telephone.

'609 Dispersal please ... Hallo, Peter (Raw), CO here. Will you tell the Flight commanders that I want to see all pilots who are not on patrol in Dispersal at 11 o'clock ... Well, get them out of bed then! Thanks Peter.'

Later in the Dispersal I found the pilots crowded round the red-hot stove. They stood up as I entered.

'OK boys, sit down but let me get near that stove! Blanco, bring me a spot of cocoa will you?'

'Now! As you all know I have been doing my best to persuade the powers to allow us trips to the Continent, and to date they are still adamant about not letting us do anything dangerous! Our coastal defence role is considered to be and is in fact vital, and nothing must be allowed to affect our efficiency in that role. However, we have achieved a step in the right direction. The AOC has given me permission to try the Typhoon in attacking transport targets by moonlight, and has hinted that if we achieve success in this we may be given permission to carry out a limited number of these operations during every moon period. Oh yes, I know that only bats and fools fly at night, but this is a very definite step in the right direction for two reasons. Firstly, it will give all you so and so's the opportunity for which you have been binding about for so long — the chance to fire your guns in anger. Secondly, if we make a success of ground-strafing by night in these so-called tricky high performance fighters, who will be able to say that we are unsuitable for similar work by day!

'Well, that's the situation. I went down to the Somme area last night; found a train in far from perfect visibility and was able to prang it properly. The thing's a 'piece of cake' and it's good fun! Van and I are going to have another crack tonight and if that is a success I can promise that any of you who are keen will be able, after a little night practice, to plan your own shows and go out during the next moon period.

'Whatever happens, in any case, everyone will have to become night-operational on the Typhoon during the next month, so that our Channel patrols can be maintained till full darkness; and as I say, anyone who is keen and confident in his night flying will be able to go over and prang the Hun.

'Well, there it is. I want the Flight commanders to arrange for six pilots to carry out "circuits and bumps" during the remainder of this moon period, starting tonight. Any questions?'

'For the information of the keen types (that was a good point: any dubious members and quite understandably there were a number, would soon feel left out of things if other pilots were doing operations that they were unable to do) the standard of training before you can go on an "Intruder" patrol will be two 200-mile cross-country flights by moonlight without wireless aid, and two sorties of low-flying practice in the Dungeness area, also by

111

moonlight. That's all, Johnny; I shall not be on patrol today, but have "*G*" tee-d up for 6 o'clock this evening.'

An excited buzz of talk broke out:

'It will be wizard to fly over France!' ... 'Sooner go in daytime' ... 'This is a day squadron ... There's no ruddy future in night ops!' I listened for a while and then said: 'All right, chaps, you won't *have* to go "Intruding" as I said before, but those who are keen will be able to.'

Outside on the broad concrete I found '*G*' trestled up and almost hidden by swarming armourers. There had been a stoppage on one gun last night, and that was not going to happen again if they could help it.

'Good morning, Sir. Just going over the guns again.'

'Morning Flight. Good, I hope to use them again tonight! By the way, the windscreen de-misting panel lowers forward visibility considerably at night, especially during the all-important few seconds of the attack. How about taking it off? Of course the gunsight will have to be re-harmonized on to the windscreen. We can keep the mist off with a rag.'

'Yes Sir, we can do that quite easily but it will take a few hours. You won't want the "kite" before dark Sir, will you?'

'No Flight, that's fine; and one more thing. The night slide for the gunsight was effective in principle last night, but it slipped at the critical moment. Can you fix that up?'

'OK Sir, I'll do that.'

Now for the office. As I opened the door the adjutant subjected me to his usual reproachful glare and I realized that I was nearly an hour late to take the 'Charges' of which he had warned me.

'Sorry I'm late Adj. How about these charges?'

'They've only been waiting an hour, Sir.'

'Good show; do 'em good!'

The first airman had overstayed his leave and had no excuse to offer. The second had committed the same offence but had many excuses, none of which was credible. The third had refused to obey the order of an NCO in terms that cast considerable doubt as to the nature and whereabouts of that NCO's parents. They were simple cases but as usual I felt uncomfortable while dealing with them. Who was I to judge and punish these men? Perhaps they felt that way too.

'Well, that's that! I'll deal with these files this afternoon. Want a lift to lunch, Hal?'

At Doon House I went into the bar for a beer and found Joe Atkinson, Frank Ziegler and Halliday Tidswell discussing the night-flying question. Ziegler, having been with the squadron during its most hectic and distinguished days of air-fighting in the Battle of Britain, was much against the idea of night work. I prepared for battle, for though the pilots were entitled to express their opinions about flying matters, I was not prepared to allow non-flying officers, no matter what their standing, to influence the pilots on operational matters.

'Have a beer, Sir?'

Tidswell started the ball rolling and after passing a can of ale said: 'Hear that you want to start the boys going on night ops, Bee.'

He seemed to feel that his position as squadron adjutant since and throughout the Battle of Britain entitled him, to small privileges like familiarity with the CO! 'Ziegy' took up the attack.

'We've always been a day squadron, you know. It's a tradition ...'

'A tradition not to fly at night?'

'No, not exactly that, but ...'

'My dear Hal, if it's a tradition of the squadron to be content to sit on their bottoms doing coastal patrols when there's a chance to fire their guns at the enemy, even at night; well, that tradition is going to undergo a change! We are going to take each and every opportunity offered to us, day or night, and if none is offered then we'll make our own; and I don't want any more insidious propaganda from you two either. Got that!'

'Yes, Sir.'

'Well, let's go and eat!'

Towards the middle of December 1942 excitement ran high in the Squadron at the approach of the new moon period. I was also looking forward to it keenly, as December was a month of clear nights and after weeks of training and encouragement we now had a squadron of pilots capable and straining at the leash to go out to strafe the enemy first at night and then hopefully by day; and this coming period could mean the success or the failure of my hopes for the Typhoon.

I watched the growing moon, night after night as it shone from clear star-lit skies until the 15th, when I decided that on the following night there would be sufficient light for operations. Throughout the next day I arranged programmes for six sorties beginning at 19.00 hours, briefed the other pilots, Van Lierde, Blanco, Johnny Wells, Eric Haabjoern and de Selys, and checked over the aircraft scheduled for night work personally. Guns, ammunition, cockpit lighting, gunsights; everything had to be just right.

A little thing like an ill-fitting gunsight night-adaptor could mean the failure of an operation, for should that little slide (a metal disc of half an inch diameter) slip out of place during the attack or at any other time during the flight, the pilot's forward vision of a difficult target would be virtually obscured by the bright orange glare of the sight ring and range bars.

This adaptor which cut out all unnecessary light, leaving only the centre sighting bead reflection on the screen ahead, had been made up to my design by the Squadron armament NCO in the absence of any cooperation or interest from Command who, when approached for assistance, had remarked merely that the gunsight as installed had always proved good enough before. Headquarters it seemed was some way from the action, at least in its lower echelons!

In fact without that small modification the Typhoon could never have been successful at night, but this was an example of many such instances of indifference in high places by which front-line pilots often found themselves frustrated during the war years.

Finally, those pilots who were nominated for 'Night Ops' were not to go on patrol after midday, and would have the following morning off-duty until lunchtime. That was the best I could do, for it was impossible to allow a pilot a complete day's rest after night flying without adversely affecting the day standing patrols commitment which was our main priority.

It was our task to maintain a constant Channel patrol of two aircraft each day from dawn until dusk, a period of eleven hours. For this 22 aircraft sorties would be required as a bare minimum, and more on occasions of engine or R/T trouble, or for operational reinforcements. I had in the Squadron 22 pilots of whom four were on leave (and under no circumstances would I cancel regular leave), and generally in the winter there were at least two on the sick list. Therefore to the remaining sixteen pilots fell the weight of the work, and now this night flying promised an additional load. However, keenness to fly Typhoon operations was now becoming universal, and for those few who raised objections, and they were very few, I had a ready answer: 'If you are tired, go to bed early!'

The pilots had begun to realize the wisdom of this and the squadron bedtime was already down to not long after midnight!

Eventually everything was ready. Van Lierde and I would be 'first off', he to the Brussels area as usual (his family lived at Gramont) and I to northern France in the Lille/Douai area. The others, detailed for routes covering most of the railways from Ostend and Brussels to Amiens and Dieppe, would await my return for final instructions in connection with the weather, flak, and any other points which might arise during my trip. As the dusk patrol roared in from the sea, wing-tip lights gleaming, and curved up and away from each other before lowering their wheels and coming in to land on the newly-lit flare-path, I drove the Hillman round to the Dispersal hut.

There I found 'Mony' Van Lierde already dressed with Mae West and flying boots and surrounded by sheets of maps on which he was busy marking courses, turning points and targets.

'Hallo, Van. You're a bit early!'

'To be prepared is best, Sir.'

Van Lierde, a quiet and even rather surly officer in the bad days of Duxford, was a new man at Manston. Always cheerful, always eager to fly and discussing or suggesting possible (and some impossible) operations with ever-increasing volubility, vehemence and Belgian incoherence, he had now become one of the most valuable men in the Squadron. For although he talked a lot, he was always enthusiastic and determined in his desire to get to grips with the enemy and could be relied on to give a very good account of himself when he did so. So often was his voice to be heard raised above all others in the Dispersal, the Mess or the Bar, that the saying: 'Old Van's getting emphatic again' had become a Squadron tradition. It was typical of his energetic, almost nervous character, to be getting ready for the flight nearly two hours before there was any chance of there being sufficient light from the moon.

I telephoned Intruder Operations: 'Hallo Controller? Good evening old boy, Beamont here. Are those jobs OK? They are? Good! How's the weather? Front NW of Brussels, otherwise clear. It should be a wizard night then! Yes, I'll be going off with Van at 7 o'clock. Good show. Thanks old boy, cheerio.'

'Van, how about bacon and eggs before we go — there's just time?'

'Fine Sir, and maybe we can organize another egg for our 'night flying supper' when we get back!'*

'You old sinner, Van! OK ring the Mess will you while I check my aeroplane.'

We drove down the winding road to Westgate with the egg-shell green of the after-sunset merging into sparkling starlight overhead, while a deep orange glow silhouetted the roof tops of Ramsgate in the east heralded the rising moon. It was going to be a perfect night

---

* With strict rationing one egg after night operations was an aircrew-only privilege.

— life was great! The pilots were crowded in the bar as we walked in and in spite of protests about flying later, cans of beer appeared as if by magic. I took mine into the dining room, where I found the 'night shift' eating heartily.

'Hallo Jean, all set for tonight?'

'Yes Sir. Do you think that the weather will stay clear?'

'Oh yes, it'll probably close down to low cloud and fog around 11 o'clock when you'll be on your way home across the sea. But that won't worry an ace like you!'

'Ah, a little fog, it is nothing for me!' This with the shrug of the shoulders so typical of Belgians. The meal continued in the same half-hilarious, half-serious atmosphere which always typified the last hour before a show.

'Well, I'll go and have a look at the moon. Don't hurry chaps, I'll let you know when I'm going down.' In the hall with its notices rustling in the draught which was always present somehow even with the door closed, I paused and looking at my watch, wondered if there was time to telephone my wife Shirley. No, that would have to wait until after the show. I should be back by 10 o'clock.

Outside it was crisp and cold but very beautiful. I closed the door behind me. The moon rising above the chimneys cast long shadows down the gravel drive as it glinted between skeleton elms and beeches. As was often the case at this season, a faint but sharp line of haze divided the night sky into two; a cup of clear starlight in a saucer of moon-reflecting mist.

Forward visibility might be poor, but in an hour or so when the moon rose higher its brilliance would provide excellent light below.

'How lovely!'

A soft voice broke this train of thought and I found WAAF Section officer Joan T's fair hair and slim form beside me.

'Isn't it.'

'I suppose it's a good night for Intruding, Sir?'

Was that a very slight note of acerbity, and why did that 'Sir' sound wrong upon a girl's lips?

'Yes, it will be wizard.'

'Are you going out yourself?'

'Yes, I'll be drifting over I expect.'

'You never think of anything but flying, do you.'

'Oh well, there's a job to be done you know.'

'I suppose so, but "all work and no play" ...'

'To the onlooker perhaps, but not necessarily to Jack, and ... I play sometimes!'

116

'Would you care to come over for a drink some evening?'

'Rather, I'd love to — when the moon is over!'

'You win! Brr, it's cold out here. I must go. Good luck.'

'Thanks. Good night.'

I stood looking at the night. Perhaps one should take the work a little less seriously, and relax more often. But with so much yet to be accomplished; the proving of the Squadron in action with its new equipment; the proving of the Typhoon itself as a successful fighter, or even, as it seemed at that time of heavy prejudice, to prove that there was at least one role in which it could be successful; and finally, the purely personal but it seemed to me equally important point of proving myself capable of commanding a squadron. With all this ahead every moment of good flying weather, both day and night, was of value.

Furthermore it was surely the responsibility of a commanding officer to take each and every opportunity of flying against the enemy, for without total effort and singleness of purpose from all involved, how could the final aim, the destruction of German armed might, be achieved?

At this thought I grinned for I realized that it was not only a high ideal which kept me at work, although that had something to do with it. But I also loved flying intensely for its own sake. The thrill of setting out alone under the moon and the stars; of flying into enemy skies, hundreds of miles from home and safety where any moment may bring a target for your guns, or else the blinding blue-white glare of searchlights and searing, snaking chains of red, green and white tracer shells; these were experiences more fascinating than any to be had in the social round which, though fun at times could be rather grim at others. But still, the spirit of a moment before had gone — oh, to Hell with women!

Little more than an hour later a sense of false security occasioned by the steady pulsing of the engine and the even grey flatness of the fields and dykes of northern France passing by in the moonlight below, was violently shattered by a loud and earnest voice on the radio: "allo! — zis is Crooner wan five. Arr you receiving me?"

A short silence, then:

"allo —! I say again, Zis is Crooner 15, Crooner 15. I wish an emergency homing. Will you please give me a vector.'

There was no mistaking that voice. It was Van Lierde becoming emphatic as usual and in some sort of trouble.

Presently Control answered him, and as I flew on deeper inland towards the Luxembourg frontier, searching for the tell-tale streak of white which as often revealed train smoke as it did a chalk pit, a railway cutting or a canal with the moon on it, Van Lierde, returned towards Manston with a steadily dropping oil pressure until at last he said:

'Okay — I am over base now. Sank you very much. Switching off.'

I knew how he felt at that moment. He had 'made it'. Fate did not intend that he should swim home — this time!

*   *   *

The remaining days of 1942 were cloudy and rain-swept and as the moon was in its last quarter and providing little light at its few appearances, I began to work upon the day problem. The Channel patrols were continuing unabated with occasional practical success, as enemy sorties had become noticeably fewer owing, most probably, to the now constant presence of our fighters near all his favourite fighter-bomber targets.

But this was not enough. Over there in that country which we saw as a hazy outline in the Channel mists, were trains, road convoys, barges, and all manner of enemy transport: targets with which we could deal very adequately with our heavy 20 mm guns, of that I was certain. The slower and more vulnerable Spitfires had for some time past carried out ground-strafing attacks in the coastal areas, but with indifferent success and comparatively high losses to light anti-aircraft fire. The Typhoon with its great speed and hitting power was the ideal aircraft for this work, and I was confident of success.

But the Service as a whole was not so confident. Did not the Sabre engine fail frequently? Was the Typhoon not an ugly, heavy and cumbersome aeroplane and hardly to be considered capable of undertaking any of the work of the lissome Spitfire? Could the Typhoon ever become a fighter? I was confronted with these questions, often accompanied by thinly veiled cynicism, whenever I approached the operations planners at 11 Group headquarters.

The answer to the first question was in the affirmative. The engines did fail frequently, but as our present role entailed combat flying over the sea there was, as I saw it, nothing to be lost and everything to be gained by flying across the Channel on occasion, instead of just up and down it. The morale of the pilot however admirable it might be under normal circumstances, naturally tended to drop when he had to sit through patrol after uneventful patrol over a cold winter sea behind a motor which was more than likely to cease to function suddenly. But if he was able to fly an occasional sortie over France and there fire his guns at the enemy, then his morale would look after itself. I could see no argument against this, and in any case how could adverse judgement be pronounced against a new aircraft, which had never been in serious action, by judges who had flown only Spitfires!

The prejudice was understandable for the Spitfire was famous for its beauty of line and for its victories during the Battle of Britain, whereas the Typhoon had a blunt, pugnacious outline, a bad reputation for engine and structural failures and as yet no major victories to its credit. Indeed there seemed such a strong case against the aeroplane that at times I wondered if my appreciation of it was at fault, and if our efforts would end in failure.

I would see the AOC again! One could continue indefinitely to telephone the Sector Commander and the Group Controller and continue to receive the stock answer: 'Righto Beamont, I'll see what I can do, but the Spits do most of that work you know.'

'So once again I flew west along the Kentish coast, over Sheppey and its bomb-cratered aerodrome, a reminder of those tense days of 1940; Chatham with sleek grey cruisers at their moorings, and the Medway at Rochester where a long white streak of foam revealed a great Sunderland flying boat taking off on test in the hands of a factory test pilot.

On up the winding Thames, past the great merchant steamers at anchor from Southend to Gravesend under the protecting balloon barrage; past Tilbury Docks under the drifting smoke haze of the hundreds of factories and millions of dwellings that spread out ahead in an even brown carpet broken only by the great river and here and there by patches of lighter colour where German bombs had left their mark.

I looked down at this greatest city on earth. Chelsea, with its extremes of population, the most ordinary and the most extraordinary. Piccadilly and the West End where the day begins at nightfall; and just plain Hammersmith. In every room of every one of that great mass of buildings were people. People, who for six days out of every seven licked stamps, tapped typewriters, stood at counters, waited at tables, or sat at desks in luxurious offices. Day after day they walked to and from their work through slimy streets glistening with damp and acrid with petrol fumes and smoke; or rattled, thundered and clanged through the bowels of the earth in the Underground, jammed against each other in a sweaty mass, breathing an atmosphere of tobacco smoke, cheap scent and hot humanity. On the seventh day most of them probably went to the cinema. Were their lives happy? How could they be; and yet could I say that mine was? Not wholly perhaps, but surely life held so much more for us than it did for them. Day after day would go by with the narrowed strips of sky between towering buildings coloured a leaden grey to those few who bothered to look upwards. Then, for a few hours the sun would bathe the streets in a cheerful glare and everyone would seem happier. The BBC would refer to a period of bright weather which brought people thronging to the parks.

But we had another world. A world which we might enter every and any day and leave the mess of civilization far behind. A world of cloud plains and mountains where the air is clean and clear; where the earth, a mere carpet of colours and contours, and all its troubles is far distant and where always the sun shines.

How frequently one heard people say: 'Those young pilots! They seem to have no respect for conventions. They are irresponsible, abrupt and quite lawless. There is something extraordinary about them — I suppose it's the flying!' Little did they know how right they were! But there ahead lay the green turf and grey runways of Northolt aerodrome in the midst of the concrete, plaster and chromium plots of Greater London, and in a few moments I was struggling to control an abject but not unjustified fear of violent decease as I was whirled down Western Avenue in a staff car driven by a beautiful and incredibly erratic WAAF.

At Group Headquarters I sensed immediately a different attitude. It was apparent that the performance of 609 squadron during the previous month had not passed unnoticed, and that our night activities had been the cause of some controversy. The AOC wished to have a full account of the 'Intruders' and of my ideas for future work of the same nature, and finally agreed to the proposal that the Squadron should operate during each moon period with the maximum number of aircraft which would not affect our daylight patrol commitment. All sorties were to be planned by me and only required approval of Group Intruder Operations staff on the afternoon before they were to take place. In the face of such a complete moral victory, for such it seemed to me, I felt doubtful of the wisdom of broaching the day-offensive question. But Air Marshal Hugh 'Dingbat' Saunders showed signs of terminating the interview, and so I plunged:

'There is one other point, Sir. The 'day' question. Constant patrols over the sea do tend to become boring, and of course boredom is the greatest enemy of efficiency in a squadron. I know Sir, that if the pilots could carry out occasional ground-strafing sorties in daylight when there is no moon for night work, it would not only serve to keep their keenness up to high pitch but would also produce some good results. There must be almost unlimited rail and road transport activity inland beyond the present range of "Rhubarbs" in the Brussels-Lille and Amiens areas, which we could deal with satisfactorily.'

Hugh Saunders had been smiling throughout my obvious effort to obtain yet another favour. Now he laughed outright: 'You know, Beamont, you and 609 can't fight this war all by yourselves! But still, if you can provide aircraft over and above your patrol commitment, then you may send occasional sections out on "Rhubarbs". But owing to the intensity of the enemy light flak in the coastal zone I have ruled that squadron commanders may not take part themselves in these operations! You know that, I suppose?'

'But Sir, I've studied the flak position and I'm sure that by changing the current procedure of flying in low across the coast in the thick of the flak, to flying low over the sea until the coast is sighted, then climbing steeply to above light flak range, say 5,000 ft, and staying there until well inland past the coastal belt, we can operate successfully without suffering many, if any, casualties.

Also, as it is quite a new thing I don't feel that it would be satisfactory to send the pilots out when I have not been myself, Sir.'

'All right, Beamont, you may do two or three trips yourself first and after that no more! Come and let me know how you get on.'

'Right Sir. Thank you Sir!'

I saluted and left the room with my head buzzing. It was incredible! I had in effect been given an almost free hand to operate with the Squadron when and how I wished against the enemy. Here was a headquarters in which individual initiative by subordinate commanders was not only tolerated but was actively encouraged by the AOC! In the meantime the Squadron was in Kent, the enemy was in France, and there was no time to lose.

Towards the end of the month as the moon waned, the nights clouded over and night ground attack flying became impractical. This was as well in a way as we had worked very hard for ten nights running and were beginning to feel the strain. I was beginning to feel tired myself, and to realize the wisdom in the MO's admonishment that one could not burn the candle at both ends for so long; that three or four sorties a day, or one or two sorties a night were quite within reason, but that sorties both by day and by night for long periods definitely were not!

At the same time our efforts had met with considerable success. Thirteen pilots had flown their first 'Intruders', and these had resulted in damaging attacks on 27 trains. My own score had reached fourteen and for the first time since 1940 the Squadron was featured both on the radio and in the Press.*

Accordingly it was with a sense of almost luxurious well-being that I allowed myself a few early nights followed by leisurely breakfasts with the newspapers. Most of the pilots needed no example in this respect, and for a few days 10 o'clock at night found the bar nearly empty and the Nook resounding with snores.

However it was not long before they were all back to normal, and after days of Channel patrols and, when the weather was suitable, a few ground-strafing 'Rhubarbs' in daylight, the bar at the Doon House mess and the Old Charles, the Bridge and the Walmer Castle pubs were soon ringing to the tunes discordant but cheerful, of 'O'Reilly's Daughter', 'The Bugger's Alphabet', 'I don't want to join the Air Force', 'Chevalier', 'Alhouette', and of course the song of the West Riding 'On Ilkley Moor bar t' hat!'

On one such evening all the Squadron's pilots and ground crews were at the Old Charles. The beer, passed round in gallon jugs, flowed as freely as the songs, and when the time came to leave there was a strenuous battle for the waiting taxis. I reached the Mess first in my staff Hillman (the passengers swearing that Boulogne flak was a rest-cure in comparison with the CO's driving) and was in the act of setting up a round of pints when a commotion occurred in the Hall. At first the turmoil was ignored as being merely the normal noises attached to any gathering of young fighter pilots after dark, until shouts of 'Where's the CO?' drew my attention from the matter in hand. So, after asking the barman to look after it for me, I walked firmly into the Hall.

There I found two perspiring constables and a worried and uncomfortable-looking police Inspector, surrounded by a melee of laughing pilots all talking nonsense at once.

'Evening 'spector, what's the trouble?'

'Serious trouble I'm afraid Sir. At 10.35 pm Wednesday 26 January, when on patrol duty near the Old Charles Hotel, Constable ...'

'All right, I'll believe you! But I didn't do it, really!'

'This is serious, Sir. It seems that one of your officers has stolen a taxi! The owner who was waiting, it seems, to drive a party of officers home, reported the occurrence to me and I have traced the missing vehicle to outside this house!'

What had happened was obvious but under the present hilarious circumstances I could hardly control myself while the mob howled

* Appendix 2.

122

its merriment until the ceilings shook.

'Oh come now Inspector, aren't you taking this a little too seriously? All that occurred was this: a taxi was ordered by me (a tactical error that remark, as I noticed one of the constables laboriously applying pencil to note-book) to drive a party from the Old Charles to the Mess, and if under pressure of circumstances the taxi took off — Shut up, you clots! — I mean departed without its driver, well surely that's the driver's fault! Fortunes of war and all that! Thirsty work this: how about a beer Inspector?'

'Not on duty Sir! thank you. Well, perhaps, if you insist! But I must have these officers down at the Station for questioning — that's all it will be, you know; the Super's got a soft spot for your boys!' This with a very broad grin, and an ostentatious wink.

And so it was settled. The criminal, Jean de Selis (it could have been no other) and his passengers were eventually driven off to the police station, where, much to the amusement of the constables they proceeded to harangue the Superintendent at great length. He, being both a reasonable and lenient man, after describing to them the error of their ways allowed them to be driven back in the police car to the Nook where the party was still in full swing. It ended up in traditional style by the playing of gramophone records at full blast, the breaking of beds and the general consumption of Canadian cakes, candies and other luxuries belonging to Moose Evans, who, lying fully clothed on his bed emitting loud snorts at intervals, knew nothing of these things.

The next day was bleak in the extreme. An icy east wind whipped heavy yellow-grey clouds overhead at less than 1,000 ft, and turned the Channel into a grey and white mill-race. At the Dispersal the faces of the 'Readiness' pilots reflected the yellow in the sky, and conversation was for some time monosyllabic and profane. But as usual by midday signs of animation began to appear; Peter Raw went out to feed Billy, the squadron mascot goat. Blanco, Cameron, and a few others began a poker game, and one or two pilots even went out to look at their aircraft.

After hiding my hangover behind the sheaf of files and casualty forms which the adjutant could always gleefully replenish at the moment when I thought the office work was over for the day, I decided that an hour or two over the Channel with the windows open and full oxygen might clear my head. But the weather had closed down in the meantime and patrols were suspended owing to low cloud on the cliffs and hills round the coast. I spent a pleasant afternoon in the circle around the Dispersal hut fire with the wind and sleet lashing at the windowpanes, drinking innumerable cups of thick cocoa, sleeping a little and talking a little of old times; beer, women, current operations, beer … in fact, all the things that go to make conversations in the Pilots' rooms of Fighter Command of the RAF often the most pointless but always the most pleasant of any in one's experience.

Soon after four o'clock with little more than an hour and a half before dark, Operations announced that the weather was clearing and that they would like a patrol to take off.

'OK Joe, I'll take this one. Van my number two? Right.'

I tightened up the Mae West straps over my overalls, and picking up helmet and gloves, ran out across the wet tarmac towards *PR-G* shouting: 'Start up "*G*" and "*L*", to the groundcrew on the way. The gale was bitterly cold and as I fumbled with the harness buckles with numbed fingers I longed to shut the door and side windows. This I did with relief as the fitter slid off the wing and then, receiving his 'all clear' signal, I pressed the starter buttons and started up. From the high ground of the East-West runway I could see the low cloud racing across Pegwell Bay and Deal. The landscape had a dreary, windswept look, and I knew that we were in for a bumpy flight. I glanced round to see if Van Lierde was ready, and seeing his gloved hand raised inside the cockpit hood, waved mine and opened the throttle.

Once airborne the aircraft began to jolt and sink rapidly in the violent air, and I was considering the direction of the wind and wondering whether there would be fewer bumps over the sea, as was usually the case, when Van Lierde's voice came over the radio.

'Hallo Crooner leader, you are leaving a white smoke trail.'

I glanced at the instruments. They seemed quite correct.

'OK Blue two. I expect it's an over-filled Glycol tank blowing off.'

This did in fact often occur as the coolant tank was fitted with a 'blow off' valve to allow for expansion with heat when slightly overfilled.

Roaring low over Deal we headed out over the wintry Channel, and well before crossing the patrol line ten miles out to sea we were completely out of sight of land in a world of low racing clouds, spray-flecked leaden sea and lashing sleet. Once again Van Lierde called up to say that I was still leaving a trail of vapour, but as we had only been flying for a few minutes I attached no importance to it other than to keep a careful check on the engine instruments; although I experienced a sudden feeling of apprehension as I thought of the possibility of engine failure over such a sea, and shivered slightly. There would be no chance of survival at all.

There was nothing unusual in these thoughts. One went through the same thing every day, but as time went by one became hardened and bothered less about unpleasant possibilities, holding rather to the comfortable theory of crossing one's bridges when one came to them. We raced on through the storm and I could just make out the dim shape of the other Typhoon a few hundred yards away in the rain. It was good Focke Wulfe weather.

'Hallo Blue II. I think we'll carry on a bit and see if there's anything doing.'

As Van Lierde's cheerful 'Okay' sounded in my earphones, I turned a few degrees on to a course which should take us to a land-fall at Mardyck in another three minutes. There was always the possibility of finding a Hun near the French coast.

Another brief glance at the instruments, and I caught my breath as I saw the radiator temperature gauge needle jump from 90°F to 100°F and then begin to rise steadily. I watched it reach 110°F and then began to act rapidly. There was no doubt this time. I was in trouble. That white vapour had been from a coolant leak and now, so much having leaked away, the remainder was beginning to boil. When it did so the motor would 'seize' and probably catch fire.

We were quite five minutes flying at 200 mph from the nearest point of Kent, and the engine was likely to stop within three or four minutes. The only alternatives were either to use the remaining power to climb up (we were flying at 50 ft) and bale out or to nurse the remaining power and fly back to as close to home as possible before ditching.

In the first case it wanted only twenty minutes to sunset, and if the chances of being picked up out of that raging sea before dark were small, those of living through an easterly March gale at night in a rubber dinghy were non-existent. In the second case I was almost certain to have to 'ditch' and the Typhoon had in nearly every case killed those pilots who had previously attempted it. However, should I get away with that I would have a better chance of being picked up, and there was always just the faint hope that I might be able to reach land before the power failed. That was the only chance. All these thoughts flashed through my mind in a few seconds as the temperatures first began to rise, and I was already turning as I called Control on the RT: 'Hallo ... this is Crooner leader. I have bad engine trouble and am heading for Deal. I'm afraid I'll have to ditch.'

'Hallo Crooner leader, OK, I've notified Air Sea Rescue. Good luck!'

Opening the radiator cooling flap, and reducing engine revolutions and throttle to a minimum in an attempt to reduce the temperatures, I climbed to 500 ft in order to have sufficient height to turn into wind when the power failed, and settled down at 150 mph to gain every yard possible while there was still time.

It was surprising how clearly and rapidly one could think out cause, effect and correct action at such a critical moment. Immediately the temperature gauge showed a drop to 108° where it remained stable for so long — in reality about one minute — that I suddenly felt a wild and unbelievable hope.

Crouched in the confined cockpit, juggling constantly with the engine controls in order to find the combinations of best pace and coolest running, with the aircraft sluggish and heavy at the comparatively low speed and nothing in sight but cloud, rain and violent seas, it was as if I held the aircraft in the air against all the odds of fate and nature. I could now well understand the cliche 'he held his life in his hand'.

Ahead the seas broke into a fury of white foam — the Goodwins! Only another eight miles to the coast but with a sickening sensation I saw the temperatures start rising rapidly. There was nothing more to be done now. With fascinated eyes I watched the needle, 115°, 120°, 125°F. Now it was jumping sharply as the coolant boiled. I tightened down the crash straps and lowering the seat, looked ahead at the sea. Better go down crosswind than attempt to do it into wind and head on to those breakers.

Van, whose normal speed of 250 mph had taken him well in front, came curving back out of the rain, and his voice, most emphatic this time, broke into the almost equally urgent remarks being made at that moment by Control.

'Hallo, 'allo, Crooner leader. You are pouring out white stuff! You will never make it! Bale out. Bale out!'

But the cliffs, for the sight of which my eyes had been straining, took shape at that moment not more than three miles distant.

With distinctly heightened pulse rate I could feel the sweat in the palms of my gloved hands. The temperature needle passed 130° and then reached 135°F with violent jerks and oscillations. Any moment now and still two miles to go.

At the bitter end it looked as if I was to lose the battle.

'Hallo Control, Crooner leader here. Rad temperature off the clock. Should ditch just off Sandgate. Off.' This was the end. I was going to die. The water would be unpleasantly cold. I felt myself saying over and over again: 'Oh well, this is it.' One was not frightened of the act, only of the anticipation. Many people had found that out before me. I thought: 'There goes the oil

126

temperature too! Clouds of smoke from the exhaust now. A bad sign that. Oh why don't you stop you bloody engine. My God, the cliffs! It's either into them or arrive among those rocks and breakers at 100 mph. She's still flying, there's just a chance. Stick back a little. We're over! There goes the motor. Fumes! She's on fire. Get the switches off. Height 150 ft. ASI 145 mph. Have to put her down straight ahead in that wood. No! Just cleared it. Oh Christ, a village! 130 mph. Mind the church! A field between those trees. Hell, it's the side of a hill. Flaps down, more rudder, but don't stall her you fool. Trim the nose back. Mind the gunsight. Back ... back ... *Crrr r ash!*'

It seemed that after the first blinding flash as my head hit the gunsight, only a few seconds elapsed before I was fumbling with the door handle and then half crawling, half sliding down onto the wing, and finally the soft brown earth where I remained for some moments on hands and knees wondering what it was that dripped slowly on to the ground in front of me.

In fact as I discovered later, some five or six minutes elapsed before I recovered sufficient consciousness to move, and it was more than lucky that the local fire which started in the engine bay had died out.

I could hear the whining of the generator which I had no time to switch off, and considered getting up to do so. But this was altogether too much effort and I compromised with myself by lying down completely and indulging in peaceful contemplation of the sky until something or someone should occur.

Presently I heard voices one of which said: 'Cor, don't 'e look a soight!' And raising my head I saw through a haze two cheerful red faces surmounting good country clothes which smelt of hay, tweed and tobacco.

I said: 'Good afternoon' — and then realizing what an incongruous remark it was under the circumstances, attempted to achieve an upright posture.

'Take it easy old man, you've had a nasty smack you know.'

'Oh, I'm all right. Just bumped my head on the gunsight you know. Be fine in a minute.'

'Ah! We must get you down to the farm some'ow. It's quite a walk too. Think 'e can manage it with us to help?'

Assuring them that I could, I clambered to my feet and stood for a moment looking at the still smoking Typhoon as it lay flat on its belly among the furrows. The little field in which I had somehow miraculously arrived sloped steeply up the side of a hill, and the Typhoon as it stalled with the tail well down had touched at an angle which coincided nicely with the slope, and had stopped dead on impact. Five tons of aeroplane had decelerated from 80 mph to nothing in less than fifteen yards as the marks in the soil displayed. It was little wonder that I had received a blow on the head! By this time my face and hands were sticky with blood from the gash on my forehead, and as a river of it was running down the bright yellow surface of the Mae West life jacket I must have presented a grim appearance.

In any case my two helpers, taking firm grips of my arms, began to lead me away down the hill.

'You'll be all right when we get 'e down to t' farm. That's it down by the wood. Think 'e can make it?'

'Oh yes, sure, I'm feeling miles better already.'

This was true for I felt quite light on my feet once more, but as I stepped out firmly to show them this I felt the heavy pressures under my arms suddenly increase and heard a faint voice in the distance saying:

'Ah! I thought he was getting pretty heavy! Well, it ain't far now!'

An exquisite coolness on my burning forehead and cheeks as I returned to consciousness turned out to be the ministrations of the good lady of the house who was gently washing my face and generally cleaning up the mess. I tried to make conversation with some apology for causing trouble, but she smiled and told me not to be silly and lie quiet, and as this seemed an extraordinarily pleasant thing to do, I closed my eyes and endeavoured to make sense of the odd sentences that occasionally came through the intense throbbings in my head.

'He's got quite a cut there ... fracture? ... cup of tea ... they'll send an ambulance I expect ...'

Here was where I could be helpful and quite triumphantly I said: 'Yes, I'm from Manston, you know. The Doc'll be here pretty soon. I wonder if someone could watch ...?'

At this moment a large blue figure loomed into my view.

'Sorry to bother you Sir, but oi must have some particulars. Must be sure you ain't a German, musn't oi! Have 'e got oidentity card?'

'Yes, officer, here in my pocket book.'

I fumbled with buttons and zip fasteners, and my hand and the wallet came out sticky with blood.

'Oh Lord. I am making a mess of your room. I'm so sorry. You'll find it all in there, officer.'

'Thank you Sir: that's all correct. Now I've telephoned the

Typical attacks by 609 Squadron Typhoons from Manston in 1943: Detal's Ju 88 (Author's Collection).

Van Lierde's Ju 52 (Author's Collection).

Author's 'M' type mine-sweeper (Author's Collection).

Roy Payne's PR-H *of 609 belly-lands with undercarriage trouble at Biggin Hill. November 1942* (Author's Collection).

Above *609 Squadron party at Doon House, Westgate, in 1943: (L to R) 'Pancho' Villa, Author, Evans, Coghlan, Haabjorn, unknown, unknown, Skett, Vanlierde, Wells, Atinson, De Moulin, Raw, Blanco (Ziegler Collection).*

Below *Author with modified face (a marked improvement according to 609) after belly-landing near Deal in 1943 (Ziegler Collection).*

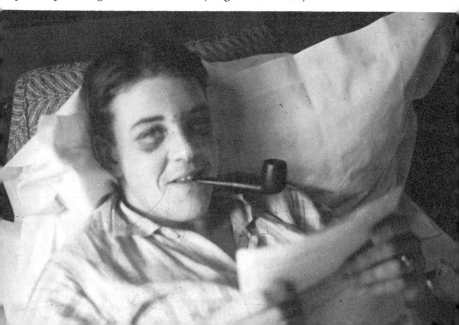

Left *Peter Raw with 609's mascot, Wing Commander 'Billy de Goat', at Manston in 1943 (Ziegler Collection).*

Below *The Air Secretary's visit to 609 Squadron in 1943: (L to R) Desmond Sheen, Sir Louis Greig, Author, Sir Archibald Sinclair (Ziegler Collection).*

aerodrome and the ambulance has already left, so oi'll go out and watch for them now. They seemed to know all about you and were in quite a state! What was the trouble; was you shot down?'

'Yes, they'd know all right, as I told them on the R/T — the wireless, you know. Just engine trouble — it stopped just the other side of the village ...'

Then a period of unknown length in which I was only conscious of one thing; a splitting pain filling the whole of my head, until breaking through it a voice said: 'He's in here ... quite a blow on the bridge of the nose.'

There was little Doc McKeckney looking rather pale and worried about the safety of one of 'his' pilots, his 'boys' as he called us. Behind him loomed the round countenance of McIver (the S/Ldr Admin) for once without a cheerful grin on it.

'Och Sir, there you are. You had us really worried that time. We thocht we'd lost ye. Now let's have a look. Ah! Just a wee cut and a dint on the skull, Sir. I regret to inform you that you're going to have a wonderful pair of black eyes tomorrow! In the meantime, just let's get at your arm ... Hypo please, Sergeant. Now Sir! I'm the Doctor here! Just a wee jab and you'll be feeling fine. There!'

'I didn't need that you know, Doc; still, you're the Boss. You didn't lose any time getting here! Hallo Mac, come to see the corpse?'

There followed a confusion of events of which I could make out only vague details through the luxurious drugged haze that crept over me.

Being lifted on to a stretcher, and trying in vain to thank the farmer and his wife for their kindness as I was carried out to an ambulance. A jolting but very peaceful journey with the MO sitting opposite saying: 'We'll give you a few days at the hospital at Deal. They'll look after you well there. Och, I know you want to be on the Station. You never will let up for a moment, will ye, but we haven't the facilities.'

More lifting and carrying through corridors with the typical hospital smell.

A small, bright room. Being undressed by bustling nurses ... embarrassing. More washing. The MO and a civilian doctor in conversation ... sutures. Jabbing and pulling at my forehead as the stitches were put in. Then peace and a delicious drowsiness.

Twelve hours later I awoke, clear headed but almost unable to see. Both eyes had swollen until the lids met and passed out a continuous stream of water. But apart from the general soreness I felt quite well and could not understand why I had to remain still in bed. This was cleared up when the Sister said that the X-rays, taken unknown to me, had disclosed a small skull fracture and that I had concussion which would take a week or more of complete rest to cure.

This was terrible. I had to get back to the Squadron. I had also to get back to the Station soon or Shirley would start to worry about my failure to telephone and then would inevitably hear through the WAAF channels that I had been hurt in a crash, and the story would not lose in the telling. This did in fact happen. The Sister smiled sympathetically and said that I must be good and rest.

After a few days during which I received many visits from the pilots in the Hillman, and from the lady who had looked after me at the farm, I realized that the concussion theory was true and that, infuriating though it was, I would have to resign myself to some weeks off flying.

The pilots brought all the Squadron news and some files and papers to sign, accompanied by gales of immoderate merriment at the sight of my afflicted countenance. The farmer's wife brought a dozen eggs and some fine apples and hoped that I would get well quickly. It was an extremely kind gesture.

Towards the end of the week I began to feel fit again and restive, and although the hospital doctor said that I could not fly for at least a month I had other ideas.

Accordingly on the eighth day after the crash I left for the camp with the MO in attendance amid a chorus of thanks and good wishes, for during the week the Press had given the Squadron and myself another 'write-up', and this had given the hospital staff the misguided impression that they had a celebrity in their midst!

Arriving back at the Mess with a dead-white face offset by two purple and yellow masses where eyelids and brows should have been, and blood-red eyeballs resulting from a haemorrhage caused by the skull fracture, caused quite a sensation; and this was surpassed on the following day when I descended upon the bosom of the family for the three weeks' sick-leave ordered by Mc-Keckney. But a week later, feeling fully recovered and with almost normal eyes, I was back at work preparing for the next moon period.

April passed by, and almost imperceptibly a misty green spread in the spring sunlight over the drab brown hedgerows of winter. 609 Squadron went on from success to success and as their commanding officer I basked in a small limelight of reflected glory locally, on the Station and in 11 Group and further afield in the Press, for under the auspices of the Ministry of Information a Press conference had been held on the squadron for the purpose of breaking the news of our new (and now clearly successful) secret fighter, to the public.

This was done with the inimitable enthusiasm of the British Press and for many weeks the papers featured photographs of dashing, dare-devil pilots propping up various corners of their aeroplanes, and portraits and experiences of Van Lierde, Peter Raw, and 'Bee' or more often, 'Bob' Beamont.

Though often nauseated and embarrassed by the publication of the incredible deeds and statements attributed to us, we obtained a great deal of amusement from the situation and almost daily the normally gloomy atmosphere of the Mess at breakfast time was livened with shouts of laughter as someone read out yet another outrageous statement about us; and I came in for a particularly heavy share of leg-pulling when Basil Cardew of the *Express* described me somewhat imaginatively, as 'Young Bob Beamont, tall, wiry and tough ...!'

On the other hand some sections of the Press dealt with our 'stories' very fairly and for a considerable period in 1943 the West Riding Squadron was in the forefront of the air news. But it was not public acclaim that made life so pleasant that spring. It was the cheerful grins of the airmen and NCOs when I arrived at dispersal. The 'Good luck, Sir' as I taxied out for a show, and the crowded groups round the aeroplane on the return. The infectious goodwill with which the ground crews worked on into the night, often in the worst of weather when I told them that such an effort was necessary, and the unanimity with which my presence was demanded at all parties held by the pilots or ground crews. For with their usual whole-hearted generosity, and after the normal period of trial 'on suspicion', the Squadron now seemed to attribute their current successes to my efforts, and proceeded to show their appreciation accordingly.

But I knew very well that although a CO could give a lead, it was the quality of all ranks that ensured the result; quality which 609 West Riding Squadron with its improbable mix of Belgians, Canadians and other 'Colonials', and bluff Yorkshiremen, had in extraordinary measure at Manston in 1943.*

* Appendix 2.

Chapter 9

THE TEMPESTS' FIRST SUCCESSES

On completion of this second 'operational tour' I was posted from Manston back to the Hawker Company in May 1943, this time as an 'experimental' test pilot to take part in an urgent programme of tests to establish the cause of a spate of tail structural failures in the Typhoon squadrons, and also for the trials of the new and much improved variants of the Typhoon, the Tempest series. This was fascinating work and in January 1944 when the Tempest trials were virtually complete, I once again asked to rejoin an operational squadron, but this time on Tempests.

Air Vice Marshal Hugh Saunders*, still commanding the Metropolitan and South East fighting area as AOC No 11 Group, Fighter Command, apparently had something like this in mind because he charged me with forming the first Wing of Tempest Vs and training the first three squadrons to operational status within two months from the end of February 1944. This made it immediately clear that the long-anticipated invasion of Continental Europe was to be expected very soon after that!

*   *   *

In April 1944 the days at Newchurch with our brand new Hawker Tempest Vs passed quickly with training formations, combat practice and occasional low and high level 'sweeps' over France; and there was no lack of keenness as I had promised the new pilots that they could take part in 'sweeps' as soon as their squadron commanders were satisfied with them. At the same time the more experienced pilots, knowing that the invasion could not be far off, made the most of this opportunity to reach the highest possible standard with their Tempests. They knew that their lives might depend entirely on their skill with the new aircraft, and they also

* Later Air Chief Marshal Sir Hugh Saunders GCB KBE MC DFC MM.

knew that there were to be no 'passengers'.

The weather remained ideal. The sun beat down between rolling white cumulus clouds, and Cap Gris Nez was visible across the glinting Channel on most days. On one such afternoon on 28 May I lay on the grass in front of the tiny cottage that served as the Wing office and soaked in the sunshine. It was so hot that I could not keep still and had to shift my position every few minutes.

'Mony' Van Lierde, who had been posted to No 3 Squadron at Newchurch from 609 Squadron was as usual, fully clothed with thick sweaters and lay asleep nearby, and the remainder of the lawn was covered with glistening pilots in various stages of undress. Buck Feldman, an exuberant American in 3 Squadron being almost naked. Six Tempests came thundering across in tight drill and one of the nudists stirred: 'Bloody ropey, must be 'B' Flight!'

I must have dozed off in the sun, for it was from a very great distance that a voice said: 'Hallo Bee, you lazy sod!' and I awoke to find Chris's irrepressibly cheerful countenance beaming at me as he threw himself on to the grass. 'Well, when are you going to do some work in this war; or are you waiting till you can get some Spitfires to escort you' said Chris who was a Spitfire pilot.

'Oh, we just don't want to put you Spit people out of a job yet. We're being saved to look after the Invasion! Oh Hell, there's my phone.'

I leaned in through the office window and reached for the telephone, knocking the 'IN' tray and a number of files to the floor in the process to the accompaniment of merriment from the nudists.

'Operations for you, Sir.'

'Thanks: Hallo, Beamont here!'

'Group have got something which they think you might like to take on. Reconnaissance showed a number of aircraft on Cormeilles airfield north of Paris this morning, and Johnny Johnson saw them about an hour ago when over there with his Wing. You can attack the aerodrome if you think it worthwhile. Of course it's in the heavily defended zone, and there's no cloud cover at all. What do you think: would you like to have a crack?'

'Don't be daft, of course I wouldn't like to; I'm enjoying the sunshine! Tell me more. Where is this place and where are the aircraft parked? You'll have the details telephoned to Intelligence? OK, tell Group I'll take 3 Squadron and we'll take-off at — let me see — 17.00 hours. OK old boy, thanks. We'll see what we can do.'

I walked back to the lawn. 'OK boys, there's work to do. How many aircraft can you muster Alan? Ten? Right, briefing in my office in fifteen minutes. I shall be leading.'

In the Intelligence Office I studied the relevant maps and plotted the track which I intended to fly on.

'Have you got a target photograph of Cormeilles, Spy?'

'Yes Sir, it's on your desk with the possible positions of aircraft marked on it, and the flak positions of course.'

'Fine, let me have the courses as soon as possible.'

I pushed through the circle of pilots round the wall map marked with the track in red tape stretching down across France to Paris, and hoped that my voice would convey the necessary confidence and not betray the butterflies in my stomach.

'Well chaps, we've been given a decent target at last. Aircraft have been seen here on this dispersal, and we are going to have a crack at them. Yes, there will certainly be flak, but we shall only attack if conditions and our approach are right for a surprise run out of the sun. We shall cross in at Le Treport at 10,000 ft and fly straight to the target area at 300 IAS. Arriving at Cormeilles up-sun on the north-west side at 7,000 ft. I shall hope to see our target in time to 'peel off' here and dive straight from the sun and away across the south-east corner of the aerodrome at about 400 mph, keeping low on the deck out of the way of flak until this point where we shall climb and re-form. Any questions? ...

'Yes, I'll give you good warning to string out in echelon before going down, but final arrangements will have to be made on the target ....

'OK then, we'll only attack if conditions are suitable, and I don't suppose that there's any need to remind you to keep on the deck after leaving the target! Cockpits at 16.45, start up 16.50, take-off 17.00 hours. Check your watches. Operations time is now 16.25. All set? Right.'

I went out to 'RB' and gave my maps, course card and helmet to the waiting groundcrew as I swung on to the wing and lowered myself into the cockpit.

The sun, intense enough outside, beat down into the confined space almost unbearably, and by the time I had buckled the parachute and seat harness, adjusted the seat and stowed the maps conveniently, I was perspiring freely. I set the cockpit chronometer — two minutes to go. What would this flight result in? Whatever it was, nothing must prevent our going. I knew that some of the pilots had felt nervous by their manner during briefing, — forced gaiety, rapid smoking, excessive fidgeting and restlessness. Did they all feel as I did? Probably it was worse for them as I was getting used to it after more than four years; but in the majority of cases their nerve tension would increase until it reached near-breaking point as we approached the enemy coastline, or the target, according to individuals. That was the crux of the matter. The average fighter pilot was always a little frightened before, and to a lesser extent during an operation. But this state gave place to excitement and in most cases to actual enjoyment as the flight progressed, according to the fighting spirit, war experience and capability of the individual.

This was no time for reflection though, and after two preliminary priming strokes I pressed the starting buttons. The great four-bladed airscrew drove a cooling gale mixed with acrid exhaust fumes round the cockpit as I taxied down the rough field to the main 'Somerfelt Track' strip. All along the dispersal grey clouds of smoke showed motors bursting into life, and one by one the aircraft swung into line behind me, with Sergeant 'F' — my 'number 2' in position close on my right. I shut the hood and held my right hand above my head, then dropped it forward and opened the throttle slowly.

Once airborne I kept the speed down to enable the remainder to overtake, and turned slowly on to course.

'Hallo Kingsley, Kelvin Leader airborne. Are you receiving me, over.'

'Hallo Kelvin Leader. This is Kingsley. Receiving you loud and clear. Listening out.' Crossing out over Dungeness with the formation drawing into their respective positions, I realized that conditions were as nearly perfect as possible. The sun blazed down from a clear sky unmarred by cloud, while from ground level up to 7,000 ft a thick haze restricted vision to less than five miles, and it reflected the glare of the sun in the south-western quarter to such an extent that I was glad of the sunglasses which I wore under my helmet. If only these conditions held until the target area!

Climbing steadily as we passed through the top of the haze and levelled out at 8,000 ft heading due south. Alan called up and, announcing that he had engine trouble, broke away from the formation and headed for home with his number 2 (the standard precautionary drill).

Almost immediately 'Lefty' Witman had to return to base, leaving only seven aircraft. Could the job be done with so few? It was our first real chance for a major action, and it was a target which would not last as, in all probability, the birds would have flown on the following day. Anyway, having come as far as this I was very loath to return without the proverbial parrot; so I rearranged the formation into a 'V' of three pairs and increased

135

speed until a steady 300 mph was showing on the air speed indicator. As usual the sea appeared to be boundless, and I found my thoughts slipping back to those lonely flights under the moon over this identical area which we had made so many times during the winter of 1942/43 in the then new Typhoons.

How different to be flying in the brilliance of a spring afternoon with the sleek, menacing shapes of these Tempests rising and falling gently at either wing, with the goggled, masked and helmeted heads of their pilots crouched in their shiny transparent hoods.

A thin white line appeared in the mist below and then developed into the low cliffs of Le Treport with the estuary of the Somme stretching out into the mist to port. Gently changing height and direction in consideration for the St Valery flak, I began to check on landmarks to make sure of the course. The target was only eight minutes away, and everything depended on accurate navigation. There was the railway passing through Aumale where a goods train had surprised me in my 609 Typhoon with some very accurate machine gun tracer one night a year ago, then the runways of Poix airfield over to port; getting deep into France now.

'Hallo Kelvin aircraft; Kelvin Leader calling, keep your eyes open now — watch the sun!'

There should be a big wood ahead — three minutes from the target now but where the Hell's that wood! France, coloured the soft red-brown of new ploughland in the haze with few sharp outlines on either side, spread out into the distance. I felt the impossibility of warfare in such peaceful scene, and immediately realized the hypocrisy of the thought.

Ah, there was my wood. In two minutes a town should appear with the Seine sweeping in a wide bend to the west. The weather was perfect and I knew now that our attack would take place. Ahead a town began to take shape and beyond it the white strips of runways on an aerodrome. There was the river in the distance to starboard — the Seine. The runways ran South-North and SE-NW; yes, there were hangars on the northern boundary and a series of concrete dispersal tracks off the western side of the field. Another long dispersal stretching away south of the field, and then 'Good God, there they are!' This aloud to myself as, while still some miles away, I saw four, five and more black shapes of twin-engined aircraft standing out sharply against dead-white concrete bays in the south dispersal area.

'Hallo Kelvin aircraft, target ahead. Kelvin Leader attacking aircraft in southern bays. Going down to port in thirty seconds.

Line astern into echelon starboard for attack, GO!'

The Tempests slid over behind me as I throttled back and turned slightly to the right in order to keep the aerodrome in sight on my left.

No flak so far! When would it start, was probably the uppermost thought in all our minds at that moment. The sun was at my right shoulder now, and those fascinating squat black insects below which were great enemy bombers were level with my left.

'OK chaps, Kelvin Leader going down to port. Make this good now. Here we go!'

I heeled over steeper and steeper until the horizon disappeared, and the aerodrome with its white concrete everywhere appeared above the top of the windshield. I pulled the nose up until the target area came into view ahead: a long white road, behind it a square concrete blast pen with an aircraft in it, and beyond it a runway and the rest of the aerodrome.

Over my right shoulder looking back into the sun I saw the Tempests 'peeling off' one after the other. They were all right.

350, 380, 400, 450 mph. The needle of the airspeed indicator swung round the dial; the din rose to a shrill crescendo and the ground, hitherto remote, suddenly rushed towards us.

'Gunsight "ON," camera "ON". Hell, it's a 188!'

Rudder the sights on to it. To hell with flak anyway. *Brrrr-rrr-rrm*. Wizard! Hits all over it; collapsing on one wing, a great chunk flying into the air from the top of the fuselage and clouds of dust and smoke. Look out man!

I had held the gunsight right on firing into the centre of the cloud of debris until, checking almost too late, we flashed across the wall of the pen through smoke and debris and on across the aerodrome at 450 mph plus, less than 20 ft high. Here came the flak — a black puff above the hood. Another off the port wing. Another, and half a dozen others behind, and then I was flashing away to the north, low over the fields — safe for the moment. I looked back; even lower than my aircraft came two Tempests: behind rose a pall of dust and two columns of smoke. It looked as if the target had been bombed at least.

The sky behind was a mass of black and grey shell bursts, and through these came two more Tempests.

'Well done, Kelvin aircraft. Kelvin Leader climbing to Angels 7. Re-form. Anyone who is hit, speak up or for ever after hold his peace.'

I looked back on either side; one, two, three, four, and way down below, five. They were all there. We climbed up, and seeing the bomb-shattered wreck of Beauvais Tille aerodrome ahead I altered course to avoid possible heavy flak. We had received some there the previous week. It was extraordinary how vulnerable one felt when climbing at a mere 220 mph over enemy territory.

'Kelvin Leader here. Keep your eyes open, there may be fighters around; opening up a bit.'

Levelling at 10,000 ft and 300 mph, the ground slipped by quickly and the coast appeared in sight in apparently half the time of the outward journey. It was a beautiful day, the boys were flying nicely and we still had ammunition.

'Hallo Kingsley, this is Kelvin Leader. Have you any trade for me?'

'Hallo Kelvin Leader, Kingsley here. Sorry, no activity for you. Have you had any joy?'

'Kelvin Leader, yes we had a good prang; listening out.'

On over the dead flat haze top with Poix, Abbeville, St Valery and the coast slipping past beneath. The sand dunes of Berck Plage on the right fading into the mist in the direction of Le Touquet — out of the flak area now.

'Kelvin Leader, throttling back a bit.'

Well, that was all over. Better watch the sun for fighters still. Out of sight of land again now, heading north. The Somme to Dungeness was 60 miles — landfall in about a quarter of an hour. The motor sounds rough! Revolutions steady; oil temperature, pressure, radiator temperature and boost pressure all correct. Funny how one always imagined trouble when over the sea. It was five years and 1,500 flying hours since my first experience of the feeling, and I had not grown out of it. Another ten minutes and while losing altitude gently at 320 mph, the green-grey tongue of Dungeness took shape ahead.

'OK Kelvin aircraft; close in now.'

Over the wide beach at Romsey and on towards the church in the wood and the green strip of the airfield.

'Aircraft echelon starboard, GO.'

A tight circuit with the others stringing out behind, and then in to land.

The sun was still warm as I sat down in the deckchair that I had only recently left. I looked at my watch: 6.15. We had flown to the outskirts of Paris and back — and had destroyed two enemy bombers and damaged two others, as the interrogation eventually indicated when the pilots became calm enough to be coherent, in a little over one hour.

The following day we learned that these Ju 188s had arrived at

Cormeilles that morning as part of the force that were to attack the Bristol area that night. In the meantime we were hot and thirsty and it was past 6 o'clock.

'The bar is open chaps! Who's for a jug?'

For the next few weeks the Newchurch Wing carried out long-range sweeps almost every day in search of enemy aircraft. I planned a series which covered every German aerodrome of any importance from Brussels to Rheims, and Rheims to Paris, and day after day we flew at tree-top height over the dykes of Flanders, past the slag heaps of Lens and Douai, the Canadian memorial at Vimy, and along the water meadows of the Somme and Marne. We often saw French folk waving from their doorways, and even more after intense AA fire as we flashed across Juvincourt, Rosieres or Achiet airfields; but never a Hun in the air.

The Luftwaffe had been driven, literally, to ground, and as we learned from subsequent Intelligence reports even local communications flights between German units based as far inland as Metz and Nancy were regarded as 'sorties against the enemy' at this time. There was little or no flying by day by the Luftwaffe and no practice-flying at all, so that our chances of meeting any aircraft were small. However the knowledge that certain units of fighters were still based in the Brussels and Lille areas, and some bombers and night fighters in the area north of Paris, provided the necessary spice of excitement. There was always the chance of arriving over an aerodrome as a Hun was trying to land!

Up to this time we had lost no Tempests, although airscrew failure had caused a number of serious — but not fatal — accidents since the formation of the Wing in March. It was a jolt to us all when Flying Sergeant Mannion and Flying Officer Zurakowski failed to return from a reconnaissance of the channel ports one afternoon in late May. I had received the order in my office. 'Two aircraft, low level recce of the harbours at Ostend, Calais, Boulogne and Dieppe', and had passed it to the Intelligence officer for transmission to the Readiness Section. It was a routine operation.

The pilots knew the French coast intimately, and had been instructed many times in the whereabouts of flak batteries and the art of outwitting them, so that missions of this nature could be allocated generally without the delay of briefing. The two Poles, both very capable and experienced pilots, had, with their usual enthusiasm, run out to their aircraft, started up and thundered away in the direction of Belgium within five minutes of the first order.

I was busy adding yet another pattern to the already intricate arrangements of red, green, yellow, blue, brown and black lines which spread out on the wall briefing map in Intelligence from Dungeness to the enemy coast, indicating our programme of 'sweeps' and other operations for the next 24 hours; and an hour or more sped by rapidly. Then the IO came in and said: 'Excuse me Sir; Green section have been away nearly two hours.'

'Hell! They shouldn't have been more than an hour fifteen. I'll see if Ops know anything.'

'Hallo Ops? Controller please. Yes it's urgent. Wing Commander Flying, Newchurch, speaking. Oh hello old boy. Know anything about these bods of mine? You haven't heard from them since they reported from Boulogne — not a word? Oh well, let me know if you do get anything, won't you. How about a search? ... Air Sea Rescue on the job already. Good show.'

Alan Dredge, their Squadron commander, had come in while I was talking. 'Do they know anything about the Poles, Sir?'

'Afraid not, old boy. Looks as though they've had it. Probably those bloody heavies at Boulogne.'

A further half hour passed by and as I walked out to my aircraft to check it for the evening show, a small and grimy 'erk' approached self-consciously, saluted and said: ''Scuse me Sir, could you tell me any news of Flight Sergeant M? He's been away over two hours Sir, and he's me pilot, an' I should 'ate anything to 'appen to 'im.' There was often a very close bond of friendship and confidence between groundcrews and their particular pilots.

'Yes, I'm afraid that we shan't see them again. They would have run out of fuel at least thirty minutes ago, so they can't still be flying. There's no other news. By the way, what's your name?'

'Anderson Sir, "B" Flight.'

'Right Anderson, I'll let you know if any news comes through.'

But I knew very well that there would most likely be no further news. It was just another of those incidents which passed almost unnoticed in this strange active service life. Two boys, living and enjoying the best periods of their lives, had flown away into the cloudless sunshine of that spring afternoon on what was probably their 200th or more sortie against the enemy, on a sortie from which they would never return.

In the Mess tent that evening someone would say: 'Poor old Zura, perhaps he'll turn up as a Pow.' And that would be all. On the following day the affair would be forgotten in the excitement of waiting for the next 'show', forgotten except by a very few who stopped for a moment to think that that incident which meant little more to us than the absence of a friendly face, also possibly meant at a stroke the end of happiness, the end of life itself as they had known it, to a wife, children and parents somewhere in the world.

Later in the evening I took the New Zealanders down to the Rosieres group of airfields which we found peacefully inactive, and we returned in the gathering dusk without firing a shot or seeing any flak. But when I telephoned Operations last thing before going to bed in my tent, they had no more news of the missing pilots — and there never was any.

On the following day there were no less than three cases of engine failure in flight, resulting in one pilot baling out near Canterbury and two others being injured in crash landings. In themselves these incidents, unfortunate though they were, were unimportant. The injured pilots would recover, and aircraft could be replaced. But at this time, when we were flying our new Tempests over long stretches of sea to enemy territory every day, my greatest problem was instilling into the pilots confidence in their new machines, and these accidents tended to aggravate the problem.

I knew where the fault lay. Philip Lucas* had worked on it in his usual indefatigable manner ever since the first airscrew had 'over-sped' on a Tempest on test in the hands of Peter Raw in the previous December, and he had finally persuaded the airscrew company to modify their 'piston transfer seal'.

This modification was at last under way, but in the meantime we had to face not only the enemy, but the constant possibility of engine failure over enemy territory, the sea, and even during the critical moments of take-off and landing. It was the early days of the Typhoon over again.

Technical troubles generally arose during the early operations of a new type, and I had learned at Langley the reasons for apparently inexcusable delays in the discovery and rectifying of defects when they appeared. An aircraft is built in three main components: the airframe, the engine, and the airscrew, and although the airframe manufacturers build the machine as a whole, the responsibility for the functioning of the engine and the airscrew remain with their individual makers.

However, frequently when a defect occurs in the engine or the airscrew the component firm states bluntly that the installation is to blame, thereby transferring the responsibility from themselves to the airframe assembly factories. The latter in their turn are certain that their installation is not to blame and, while investigat-

* Hawker's deputy chief test pilot.

ing it for their own peace of mind, attempt to 'pass the buck' either back to the engine makers, or if there's the slightest evidence in that direction, on to the airscrew company.

Thus each and every new problem which arises has to undergo weeks of separate investigation by the various firms, all anxious to prove that their products are blameless in order that 'Production' — god of management and enemy of development — should not be affected; until at last the responsible Ministry steps in and, co-ordinating the investigation, finally apportions the responsibility.

In this particular case the problem had long been analysed as over-speeding of the propellor which allowed the engine to achieve uncontrollably, in a space of seconds, two or three-thousand rpm more than its maximum. Thereupon the bearings failed, the oil system collapsed and the engine ceased to function abruptly. But the propellor manufacturers saw the matter differently! They held that the bearings failed, causing the engine and therefore the propellor to lose its oil pressure and the propellor in turn would naturally become out of control and 'over-speed'.

The argument continued for months and it was not until June 1944 — six months after the first reported failure — that we began to receive the modified propellers which solved the problem.

In the meantime the pilots were naturally becoming worried as almost every day brought news of another crash, and on each flight the possibility that this time it could be their turn. This had the effect of revealing the weaker brethren: a very few pilots who had shown a brave front under easy conditions now failed to maintain it as the going became rough. I knew the symptoms well by now; lack of enthusiasm for flying, heated arguments with Flight commanders about 'days off', and 'early returns' with aircraft suffering from purely fictitious troubles; and I welcomed the opportunity of removing some unreliable elements and replacing them with new pilots while there was yet time to train them.

Then, at the psychological moment, came a day of just the sort of intense action which was needed to test the quality of the Wing and its standard of training, and to restore to the pilots confidence in themselves and their aircraft. During April and May we had swept the skies and countryside of France and the Low Countries almost daily with small and large formations, and during that time had sighted hundreds of enemy trains. But we had been forced to ignore these tempting targets in compliance with a High Command order in force since December 1943, banning further attacks on continental railways for diplomatic reasons. No doubt a matter of high policy but very irksome to us as the enemy took great care to leave little else of value uncovered, and the railways were obviously a vital part of his logistic system.

Occasionally we had been able to circumvent this order by submitting carefully-worded intelligence reports. These were received with amusement by Group, and we had got away with it. On two occasions earlier in the month I had attacked trains, one at Guines near Boulogne and the other near Rouen, both by moonlight, and had justified the attacks by first flying low over the trains without firing. This action had resulted, as anticipated, in streams of tracer shells from the flak wagons, and as this was obviously a hostile act I was now lawfully entitled to return the compliment!

But Van Lierde had, inevitably, gone one better. Not content with returning one day and reporting to Intelligence that he had been 'attacked by a hostile train while flying peacefully along at 1,000 ft and had therefore been forced to destroy it', he had found a magnificent target near Brussels a few days later.

While leading a section of four Tempests on a patrol of the German airfields of Melsbroek, Evere and Le Culot, he had sighted a long train of flat wagons heading north-east which on closer inspection had proved to be carrying between forty and fifty camouflaged staff cars. This was obviously a legitimate target and the fact that there happened to be a train underneath the automobiles 'was merely unfortunate', as Van Lierde expressed himself forcibly upon his return having strafed the target until all his formation's ammunition was expended and the train in flames! There had been no flak; the target had been almost too good to be true, and they were sure that they had destroyed at least forty vehicles.*

Van Lierde had done a good job, and when, only a few days later he had found another train loaded with a dozen more military vehicles and destroyed that, 3 Squadron began to behave much more cheerfully.

But we needed still greater encouragement, and it was not long in coming. On 21 May 1944, the telephone shattered my sleep in my tent at 3.00 am and the somnolent voice of Knight, the duty IO said: 'Big show on tomorrow, Sir; they've lifted the train ban.'

* This claim was supported by excellent 'combat films' of the attack taken from the cine camera of Van Lierde's Tempest, and it was finally confirmed to me some months later at Stalag Luft III by Flight Lieutenant Geoffrey Rice, who had passed by the blazing wrecks on his way to Germany as a PoW and had counted 52 Renault saloons, all of which were burnt out or still burning.

A few moments later a despatch rider clattered up and thrust his way under the tent flap: 'Wing Commander Flying, Sir? Form D* for you Sir.'

'Thanks: will you go back to Intelligence now and wait there. I shall want you to carry orders to the squadron commanders in a few minutes.'

'Right Sir.'

I peered at the signal form in the dim light, and then whistled involuntarily. This was terrific!

'Hey Digger!' I shouted across the tent to where the dim form of the Airfield commandant lay snoring upon his camp bed.

'Christ! What's the blooming row!'

'Listen to this Form D old cock. It's addressed to every wing in all three groups and to the American fighter groups ....

'Intention: To attack and destroy with all available squadrons enemy rail transport from Germany to the Atlantic coast from First Light 21 May. Planning, routes and timing in allotted areas at Wing Leaders' discretion ...'

'Gosh! This gives us a completely free hand and the allotted areas's right up our street too! The area bounded by Ostend-Louvain-Valenciennes-Douai-Gap Gris Nez! We know every yard of it. This is just what we've been waiting for!'

'For Gawd's sake, stop being so ruddy enthusiastic at this horrible hour. What time are you off? I'll fix early breakfasts.'

'No, it's OK, zero for the Wing is eight o'clock so the boys can breakfast in the Mess at seven quite comfortably. Afraid I'll have to work all this out now though — sorry to keep you awake.'

I studied the orders for some time with a map of northern France and Belgium on the ground by my camp bed, and then reached over for the telephone.

'Intelligence please. Hallo Spy. Got some paper? Right, here's the programme. Area divided into four sectors, Ostend-Brussels, Brussels-Mons, Mons-Valenciennes and Valenciennes-Douai. Each sector to be patrolled by four aircraft at a time. First sortie 3 Squadron four separate sections at 08.00. Second sortie 486 Squadron at 09.00 and so on at hourly intervals until midday. Submit that to Ops will you Spy, and if they ask why we're not just sweeping in squadron formation, you know the answer! Briefing at 7.30 and you'll have the squadron commanders warned now? I'll lead a section of 3 Squadron in the first sortie. Righto, Spy. Thanks, goodnight.'

* Group Operations order form.

This was where the accumulated experience of some years of this type of work became useful. I intended that on this coming operation we would cause the maximum amount of destruction for the minimum loss to ourselves, and had planned accordingly. Small formations covering the whole area would produce better results and present less vulnerable targets than one large one, and now there remained merely the briefing of the Wing in the flight plans of which I already had formed an idea before finally dropping off to sleep again.

It seemed almost at once that that many-times-cursed telephone awakened me, and for the first time for many weeks I felt quite enthusiastic about rising at dawn. There was a chill in the air. I stepped out of the tent and the Ford's windscreen was opaque with dew. The air throbbed with the sound of fifty or more 2,000 hp Sabre engines 'running up', and in the grey light of before sunrise I could see brighter patches in the cloud sheet above which augured well for later in the day. After driving round the squadrons I returned to the Mess tent where the pilots were consuming bacon and eggs in a high state of excitement. They knew that something big was afoot but were tantalized by not knowing what it was, and I was greeted by a chorus of questions to which I responded by grinning and saying: 'I'll tell you all about it — at Briefing!'

The weather was clearing as I had hoped, and while waiting for the squadrons to assemble for briefing I telephoned Operations for any final information.

'Hallo Controller? Beamont here. Yes, we're all set for 8 o'clock. Group have been asking why we are not flying in squadron formations? Well now! I think they will find our system satisfactory. How have the first shows gone? Plenty of trains but losing some Spits? Do you happen to know how the squadrons concerned were flying — in big bunches! It just doesn't pay with all the light flak the Hun has in the coastal belt. Well, we're off in half an hour. Thanks, old boy. Cheerio.'

The Intelligence officer's head appeared round the door: 'The pilots are ready Sir.'

In the marquee the squadron order and times of take-off were already chalked on the blackboard, and the target areas and courses marked in different colours on the wall map. I read out the Form D, ran over the main points of tactics, such as remaining at above 'light flak height' (up to 5,000 ft if the cloud-base permitted) at all times except during actual attacks; maintaining a cruising speed of at least 300 mph throughout the flight, diving to tree-top height to evade intense light AA fire, and finally crossing the coast, both on

145

the way out and when returning, at sufficient height to be safe from the dangerous coastal heavy batteries. And then: 'Finally chaps, nearly every squadron in Fighter Command and the American Air Force, in fact about 2,000 fighters, are on this show. Its significance is obvious for there can be only one reason to paralyse the enemy's transport system. The results of this show will soon get round and I see no reason at all why we should not top the list of scores. We ought to be able to see off all those Spit merchants anyway! So let's get cracking, but don't forget to look out for flak wagons on any of the trains. They can be dangerous, so if you find one firing at you (they are generally on the last truck) as you attack, leave the engine to the bloke behind and knock out the gun! OK Alan*, cockpits for us in five minutes!'

For once I was feeling quite happy during these last few minutes of waiting for take-off. The knowledge that I was going to do this operation, one which I had long wished to carry out, in my own way, did much to obviate the doubts which one sometimes entertained about the planning of other people (ie, staff officers not directly involved).

Moreover 'train-pranging' was a very satisfactory occupation and, if carried out circumspectly, relatively safe; so that it was with feelings of pleasant anticipation that I settled into the cockpit of 'RB', placed the course card into the bracket on the instrument panel, and started up.

Visibility was almost unlimited, and as we turned away from the coast we could already see the hazy outline of the French coast forty miles away across the sea. But the cloud base was too low to allow a safe crossing of the enemy's coastal defences below cloud, so I eased into a steady climb and in a few moments the gently rising and falling shapes of the other aircraft became blurred as the mist closed round them. At 4,000 ft we broke with startling abruptness into the above-cloud brilliance where visibility is limited only by the human eye. For a few seconds we hurtled over the surface of the cloud sheet, enjoying the sensation of very high speed as glowing wisps of mist flashed by, and then as I eased back into a climb again the white sheet fell away below, and by comparison we appeared to float immobile in space ...

Results of this sortie on 22 May 1944 — seven trains shot up for no loss. 150 Wing score during day 50+ trains attacked for no loss, and 100 in two days. Highest Wing score in all Commands, and personal congratulations from AOC. Good camera gun photographs available.

* Alan Dredge, CO of 3 Squadron.

At Newchurch on the afternoon of 4 June 1944 I flew over the hill to Hawkinge to collect prints of my combat film of Cormeilles. They reproduced well and showed clearly the Ju 188, the faint shell bursts round it, and then the concentration of fire almost obliterating it. They would look well in my log book.

Taking off and pulling low round the boundary in a tight turn, I looked idly at some parked Fleet Air Arm Swordfish torpedo bombers as I flashed by them, and suddenly realized a most significant fact — they were painted with broad black and white stripes, the secret scheme for the Invasion!

Could something have gone amiss or was it really going to happen at last? A chill feeling ran down my spine as I dived for home. Reaching Newchurch airfield at 480 mph I held 'RB' down to 20 ft from the runway and then pulled her up to a 60° climb holding it as the speed dropped slowly off and the altimeter needle spun round the dial as if it were mad. At 7,000 ft the speed was dropping below 180 mph and I rolled the Tempest lazily inverted, then allowed the nose to drop until the horizon, at first above my head, disappeared below (or rather above) the now inverted nose, the fields and woods steadied into the centre of the windscreen and then whirled around as I put the stick hard over and rolled round the vertical dive. Steadying again I pulled out over the tree tops at 500 mph, throttled back and pulled hard over towards the airfield in an over-the-vertical climbing turn, lowering the wheels and flaps in a roll as the speed dropped. What a magnificent aeroplane! They could have all their Spitfires and Mustangs!

The IO said: 'Ops have been calling you Sir' as I entered the office.

'OK, I'll ring them.' I shut the door and picked up the telephone. 'Hallo Operations, please. Hallo, Beamont here — Operation 'Overlord' in effect 12.00 hours tomorrow. Aircraft to be repainted with Overlord code scheme by midday. Well now! Report to where? Tangmere at 10.00 hours tomorrow. AOC's Briefing. Good show!'

It was really going to happen after four long years of waiting! I wanted to break into the crew room and shout the news, but absolute secrecy was necessary and not even a rumour must be allowed to spread until the briefing which would take place late on 'D—1' — the day before Invasion Day. So I just said: 'Things are warming up, chaps' as I went out to find Digger* and arrange the immediate job of painting all the aircraft.

* W/Cdr 'Digger' Aitkin, Newchurch airfield commandant.

Nevertheless by midday the whole camp was talking, although most people considered that the black and white paint was for just another exercise. After tea one of the usual 'flaps' occurred. Group required a fighter sweep of three squadrons at five o'clock. I enquired if I should equip each aeroplane with a bosun's chair so that the groundcrews could continue painting during the flight. The order was cancelled, and the work went on.

Over a jug of beer in the Mess tent, squadron commanders Alan Dredge and Bobby Hall both attempted to sound me on the current rumours. 'What's cooking, Sir?'

'Can't say old boy (which was quite true) but we shan't be flying tomorrow, so see that you get maximum serviceability by tomorrow night. Well, I think an early night is indicated. Goodnight, chaps.'

Outside, the night was clear and starlight and a pale glow in the East heralded the approach of the moon; while the West still showed a glimmer of sunset.

A soft breeze rustled through the trees behind my tent. A little owl screeched as it terrified a mouse or a vole in the next field. Then stillness which could be felt.

I rolled up the tent flaps and climbed into the camp bed, but it was some time before I slipped into a restless sleep.

Now that the great day was at hand, was every link in my part of the chain as strong as it could be?

The pilots yes, the pilots were as good as I could wish for. They had moaned and grumbled during training of course, but they flew extremely well now and at Cormeilles and the 'train' days of May 20th and 21st they had proved their worth in action.

But supposing we had bad weather and night operations to contend with? There again the extensive training which we had put in in the preceding months would stand us in good stead. How would they stand up to hard flying and hard fighting? The next few weeks might well bring the hardest air fighting since the Battle of Britain. There again I had managed to have the establishment of pilots increased, and there was a sufficiently adequate surplus of trained pilots to allow frequent 'days off' for everyone, and to fill in any gaps in the ranks. 'Doc' Morell and I had discussed the nerve strain possibilities many times, and anyone showing signs of cracking would be removed immediately and ruthlessly. It had to be that way. However, I had already weeded out some weak links and did not anticipate trouble on that score. No, they were a grand bunch of boys: the average age was 21 years and I was lucky, and, when I thought of it, extremely proud to be their leader.

Ah, that was more to the point. Was I fit to lead them to what might well be their deaths if I failed them. I felt (probably over-confidently), that I could outfly any man in the three squadrons and for that matter any enemy pilot in the air. I was sure of that and happy in the thought, but had to grin when I thought of how the pilots would react to such a 'line'. But moments of nerves still occurred before take-off — how could I be sure that one day I might not be able to overcome one of them; and more important still, would I be able to continue to inspire confidence in the Wing?

'Good God, you introspective idiot, you're achieving an inferiority complex. If other people can do this sort of thing, so can you — and better!'

With this more cheerful thought I turned over, but sleep did not come until I had wondered how I should feel when sighting enemy fighters for the first time for over two years. For in spite of intensive ground-strafing operations in that period, I had not even seen an airborne Hun close enough to fire at in daylight since the Battle of Britain.

The answer to this problem was to transpire in two days' time — and it was to be a satisfactory answer. In the morning I called the squadron commanders to the office and told them that no pilots were to leave camp until further notice. There was to be no flying that day except essential air tests, and a maximum effort was to be made to have all aircraft at 'readiness' by nightfall. Sergeant Priestly (an old friend of 609 days) came in to say that 'RB' was ready, bright with its new invasion stripes, for my flight to Tangmere.

I looked at my watch. Ye Gods! 9.30 and the conference was at 10.15! Two minutes later we were heading low over the South Downs at 345 mph. Battle, Polegate, Brighton and Arundel disappeared astern, and at 10.00 I pulled the Tempest round the Tangmere circuit in a vertical turn which tore white vortex trails from the wing-tips, ten minutes after leaving Dungeness.

Ranged outside the Watch Office were Spitfire IX's, XII's and XIV's Typhoons with bomb racks and with rocket projectile rails, and Mustangs, all with the initials of their various owners painted on the fuselage — the prerogative of Wing leaders only.

Parking 'RB' I noticed two Typhoons, one marked 'DUS' and the other 'MB' — Scotty (Desmond Scott) and Mike Brian had arrived. At the Theatre hangar my credentials were checked by an ominous Redcap who was obviously not amused and I was directed to the courtyard around the entrance. There I found a galaxy of talent seldom, if ever, equalled at one gathering of fighter leaders.

All the Wing leaders of Fighter Command in the United Kingdom were present, to say nothing of most of the sector commanders, themselves veterans of the Battles of Britain and France.

Johnny Johnson (still the top-scoring pilot of the Air Force), Peter Simpson, Don Kingaby, 'Hawkeye' Wells, Johnny Baldwin, 'Scotty' Scott, Jamie Rankin, Johnny Walker, Jamie Jamieson, Robin Johnston, Ray Harries and Charles Green, were but a few of them: Not a man with less than three decorations and many with four, five and even six, all won in combat with the enemy.

'Hallo Bee, you old sod; how about that fiver?'

'Thanks Hawkeye, pay me when you like!' (I had wagered Hawkeye Wells five pounds that I would land my Wing on the Continent before his.)

All round the conversation was animated — and the 'hangar doors were wide open'.*

'Isn't it grand that it's here at last.'

'I wonder how it will all go?'

'Eisenhower says ...' 'Montgomery says ...' 'Churchill says ...' 'I reckon ....'

'Shouldn't think there'll be any fighter opposition, the Hun has only a few 190s and 109s left on this front.'

'They've got 1,500 fighters in the West and more in Germany' ... and so on, until a sudden hush indicated the arrival of the Air Officer Commanding No. 11 Group — Air Vice Marshal Saunders.

We took our seats and watched a sheaf of maps being unrolled and pinned to blackboards on the stage.

This was it right enough, for the maps showed red, blue, yellow and black lines stretching out from London, Dungeness, Portsmouth, Southampton and the West to a point south of the Isle of Wight and thence straight across the Channel to Normandy. The AOC came straight to the point:

'Gentlemen, tomorrow is D-Day. I will describe to you briefly the plan as far as it concerns us, and then I wish you to return to your units, open and study your sealed files on Operation "Overlord" — brief your Wings at dusk and be instantly available from midnight onwards. The first four days will be extremely hard work, but after that we can expect to be able to revert to a regular programme.'

He went on to describe how the armies had been safely embarked, and were at that moment moving out from the

* RAF term for 'talking shop'.

concentration point off the Isle of Wight.

By midnight they would be forming for the landing a few miles offshore between Ouistrahem and Bayeux, and from midnight onwards airborne landings culminating in the landing of a large glider force at 04.00 hours, would be taking place throughout the area in preparation for the main assault. It was a colossal undertaking but there was no doubt that it would succeed if all the services could meet their commitments.

For our part the tactical Air Force would have a close supporting role (to the Army) and would keep every available aircraft in the air all the time. Over and above that, it had been found that to allow for all possibilities it would be necessary to maintain a constant patrol of 200 fighters over the beaches from thirty minutes before sunrise until thirty minutes after sunset. With the forces available this would mean four patrols a day from each squadron: a heavy responsibility, but one which would be lessened in all probability after a few days. The enemy was not expected to react in the air in great numbers on the first day, but might appear in strength (up to two or three hundred) in three or four days: that would be our opportunity.

'Finally, gentlemen, I need hardly remind you that the Royal Air Force has never failed in a mission. Many of you took part, years ago, in famous victories against great odds: victories which set a standard that has been maintained ever since. You are now on the brink of the greatest adventure of all, and I have no doubt as to the outcome of your part in it. I sincerely wish you Good Luck, Godspeed, and Good Hunting!'

A beer or two in the Mess with Johnny Walker, and then: 'See you at Le Touquet!'

On the way home visibility had improved, and off Bognor I could see great shapes like blocks of flats standing up from the water: another concentration of concrete caissons for the Invasion's mobile harbours. Ten minutes later Tempest *JN751 'RB'* was rolling down the grass strip on Dungeness again. I went straight to the office and called the Intelligence Officer: 'Spy, get me the 'Overlord' file from the safe, will you? Thanks. Oh and will you tell the squadron commanders that I want to see them here at 2.30 pm with their orders. I'll brief the Wing at 6 o'clock. One more thing: will you have tracks and times made out for my reference from Dungeness to Le Havre, Caen and Bayeux, at 10,000 ft, average cruising speed 270 mph. Fine.'

I spent the next two hours poring over the Invasion orders. There was no time for lunch.

Every detail was there and had been worked out with a finesse and foresight which, though expected, was amazing. Coloured plans and charts showed the convoy routes; the landing areas and the formations using them; the immediate battle areas and the disposition of main formations; the positions of naval units and the areas of naval action; the naval and army anti-aircraft zones; the fighter patrol areas divided into convoy protection, beach cover, close support and forward support areas, and beyond that armed reconnaissance, and over the whole area, high cover; the position of fighter control ships and Air Sea Rescue services. Page after page of rosters assigning wings and squadrons, both RAF and American, to their various roles, and further to that their actual times of take-off throughout the day. The whole plan was a masterpiece of organization — if it worked.

There was a knock at the door: 'Wotcher Bobby, come in Alan, Johnny. Take a pew. Isn't this great! The AOC briefed the Wing leaders at Tangmere this morning. I'll give you the gen and then we'll go through all this bumf. Yes, Bobby, you've got the laugh with your Spits!* I see you're down for escorts tomorrow and the Tempests are in reserve! Never mind, we'll still get the first Hun!' The time flew by as we worked out every detail that applied to the Wing, and it had turned five o'clock before I was able to discuss more intimate problems such as aircraft serviceability, guns, numbers and health of pilots, and feeding under emergency conditions. But here previous work and planning showed up to good effect. There seemed to be no problems and the wheels were turning smoothly.

'Excuse me Sir, the pilots are ready in the Briefing tent.'

'Righto Spy, I'll be there in a minute. Well this will give the boys something to think about! Let's go.'

I knocked out my pipe as we walked through the pilots' room with its mildly pornographic decorations, and ducked into the gloom of the marquee crammed with more than fifty pilots.

'OK, don't get up, there's no room. Let's have a little more breathing space, please.'

I glanced at the map on the blackboard behind me. It was the one that I needed.

'Everyone here? Yours here, Alan? Johnny? Bobby? Right. Well, gentlemen, tomorrow is D-Day! — The first British and American troops will be fighting on French soil in six hours from

* 56 Squadron still flew Spitfire Vs pending arrival of more Tempests from the M.Us.

now: H-hour is midnight ...

The AOC briefed the Wing leaders of Fighter Command this morning and I'll go over the points he made briefly.'

I showed them on the map the general outline of projected events, and told them of the tremendous commitment which the RAF had to meet. Then: 'The Tempests' job is most likely to be fighter cover purely and simply, but as yet we have not been allotted anything for tomorrow. Oh, you needn't worry! We shall fly all right! 56, however, have pulled a fast one; they are down for close escort with their Spitfires to airborne forces at dawn and in the afternoon. Quiet!'

The boys were reacting magnificently. There appeared no half-heartedness in the general enthusiasm and I could not see a face without a broad grin on it.

I read out the messages of Sir Trafford Leigh Mallory and General Eisenhower, and then:

'Finally, I want to remind you of the following. Tomorrow is the day that you, I, and the whole Service have been training for, for more than three years.

'The next few days may well bring with them the hardest air-fighting of the war; and those of you who flew in the Battle of Britain will know what that can mean.

'If the enemy does react in great numbers, and there is an even chance that he will, it will be our job to smash him and drive him out of the sky. From now on we shall not be flying round in the off-chance of meeting a Hun just for the fun of it: from tonight our men will be fighting day in and day out on the ground below us. They will cope, and more, with the Hun on the ground, but they rely on our protection from the air entirely.

'If we are given ground targets then we'll go right in whatever they are and to Hell with flak! If we meet large circuses of fighters — well, we know what to do about that! the Royal Air Force has never yet failed on a job, and we have the honour of being part of the spearhead of the Service in the greatest undertaking in the history of warfare. I am confident that, come what may, in the next few weeks you will prove the Wing to be more than worthy of that honour. That is all I have to say, gentlemen. All three squadrons will be at Readiness at 03.15 hours. Good luck and good hunting!'

It was nearly seven o'clock and there was still much to do. I went out to my Tempest, which was on the gun-harmonization base, and informed the groundcrew and armourers of the main facts as I squinted through the big rifled barrels of the oil-glistening cannon. Unreasoning anger surged over me when I found that without my knowledge the guns had been changed, and that I would have to fly with untried guns on the Invasion day.

Having seethed at everyone in range and a number out of range over the telephone, I climbed into the Ford brake and accelerated viciously across the rough field, leaping from bump to bump.

After checking each squadron's aircraft and making sure that the transparent sliding hoods were spotless, I drove round the winding lanes to 'Plumbers Hall'★ — the headquarters of the Wing engineering officer. How was the spares situation? OK! Refuelling – could they deal with the possible requirement of 20,000 gallons a day? All laid on: Good show!

On to the barn housing the armoury: 'Still working, Tubby?'★★

'Twenty-four hour service here, Sir!'

'Good show. How are you set? Can you cope with a three-squadron re-arm in twenty minutes? Fine, and how about belted ammunition? Plenty in hand? Good show. Hope we'll be giving you some more business soon!'

As the sun set I reached the Mess tent which was empty except for the airfield commandant and the Intelligence Officer.

'Hallo Bee, everything ready? Have a drink.'

'Thanks, old boy. Yes, I think everything should run smoothly. Readiness is at 3.15 am, and for the first day or so I doubt if the pilots will be able to come to the Mess for meals. Can you arrange for all meals at Dispersal?'

'That's all organized, old chap. Tea and bacon and eggs at Dispersal at 3.15: you aren't likely to be off before 3.45 are you? Well, here's to tomorrow!'

'Cheers. No, that's about the form, I think. I see that the boys have all gone to bed. They're a good bunch, and by God they're excited!'

'Well, aren't you?'

'All right, you big lump, so I am! Well, I must get some sleeping hours in. Spy, ring my tent at 2.45 will you; and of course if anything comes through before. Good night Digger: 'night Spy.'

'Goodnight old boy. Good luck tomorrow.'

Outside the darkening sky showed heavy patches of cloud — it must be fine for tomorrow.

I took off my jacket and rolled into the camp bed fully clothed; there were only four hours of sleep for us anyway.

As I lay listening to the night sounds of the marshes, I no longer

★ A Royal Air Force engineer is always a 'Plumber'.
★★ S/Ldr Cottingham, Wing Armament Officer.

felt as strained as I had the night before. There was nothing much to worry about now. The organization had operated perfectly at the critical moment, and there remained merely the fighting.

The fighting. Now that the day had come it had got to be a success. We would make it a success. By God we would. When would the BBC announce the landings? Probably quite early in a special bulletin. My wife wouldn't hear! She wouldn't know about it till the postman or the Ellis's told her. She'd probably worry about it, but she wouldn't show it. Mother would worry too much, much too much and it would not do any good. How about the 190s. They should be easy for our Tempests — and 109s — if only we could meet them! If only we could have a really good 'bounce'* one day. Other people had that sort of luck but I never seemed to.

But why did I want to shoot down a Hun again so much? I never wanted to kill a man. Good Lord no! The thrill of the chase I suppose. Yes, that was it. The boundless skies with rolling white clouds. Specks in the distance, getting larger every moment. What on earth are they? Huns! Get above them; round into the sun. They're coming in. Turn into them; tighter, tighter; now down, down, faster and faster. Almost in range. Black crosses. Get him before he gets you. He's weaving from side to side at full throttle, streaming black exhaust smoke. Get that sight on max deflection; more. Now! *Brr-rr-rrm*. Got him! The hunt in its most magnificent setting.

* 'Bounce': the act of achieving surprise upon enemy aircraft — sighting them below and being able to dive on them.

Chapter 10

TEMPESTS OVER THE INVASION

It was 6 June 1944, D-Day, the Invasion of Europe.

'*Kling-ing-ing-ing-ing.*' Good Lord have I slept?

'*Kling-ing-*' 'HAL-LO! 2.45? OK. Thanks very much.' I felt terrible. What a ghastly hour! I blundered out of the tent and breathed in gulps of cool night air, and felt worse.

The windscreen of the brake was covered with mist, and driving round the narrow lanes to 3 Squadron dispersal was a hazardous business as the night was dark and cloudy. I stepped out of the car into a dark world of harsh resonant sound as, unseen behind the trees, between forty and fifty aircraft engines were warmed up. While walking up the flagged path to the cottage the wild shoot of rambler rose which hung down from the pergola round the door again tore at my cheek. Why didn't someone cut the damn thing off!

In the 3 Squadron crew room there was a confusion of booted and life-jacketed pilots, and a glowing petrol cooker, on which was a large pan of sizzling eggs.

Talking was an impossibility, and as there were still ten minutes to go before Readiness I walked out across the plank bridge over the ditch which bounded the dispersal, to check '*RB*'.

Ahead the darkness was broken in a dozen places by little blue lights dancing backwards and forwards over roaring exhaust ports, and occasionally a corner of the field would flare into orange light as sheets of flame leaped back from a newly started motor. The strong tang of high octane exhaust smoke hung in the air. The scene was so familiar, and was little different from any other morning on an active fighter station; yet there was a difference.

Dawn would break over the greatest military struggle the world had ever known, and within a few hours we would be flying those thundering, straining machines, taking our part in it. One after

156

another the engines spluttered into silence, until only one remained running in the distance. Back in the crew room breakfast was in progress, but tension hung heavily in the atmosphere. Some of the pilots toyed with their food and others would not eat at all, saying that it was too asteriskly early. 'Too ruddy true! Who the hell could eat at this ungodly hour! Certainly I'll have your egg if you don't want it!' So far my nerves were behaving and not interfering with my appetite.

'Anything doing yet, Sir?' This from New Zealander Spike Umbers, 'B' Flight commander of 3 Squadron.

'No. Ops have not been through yet. Perhaps they don't know about the Invasion. I'll phone them.' The office was very dark and while fumbling for the instrument I collided with the long air-cushioned 'aircrew rest-chair' which I kept there. That was an idea; if nothing was going to happen I might as well sleep some more. I settled comfortably, and lifting the receiver asked for Biggin Hill Operations.

'Biggin? Controller please. No, the Ops B will *not* do. Will you get the Controller please. Good morning, Beamont here. Everything going to plan? Good show. Fighting reported already at Ouistrahem. Well, that's fine. Have you got anything for us? Just a section weather-recco for 56 at dawn from Dieppe to Le Havre. Nothing else yet? OK, well we'll just have to hang on I suppose. Thanks, goodbye.

'Spy, pass that on to Squadron Leader Hall will you. He's not to go farther west than Havre for obvious reasons. I'll be in here having a quick sleep if anyone wants me.'

However, a few moments later Biggin came through with an order for 56 again, this time to escort a glider train at 05.30 hours.

The sky was grey as I drove across the runway tracking to the other dispersal and 56 Squadron, and the air was full of the hum of distant motors as the American Thunderbolt groups from Ashford and Headcorn set off on their scheduled patrols of the assault area. Occasionally they could be seen as bunches of red and white lights against the stars, in breaks in the scattered cloud.

Bobby Hall landed his section at 4.30 am, by which time the light was good enough to see the weather from the ground. It was not too good, and Bobby reported having flown on instruments most of the way out and home. He had however seen signs of battle near Ouistrahem, and said that the shipping in the Channel had to be seen to be believed. He was very excited at the prospect of the coming escort, and after warning the pilots to stick with their gliders at all costs I left the rest of the briefing to him.

The sun was edging the eastern clouds with gold as Bobby Hall led his Spitfires off, formed them up rapidly and climbed away to the rendezvous at Bognor. He was doing a fine job with that squadron. For a moment I wished that I was with them and felt that I ought to be. But one could not do two different types of operational flying at one time: it would be a case of Jack of all trades, master of none, and the Tempests were my job. I drove on round the field to 486 where Johnny Iremonger and his New Zealand pilots were sitting outside their tent in the open, round a bright log fire. No, I could not tell them when we would fly but it would not be long.

I could never quite make out the New Zealanders. They flew better than any of the other squadrons, even better formations than my own old 609, though I would never admit that to them. I was happy flying with them and they, I think, with me, but there it ended: perhaps they could not forget their old New Zealand CO, wing leader and idol, Scotty*, to my disadvantage.

Soon after eight o'clock 56's Spitfires came over in perfect formation, and breaking away one after the other in quick succession, came in to land. I counted them quickly: they were all there. I drove up to meet them as they climbed from their cockpits.

'How did it go, Bobby?'

'OK Sir: nothing doing though. Streams of Stirlings and Albemarles towing gliders as far as you could see. They were going in round the Caen canal. Masses on the ground, only isolated light flak firing. We saw two aircraft shot down. No Sir, no fighters reported at all. There's a lot of shelling going on around the shipping. We saw a cruiser go up with an incredible explosion. It was an amazing sight.'

'Oh well, never mind Bobby. Better luck next time: but I'll get that first Hun for the Wing!'

The morning dragged on. At 9.30 the newspapers arrived as I sat in the fitful sunshine on the lawn. No mention of Invasion. I was tired and depressed, and everything felt flat and an anti-climax.

Finally, at three o'clock in the afternoon, Biggin Operations rang through.

'Wing Commander Beamont? We have a job for you. Convoy escort at squadron strength. Your convoy is moving down Channel to the rendezvous point, and is now south of Dungeness. Can you arrange for your squadrons to relieve each other at hourly intervals? Sorry there's nothing more exciting at the moment.'

* W/Cdr D. V. Scott, DSO, OBE, DFC & Bar, RNZAF

It was better than nothing, and on a day like this the Hun might try and attack the convoy.

Our twelve Tempests wheeled out over Dungeness to where the convoy plodded steadily west with the fast escorts leaving white streaks of wakes and two MLs trailing great banks of white smoke to seaward to blind the watchful enemy on Cap Gris Nez, and we resigned ourselves to the monotony of patrolling backwards and forwards for an hour. So this was our part in the Invasion; and after my speech the previous night too! But the patrol time was soon gone and three parallel lines of specks over Dungeness revealed the 486 New Zealanders climbing out to relieve us. With the deliberate intention of keeping the squadrons occupied, I agreed to carry on the patrols without assistance until the evening, as there was nothing else for us. Anything was better than sitting on the ground on such a day.

In the meantime Bobby Hall had another mission, escorting the second wave of airborne troops in to the Caen-Oustrakem area. I was really jealous then. The news of the assault was good. The British were ashore and pressing inland. The Americans on 'Gold' beach were having a fierce battle. Generally speaking everything was going according to plan, according to the information that Operations had. No, there had been no reaction from the Luftwaffe yet. Oh well, we were not missing anything. The remaining convoy escorts were uneventful and I was watching the sunset while awaiting the return of 56 and worrying a little about them because of a deterioration in the weather, when the Operations telephone rang.

'Beamont. What! Say that again will you. All available aircraft "scramble" to Le Havre-Lisieux area. Enemy bombing the beaches, eh! You know that it's nearly dark now, and that I can't get there in less than thirty minutes as it's a good 150 miles? It must be done? OK, fair enough.'

'Spy, tell Squadron Leader Iremonger I'll meet him on the runway in five minutes — all aircraft. Alan, I'll lead your squadron. No briefing, get on out to your aircraft, everyone!'

I grabbed helmet, gloves and Mae West, and ran out to 'RB'. In thirty seconds I had pressed the buttons and started the motor — the first by two seconds.

While taxying to the take-off point I set the compass and trimming tabs and the cockpit lighting, and then glanced at my watch. 10.23 pm. To attempt to take a Wing to Normandy at this time of the evening was crazy. I should be lucky if I succeeded in forming the whole lot up in this murk, and it would be full darkness by the time we reached the beach-head. The last men were still taxying out as I opened the throttle and, switching on the wing-tip lights, released the brakes.

'Hallo, Kelvin aircraft, Kelvin Leader turning on to two one zero.' There was no time to circle base and in this poor visibility a straight course would enable the others to pick up formation more easily by following the lights of the next ahead.

The weather was quite unpleasant and I became even more apprehensive as we crossed out over Rye and left the coast still faintly visible in the murk behind. Ahead and on either side, mist and rain merged into cloud forming a blank wall through which could be seen no sign of the horizon, or even the light of the sky. Below, the sea was invisible in the darkness, and an occasional patch of light passed overhead indicating holes in the cloud sheet.

By now I was flying by instruments and occasionally glancing round at the dark shapes and bright red and green lights on either side. I was on instruments not merely to keep '*RB*' flying on a steady course, but each one of the twenty or more pilots behind were flying purely in formation with their next ahead and after fifteen minutes or more of concentration upon that aircraft a few yards away, with no ground or horizon to glance at — only grey opaqueness — many of them must have been experiencing that misleading feeling of certainty that their aircraft was turning, diving, climbing or doing anything but flying a level course. I was their horizon, and an error on my part could mean tragedy. A few more minutes of concentration on altimeter, airspeed indicator, artificial horizon, turn and bank indicator and compass in steady climb and then:

'Kelvin leader, opening up a bit. We'll try and climb out of this.'
'Hallo, Kelvin leader; this is Blue 1. I have not found you yet.'
'Hallo Blue 1, climb on two one zero and meet me above cloud.'
Then the Controller:
'Hallo, Kelvin leader, this is Kingsley. All aircraft not yet with you are to return to base. How are your oranges*, and what is your position?'

Operations had probably realized how unpleasant things were becoming. But that cleared up one problem.

'Hallo Kingsley, Kelvin leader. My oranges are bloody and I am estimating twenty miles NW of Le Havre.'

'OK Kelvin leader. There are still plenty of bandits near Lisieux.'

* R/T code for 'weather'.

160

Right *The Hawker Typhoon came through its trials in 1942/43, and went on to become a major scourge of the enemy ground forces in the Battle for Europe in 1944/45* (RAF Museum, Charles Brown Collection).

Below *'Tip and Run' raider adversary of the Manston Typhoons. This FW 190 landed intact at Pembrey and was later tested by the author at Farnborough* (IWM).

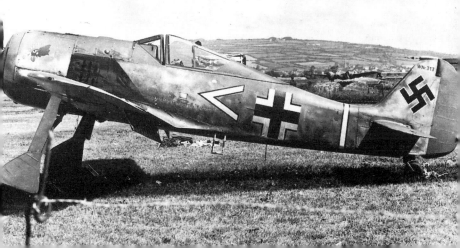

Above *A production Hawker Tempest 6 at the Langley Factory (British Aerospace).*

Left *A Tempest on test, flown here by Bill Humble in 1944 (RAF Museum, Charles Brown Collection).*

Above right *The first Tempest V squadron, No 486 (NZ), forming at Castle Camps in February 1944 (IWM).*

Right *Johnny Iremonger, the first Tempest Squadron commander, in front of the author's Tempest at Castle Camps in February 1944 (IWM).*

Far right *The new Tempest — the 'Hawker Spitfire' — in 1944 (British Aerospace).*

Left *Castle Camps: HQ of the first Tempest Wing in March 1944. Author's 'R-B', serial JN751 in the foreground* (IWM).

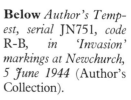

Below *Author's Tempest, serial JN751, code R-B, in 'Invasion' markings at Newchurch, 5 June 1944* (Author's Collection).

At this point the darkness lessened and the first quarter moon took shape mistily ahead until, with a sudden impression of great speed as final wisps of cloud whipped by, we broke into the clear above a flat cloud sheet stretching to the horizon.

This was better. In the West a few streaks of cloud were still tinged with red sunset and ahead was the clear moon. The June night would not get really dark anyway, and at the worst I would be able to take the formation back to England above the weather, and send them down through it to land one by one. I had always enjoyed night flying by myself and in small formations, but a Wing Sweep by night was a little unheard of to say the least of it!

Presently a cluster of lights appeared ahead, apparently remained motionless for half a minute, then suddenly developed into a group of P-47 Thunderbolts of the USAF returning to England as they flashed past and disappeared astern. 10.55 pm read the cockpit clock as I flooded it with warm red light by the rheostat. We should be somewhere near the Seine bay by now. The even cloud top became broken below and I was momentarily able to make out the dim outline of Le Havre on our left. If the Huns were attacking the beaches, they were obviously not doing so from above this cloud.

'Hallo Kelvin squadrons, Kelvin leader going down now.'

The haze absorbed us as we slid down into it at 300 mph and for a few moments I was again concentrating on the instruments. Then ahead and below occasional flashes and two or three red fires showed where heavy fighting was going on between the coast and Caen, but if there were enemy aircraft it was quite impossible to see them, and there was a far greater chance of head-on collision with other fighters than there was of shooting the enemy down.

'Hallo Kingsley. Kelvin leader here. This is quite pointless. It's as black as the proverbial miner round here, and we're not ruddy night fighters!'

'Kingsley here, OK, steer three five five. You are diverted to land at Harlequin base.'

'Kelvin leader. OK, understand, three five five. Thank you. Hallo all Fairway and Spider aircraft, hang on tight and we'll climb out of this again.'

The battle faded into the mist to port, but before reaching the clear sky Fairway Red leader called to say that he had lost contact in the murk.

'OK Red leader, climb above this and then head three five five for Harlequin base. It will take you about 25 minutes.'

'Hallo Kelvin leader. Red leader, Roger, out.'

Once clear of cloud at 10,000 ft and heading north with the scattered formation closing in behind it was possible to relax for the first time for forty minutes and I suddenly felt fatigue and was forced to shake my head quickly to keep away drowsiness. This was not surprising perhaps as we had been at Readiness or flying for the past 22 hours, and that after only three hours' sleep in the previous night.

The sunset had faded away by now and given place to the moon which made the night beautiful above the endless white cloud sheet. But below it, if the weather at Harlequin base was as bad as it had been at Newchurch at take-off, we were due for a difficult time. That reminded me of a further problem. Where was Harlequin base? I knew that it was one of the Tangmere group of airfields in Sussex, but which one? They were all so close together. Johnny Iremonger had been stationed there; he would know.

'Hallo Fairway leader: this is Kelvin leader; do you know Harlequin base?'

'Hallo Kelvin leader: yes, I know Harlequin base.'

'OK Fairway leader. Will you take over the lead and show me the way.'

'Right, Sir.'

The clouds were breaking below, and I led the formation down through a hole to find that the weather had cleared completely. From cloud-base at about 7,000 ft a flashing beacon could be seen somewhere in Sussex at least twenty miles ahead, and below, the sea showed up sharply, mottled by cloud shadows in the moonlight.

I received a final check bearing from Control and then changed R/T frequency to call Harlequin base.

'Hallo Harlequin, Kelvin leader. I am approaching your base with twenty aircraft. Shall be with you in four minutes.'

'Hallo Kelvin leader. Harlequin. Your turn to land is 24. There are two squadrons ahead of you. Come into the circuit and orbit at Angels 8. The weather is clear.'

This was good news, and after a few minutes more a thin line of white could be distinguished against the cloud moon-shadows ahead. We drew nearer rapidly and I recognized the beaches between Worthing and Littlehampton as we crossed in towards the great circle of lights which marked the perimeter of Ford aerodrome. Visibility had improved greatly and ahead could be seen countless red and green lights at all heights up to the base of the clouds, as fighters which had returned late from Normandy circled while waiting their turn to land. In the centre of the light circle round Ford the parallel lanes of the flare-path shone like some great pre-blackout highway, and every few moments the navigation lights of a fighter would appear travelling down the lane after a bright green Aldis signal light had shone from the Aerodrome Control Point, just like a car passing the traffic lights.

I reduced speed to the lowest cruising conditions as it was certain to be some time before our turn to land came round, and we were already low in fuel.

We made circuit after circuit, round and round with eyes straining to pick out other aircraft ahead; for apart from the thirty aircraft landing at Ford there were a number of squadrons circling Tangmere only five miles away and their circuit frequently clashed with ours. Head-on meetings at night between fighters travelling at 250 mph give little time for evasion, especially when the pilots' reactions are dulled with fatigue.

After what seemed an age, but which was in reality about 25 minutes, Control said: 'Kelvin leader, Harlequin here. You may land now.'

'Kelvin leader, OK. Hallo Kelvin aircraft. Kelvin leader going in now. Open out for landing. Throttling back, wheels down.'

I curved in from the circuit lights and through the 'funnels' to line up with the flare-path and so down hard on to the runway, bouncing heavily twice. I was too tired to care. The others came safely in, in turn. At the end of the flare-path an ATC vehicle with an illuminated arrow mounted on top guided us along the sinuous perimeter road, past great dark shapes of Stirlings. Albemarles and Hamilcar troop-carrying gliders, to a grass dispersal where a torch-waving marshaller signalled me to switch off.

Another difficult job had been accomplished. Safe on the ground it all seemed to have been much simpler than was actually the case.

The cool air was refreshing as I walked over to where Johnny Iremonger was climbing from his cockpit.

'What sort of a view did you take of that Johnny?'

'Pretty bloody, Sir!'

'I thought it was a bit grim in patches myself. We'd better fix up servicing now before anything else. We may be off again at dawn.'

A further thirty minutes were spent in arranging for fuel, oil and oxygen, and in instructing the unaccustomed ground crews as to the whereabouts of the filler caps on Tempest aircraft; and it was past 1.00 am before I was able to say: 'OK Flight Sergeant, you'll have crews available in case of a dawn take-off? Otherwise we shall start up at 08.30 for Newchurch. The pilots will do their own preflight checks in the morning. Thanks Flight. Good night. Johnny, collect the bodies, will you?'

We drove round the aerodrome to the Watch Office, where, leaving the pilots in the coach, Johnny Iremonger and I climbed the stairs to the Control room. After reporting and thanking the Controller for his excellent handling of a difficult situation, I telephoned Operations. 3 Squadron had landed safely at New-church, all but two aircraft. Were they with me? Yes they were. Then I had fourteen aircraft here? No, only twelve, I remembered, Blue section becoming separated.

'Johnny, have your Green 1 and 2 landed here?'

'No Sir, I thought they had gone back to base.'

There were definitely two aircraft missing. I looked at my watch: 12.45 am. It was certain that they could not be flying now, as their fuel would have run out fifteen minutes ago. Could they have landed here unnoticed? The Flying Control Officer was certain they could not. However a further twenty minutes of telephoning producing the information that both pilots were safe at Dunsfold, 25 miles to the north. They had committed the all-too-easy error of under-estimating their speed, had crossed the coast over cloud and had descended to find themselves over a lighted airfield which they took to be 'Ford' base. I passed instructions for them for the morning.

After a struggle with my conscience I informed Operations of our preparedness for a dawn take-off if necessary, but they replied that such a contingency was unlikely and that we could return to Newchurch in the morning at my discretion. The coach drove through the camp and thence down a winding lane to the 'Visiting Aircrew compound' where, in the Mess Hall, we were welcomed by the sight of hot tea and bacon and fried potatoes. It was 1.30 am and the girls who served us had probably had one of the most strenuous days of their lives and already served meals to thousands of parachute troops (who were even then fighting on the Conti-nent), as well as to hundreds of visiting pilots. All things considered it was amazing that most of the girls were still very cheerful. But there was yet another duty to be carried out before I could eat.

I reported to Intelligence the details of the sweep. No, we had seen no EA. Had anyone else during the day? Some Spitfires had run into a formation of Ju 88s over the beach head late in the evening, and shot most of them down. The Hell they had! Oh well, our turn tomorrow! There was only one more thing to remember, I thought as I sat down to supper almost too tired to eat. If the pilots were not called in the morning they would never get up!

'Johnny, if we're not called for an early show we'll have breakfast at 7.30 and start up at 8.30. OK, let's go and find these bunks!'

We walked down the lane in the moonlight to a group of huts, and were shown into one of them filled with row upon row of double-tiered bunks. I went back with the orderly to his hut to make sure that he wrote down the calling times, and three minutes later when I re-entered the hut there was only one other pilot not yet asleep.

I looked at my watch. It was 2.45 am. Twenty-four hours had elapsed since I got out of bed on D-Day. It was now the second day of the Invasion and I had only slept three hours out of the past forty.

I had time for one more thought — we had flown over the Invasion on D-Day; then my head touched the pillow and I slept.

At breakfast on 7 June, five hours later, the Mess was filled with pilots of other wings who, more fortunate than ourselves, had landed earlier on the preceding evening. Johnny Johnson with his Canadian Wing was amongst them, and in his usual good spirits.

'Hallo Bee: I hear you had a prang at those 188s on Cormeilles the other day.'

'Sure, you want to fly a decent sort of aeroplane one day Johnny! You can attack things with Tempests!'

Johnny had sighted the Ju 188s with his wing but had wisely refrained from taking his slower, less heavily-armed Spitfires down to such a heavily-defended target, as it would almost certainly have cost him the loss of some of his pilots.

On the aerodrome a constant stream of Spitfires roared off for the Continent. Our Tempests had been standing uncovered during the night and the engines would be cold, so I gave instructions for running up.

'Johnny, gather the boys together will you? — OK boys, check your aircraft right away. Start up in ten minutes, that is 8.35, and run them till they are warm. I shall be taxying out when my motor is warm and we will fly in the usual formation of three line-astern fours. Anyone whose aircraft is unserviceable will stay behind, have it fixed, and return as soon as possible.'

On the way home the clouds hung low over the Downs behind Lancing and Brighton, and as we thundered over streets and housing estates at 300 mph I could see many upturned white faces staring at us. I looked round at the formation. At each hand less than twenty feet away flew four Tempests, nose to tail and gently rising and falling in relation to each other. Looking below and behind, I could just see the wing-tips of the three aircraft in my section. The boys were flying well, and they were worth looking at.

All was quiet at Newchurch. Digger Aitkin and Bobby Hall were in the Mess tent having a before-lunch beer when I walked in.

'Hallo, old boy. Hallo, Bobby. Certainly, I'll have a bitter.'

'How did you get on last night? I was just getting worried about the weather — for Bobby was coming back, when you went hurtling off! I thought it seemed crazy,' said Aitkin.

'So did I, Digger! Still, there was a chance of getting the odd Hun so I didn't stop to argue. It was pretty bloody though, and when we did get back to Ford we had to chase our tails round the circuit until at least two other squadrons had landed in front of us!'

During lunch a Form D arrived for a wing sweep of the area Rouen-Lisieux-Caen, height and withdrawal at Wing Leader's discretion. The left flank of the assault. This was a good sign as it meant that we were being given every chance of meeting the enemy, and were not being held for convoy escort duties — a possibility that I had feared. I drove the brake fiercely to 3 Squadron dispersal, incurring once again the extreme displeasure of the transport officer as I skidded past his motorcycle. Monks was a very good MT officer, but he had two failings. The first, the theory that pilots and least of all Wing Leaders should never be allowed to drive Service cars, and he was probably right! The second, the opinion that the place for all Service vehicles was in his transport yard, and that none of them should ever be allowed to leave it!

The Intelligence Officer was already working out courses, and after a few slight alterations of track with regard to coastal flak and the position of the sun, I was ready for briefing.

The hum of conversation died down as I ducked under the tent flap.

'Everyone here Spy? Right. We've got a nice little job on this afternoon boys. A fighter sweep over the assault area on the enemy's right flank between Rouen and Caen. Height and timing is at my discretion, and the object is to destroy any enemy aircraft that are foolish enough to be flying there. There may quite easily be Huns incidently, as Ops say that 190s have been seen in the Lisieux area this morning — here — (I pointed on the map). So keep your eyes wide all the time, and don't straggle. Report all aircraft seen to me, and don't break formation without permission. If we sight Huns below us I'll take the leading squadron (486) down, and Alan – you'll fly 2,000 ft over me as cover, OK?'

'Yes, Sir.'

'Finally, anyone in trouble from the time we've crossed in till we cross out at the French coast, remember that between Ouistrehem-Caen-Bayeux the land is ours — or more or less! So force-land there if you have to and you'll get back OK. By tomorrow we should have a landing strip operating which will make things even easier. Usual formation and take-off arrangements (here our constant training and practice were bearing fruit). Any questions? OK, start-up and take-off times are on the board here. You have twenty minutes to get ready. One more thing — don't forget that it's Training Command for any blighter who shoots down the first Hun before me!'

It was with a thrill, part excitement and part pride, that I looked over my shoulder as we headed out to sea and saw both squadrons — 24 aircraft in all — drawing into position. The New Zealanders with me, in fours on either side, 3 Squadron, with Alan leading, a quarter of a mile to starboard and 1,500 ft above, still a little behind. They would have plenty of time to close in over the next 100 miles or more of sea. Climbing steadily we began to pass through small banks of scattered cloud which rushed up, enveloped us, and were gone again in a flash. The tops were reached at 8,000 ft, and as I levelled off gently at 11,000 ft the Channel could be seen sparkling brilliantly in all directions, spotted with small white clouds.

Presently the French coastline took shape, and I was soon busy in trying to make out landmarks. We were to cross in over Pointe d'ailly, and it would be unpleasant to misjudge the track and fly within range of the Dieppe guns only two miles to the north east. A Wing formation could not be turned very quickly and the safest policy with regard to flak was always 'avoid, not evade'. Yes, there was the headland, and down there to the left the front, Casino and harbour entrance of Dieppe. The old Casino! It was number 2 Base Hospital of the BEF when I knew it in that grim winter of 1940. Did that little cafe near the harbour still offer superb langouste?

We crossed over the coast and flew steadily inland. The clouds were thickening below and the ground was visible only in patches. The sun was intensely bright.

'Hallo Kelvin aircraft, keep your eyes wide open now.'

'Hallo Kingsley, this is Kelvin leader. Anything doing?'

There was a crackling silence for a moment, then:

'Hallo Kelvin leader; this is Kingsley. Sorry, have nothing definite for you. There might be something in the Lisieux area, over.'

The rolling cumulus towered over us to 15,000 ft or more. There was no point in flying around above this.

'Hallo Fairway leader, Spider leader. Kelvin going down below this stuff.'

Ahead was a long cloud valley with the winding Seine its floor; its sides sheer from nearly 20,000 ft to 1,000 ft where grey sheets of rain extended these walls to the ground. We thundered into the gorge at 500 mph with an impression of tremendous speed as the cloud-walls sped by. Below, the ground, previously remote and not of our world, was now seen as a small patchwork of fields, woods and villages two miles down between two sheer grey cloud cliffs. Neither landsmen nor seamen could ever experience this magnificence of nature so often disclosed to flying men.

The city of Rouen was half concealed on our left, and ahead to the south the valley ended in towering cloud. There was a break in the direction of Lisieux.

'Kelvin leader turning right sharply, Spider leader if you lose me in this cloud ahead, fly towards Caen and I'll wait for you there.'

'OK Kelvin leader.'

So it went on. Often I lost sight of Alan's squadron as he strove to follow in and out of the cloud valleys, but always in the next clear patch his formation would appear on my right.

We were heading for the Caen area, but when within ten miles of the town the weather closed into a solid wall of cloud and I was forced to turn about and head for Le Havre.

By this time we were low — too low; for as we passed over the Seine estuary came the call, 'Flak at 8 o'clock, Kelvin leader.' The warning was unnecessary. Black puffs appeared in twenties and thirties among the aircraft on my left, and faintly glinting tracer shells streaking between mine and the next machine showed that we were under fire from a Bofors battery of some strength.

Damn! The estuary was an obvious place for flak.

'OK Kelvin aircraft. Opening up and climbing. Turning left.'

It was hot for a few seconds, but no word came from the pilots as they held formation with shells bursting among and around them. Then we were clear and approaching Le Havre at 5,000 ft.

Alan Dredge, seeing the flak, swung his squadron across to starboard and avoided it. We skirted Le Havre to the north and headed back across the bay towards the battle area.

There was much evidence of fighting along the Caen-Ouistrahem canal, but ahead the weather closed down to very low cloud with rain beneath and I was forced to turn the Wing back over the beaches and out to sea. 'Hallo Kingsley, this is Kelvin leader. Anything doing yet?'

'Sorry Kelvin leader. Nothing for you at all.'

It was a pity, but we had already overstayed our planned patrol by ten minutes and it was time to return. I began a gentle turn away from the coast and over the assembled shipping with their hundreds of busy landing craft streaming to and from the beaches.

'Hallo Kelvin leader, aircraft coming in at 11 o'clock.'

'Yes, I've seen them, they're friendly. Turning right but watch those aircraft.' The Wing of Spitfires on beach-head standing patrol flew past at our level and then swung hard round towards our tails, with smoke trailing as they opened their throttles.

'Kelvin leader here. Spider leader, watch those Spits. The clots haven't recognized us.'

'Spider leader here. They are shooting from long range.'

'Bloody fools! Why couldn't people learn aircraft recognition!

'Kelvin leader here. OK, open up to full throttle.'

Immediately we began to draw away with our greatly superior speed until the Spitfires were a group of specks against the sea behind. That would give them something to think about!

As usual when Dungeness came in sight again I drew the formation into tight drill.

'Hallo Kelvin squadrons. Aircraft line astern, squadrons line astern — Go!'

Then as we approached the airfield: 'Steady now. Make this good. Very nice indeed. Spider squadron echelon starboard — Go. Aircraft echelon starboard — Go. Open out for landing.'

A close circuit, ending in a tight turn down on to the rough matting runway to give succeeding aircraft room for their approaches, and another show was over.

I slept heavily on the night of 8 June and for once uninterrupted all night, and after a late breakfast strolled back to the tent with a pail of hot shaving water from the field kitchen. It was a luxury to be able to take one's time after the hurry and tension of the past days of crisis. I propped the mirror on the folding washstand, brought a camp chair outside and sat down to shave in the comfort of the warm morning sunshine. Camp life certainly had its moments, but this one did not last long. I had completed the operation upon the port side of my countenance and was about to begin on the starboard, when the field telephone in the tent broke into shrill clamour.

'Beamont here! Oh, hello Spy. Rouen-Caen area? That's the same as yesterday. OK, check yesterday's courses for today's wind, and I'll be down in a couple of minutes. Squadrons for briefing in ten minutes. Got that?'

I threw my shirt over my head and my battledress jacket over it, and then swore as I remembered the lather on half my face. A quick rub with the towel, and then away out of the field and down the road over the bridge with screeching tyres. The transport officer never would believe that I was often in a legitimate hurry.

There had been a number of enemy fighters in the area during the morning. Would this be our chance? Time after time this happened. You tensed yourself for that moment when it would be either the enemy who fell or you yourself, or your friends. You thought out over and over again the maxims of air-fighting and staged imaginery combats in your mind. Recognize the enemy before he recognizes you! Get into the sun. Gain and maintain height advantage. Always turn towards and never away from the enemy. Fire all the way in to point-blank range and break away only to avoid collision. Always leave an element of your formation above you to cover your tail, and above all when manoeuvring with the enemy, fly to enable your formation to remain compact behind you. The Hun in the sun loves stragglers! Every day these thoughts occurred, and every day seemed to bring the same result — no enemy sighted! In the meantime there was this cold feeling in the stomach again. Thank God it was a simple matter to grin at the pilots and make aggressive remarks while briefing them.

'Everyone here? Right. Well chaps, we've a nice little fighter sweep in the battle area again at medium altitude. No light flak or anything dangerous like that! Anyone flying who was not on yesterday's show? No? Well, it's in the same area again, but with a difference. There have been more Huns about this morning! I'll be leading your squadron Alan, with Johnny as cover. Otherwise the same arrangements as yesterday. (Again it was very satisfactory to feel that they all knew exactly what to do without my having to go over details.)

'Any questions? OK. Start-up 10.30. Take-off 10.40. Get cracking!'

As I walked out to 'RB' the Intelligence Officer came running from the cottage.

'You're wanted on the 'phone, Sir.'

'Oh, go to Hell!'

A churlish attitude: after all it was not the IO's fault. Did they realize that this sort of response was merely the result of taut nerves? Not that it mattered either way, really. The fitter helped with the harness straps and handed me the course card and map.

'Anything special doing, Sir?'

'No, just a sweep round the battle area. But there's always the chance of a Hun.'

'This machine has got to get the first one Sir. All clear Sir.'

We were not pressed for time so I began a leisurely circuit after take-off and looking back watched the aircraft as, pair by pair, they sped down the runway and, once airborne, curved left to cut off the corner and join formation. Johnny Iremonger's 486 NZ Squadron was formed up and drawing into position on my right before 3 had even settled down around me. Those New Zealanders were good, but it would not do to tell them so too often.

Dungeness dropped astern as we once again headed for Normandy. From now until our return, engine failure, flak or fighters could mean to each one of us death or captivity as a prisoner of war. Unpleasant prospects either of them, but somehow that sort of thing never did actually happen to you; it was always the other fellow. In the meantime the day was far too beautiful to be spoilt by worry. The sun shone from a brilliant sky on to a blue sea dotted with puffs of 'fair weather cumulus' cloud that reminded one of cotton wool snow in a Christmas shop window.

The squadrons spread out behind like skeins of wild geese, and the sun glinted on wings and windscreens. It was good to be flying on such a day, and to be leading such men.

There was the French coast again with the clouds thickening over it.

'Kelvin leader increasing speed a little. Keep a good look out now.'

Crossing over the enemy coast was still always a slight thrill.

'Hallo Kingsley, Kelvin leader here. Anything doing?'

'Kingsley here. Yes: information is uncertain but there are some unidentified aircraft in the vicinity of Lisieux. Will you get there as soon as possible?'

'OK Kingsley. Kelvin leader opening up a little and turning right ten degrees.'

Lisieux was a few miles south of the Seine, and there was the winding river now: another three minutes at 330 mph would see us there. Johnny Iremonger was a little behind his position.

'Hallo Fairway leader, you're too far behind. Come up a little.' Then further vectors from Kingsley control giving information of 'probable Bandits'.

'Hallo! What's that!'

Yes, there were aircraft down there about two miles away and five or six thousand feet below, just specks against the cloud. No-one else reported seeing them.

'Hallo Kelvin aircraft, there are five or more aircraft at seven o'clock low-ahead. Watch them.'

I turned the formation gently to port. The specks grew larger as the distance closed, and I could now see clearly five or more fighters weaving in line astern about a course roughly parallel to our own.

What on earth were they? They could hardly be Germans as close to the coast as this — we had not yet reached Rouen even. Yet they were not Spitfires, Thunderbolts, or Typhoons.

We were overtaking them quite rapidly so that it would be simple to dive down to close range to make certain of their identity.

'Kelvin leader going down to investigate aircraft ahead below. Be very careful, I think they are Mustangs.'

The speed crept up: 350, 370. 390 mph as we lost height at cruising throttle. Our Tempests were magnificently fast, and the formation ahead was less than a mile away now. Their weaving flight and general appearance was somehow suspicious. Yet they surely could not be Huns.

At that moment they broke away from their previous course one after the other in a gentle diving turn to the left, and in doing so displayed narrow straight tapered wings with round tips and long thin fuselages. God!

'They're not Mustangs you know, they're 109s. Fairway leader, stay up and cover. Spider squadron attack with me. Come on down and make this good!'

Why did one always say that? They would make it good anyway. Even as I gave the orders I rolled over to port into a steep dive to cut off the Messerschmitt formation that, by turning left had reached a position almost directly below us on the port side.

The sun was behind us. It was a perfect 'bounce' — or was it? Could this be a trap? If there were more Huns above Johnny would take care of them, and we were fast enough to deal with these 'Joes' ahead first and then think about the others.

Gunsight 'ON'. Camera gun switch 'ON.' About 800 yards now and overtaking in the dive. No need for more throttle: they would be in range in a few seconds.

This was it! The moment I had thought of and planned for for so long. Those sleek dark fighters ahead were the enemy. Yes, there were the black crosses! I had got to get this Hun. We had to get all these Huns. A quick glance over my shoulder. There were the rest of 3 Squadron haring down the sky after me.

Ahead again. They've seen us! Suddenly black exhaust smoke trailed from the 109s as they opened their throttles wide and reversed their turn violently across our path and down for the cloud.

Too late. I rolled easily down behind them and ruddered the gunsight on to the last aircraft in the formation. Bead slightly above the cockpit and half way along the wing for 15° angle off. Now! *Brrrr*. Hell — missed! The 109 pilot was well aware of the situation by now and was doing his best to alter it.

Still with black smoke curving back, he rolled half over to the left, then back violently to the right, with white vortices streaming from his wing-tips, and then he dived for the cloud, some 3,000 ft below. But while making that fatal mistake of changing the turn he came straight into my gunsight at point blank range. I throttled back sharply to avoid overtaking and opened fire again with the sight bead on the enemy's cockpit hood.

There was no mistake this time. The range was less than 200 yards and closing rapidly, and as I fired I could see the dusty puffs of shell bursts on the tail, fuselage and cockpit. The Tempest was still travelling at 400 mph in spite of having the throttle completely closed, and the Messerschmitt grew larger and larger until it filled the windscreen and a collision seemed inevitable. Whether we were diving vertically or climbing I knew not and cared less. The world was a gunsight and a sleek dark, violently-twisting fighter a few hundred feet ahead against a dazzling white cloud background.

Fighting against the turbulence of the Me's slipstream I held the sight on, and with thumb hard on the gun button pumped shells into it until the last possible moment, and then, as I had to pull back on the stick to avoid collision, the sleek lines of the enemy became blurred and almost obscured. Smoke! It was in flames!

Hell, that was close! I had broken away almost too late and the Messerschmitt's tail flashed by my port wing as I curved up and over it.

I rolled half over to the left immediately and looked below. There not a hundred yards away was the 109, still on the same course but with its mottled brown camouflage partly obscured from in front of the cockpit to the tail by streaming yellow flames.

As I watched the port wing crumpled and folded back, and the 109 dived away on its back leaving a thick trail of oily smoke against the cloud.

Got him! Now, where are the others?

Bang! I felt the concussion of an explosion, the cockpit filled with dust which stung the eyes and the aeroplane began to shudder violently.

Without waiting for further developments I pulled the Tempest out of its dive with all my strength and used the excess speed to zoom vertically towards the sun for two or three thousand feet, and then as the speed dropped, rolled out into level flight and took stock of the situation.

There was a large hole in the starboard wing where a shell had hit, and so this shuddering vibration and reduced performance must mean that the starboard undercarriage had been blown out from the wing! Supposing the Hun that did that is still behind!

Sliding the tail from side to side I looked around, below, behind, ahead, into the sun. There was nothing in sight except a smudge of black smoke against the white cloud behind. Suddenly, my part of the sky, crowded with aircraft a moment before, seemed serenely empty.

'Hallo Fairway leader. Spider leader here. Are you receiving?'

'Fairway leader, OK Sir. I'm just approaching Rouen.'

'Hallo, Spider leader; this is Kelvin leader; reform your squadron when you are disengaged and join Fairway west of Rouen. Angels ten. I have been hit and am returning to base. OK?'

'Spider leader, OK Sir. Is your number 2 with you?'

'Kelvin leader here. No. I've got separated, but I think I'll be OK.'

'I called my 'No 2', Canadian 'Lefty' Witman.

'Hallo, Spider Blue 2. Did you see my flamer?'

'Hallo Kelvin leader. Yes, I saw it disintegrate! I got one of them myself.'

The tension was over and the wireless crackled with excited chatter: '— I got one!' '— did you see that _____ blow up?' and so on.

'Kelvin leader calling all Kelvin aircraft. Shut up!' 'Fairway leader, when you are set, take over lead and continue as planned.'

'OK Kelvin leader, listening out.'

That looked after the Wing. Now, how about getting home. I was alone with a damaged aeroplane. Speed much reduced and the possibility that the wing tanks on the starboard side were holed; and, what was more important still, I had some miles of hostile sky to fly through before reaching the coast; there was Rouen now through a gap in the clouds below.

Weaving and skidding constantly I lost height quickly to 7,000 ft where wisps of cloud enveloped the Tempest for a while, and with a sigh of relief as one problem was solved I began to look for further damage.

The engine was functioning normally, though the airspeed was down by about 50 mph and the whole aeroplane was vibrating.

That wheel and fairing must be hanging down. Oh well, always providing that the fuel tanks were not hit we should be able to make

Base. But it would probably mean a belly landing.

The R/T shouted into life: 'Hallo Kelvin leader. Spider Yellow 4 here. My engine is failing and I'm south west of Rouen.'

'OK Yellow 4. Try and make the far side of Caen–Ouistrahem canal. You'll be OK there. Good luck.'

'OK Kelvin leader; I think I can make it.'

Meanwhile as I slowly neared the coast, the clouds which had formed such welcome cover became thin, finally dispersed and left me feeling rather naked and alone. Ahead I could see the coastline and the sea. Would I never reach them? Then the cliffs and beaches were passing below and there was over 100 miles of sea to be covered before sighting friendly soil. Not out of the wood yet by any means though I should make it now, but of course there was probably a crash-landing to be dealt with upon arrival.

'Hallo Kelvin leader, this is Kingsley. If you need assistance, transmit for a fix.'

'OK Kingsley. This is Kelvin leader transmitting for fix. My aircraft is damaged and I am returning alone. I think I can make Base. (If the fuel didn't run out in mid-Channel.) Over ...'

'Kingsley here. Steer zero one five for your base. You have ninety miles to go.'

They were ninety very long miles with nothing in sight but sea and sky, and my imagination playing tricks with the shuddering of the damaged wing.

The ground station continually called up with new courses, and with comforting remarks such as: 'Air Sea Rescue are standing by.' At long last the coast at Hastings took shape in the haze and I crossed at the nearest point directly over the town before turning down the coast in the direction of Dungeness.

Home again! The sight of land after the long return over water was always accompanied by a feeling of relaxation and relief; a feeling of satisfaction in another job completed. This occasion was no exception, but there was still trouble ahead.

'Hallo Newchurch: Kelvin leader here. My aircraft is damaged. I will fly low over you and I want you to confirm the condition of my starboard wing and undercarriage.'

Receiving acknowledgement, I throttled back and, decreasing height to a few hundred feet as I passed over Rye, levelled the Tempest for a run directly across the Watch Office tent of Flying Control.

'Hallo Newchurch, Kelvin leader approaching you now.'

I was still travelling at more than 200 mph as I flew at the Control tender at 20 ft, and lifting the wing at the last moment in time to clear the group which I could see staring up, curved up and away into the circuit.

'Kelvin leader your starboard wheel fairing is projecting below the wing, but the wheel is not out.' As I thought. It should be possible to lower the wheels and land normally. There was still the possibility that the damaged leg might not lock in position and might collapse when it touched at 100 mph. We would soon see. I operated the lever and with a series of jolts the wheels came down, and the cockpit lights flickered to the 'LOCKED' position. A final check run across the field.

'Your wheels are right down, Sir.'

A careful approach. There goes the blood wagon, 'just in case.' Hold off with the port wheel touching first, and no bouncing. Down!

At the dispersal the groundcrew crowded around as I swung the tail round and switched off the engine.

'Any luck Sir?'

'Yes, I got a 109 in flames. The boys got two or three others, I think.'

'Bloody good show, Sir.' 'Hey! The Wing Commander's got a 109! — Where were they?' — 'How many?' 'Who got the others Sir?'

It was the first enemy aircraft to be shot down by a Tempest and by 150 Wing, and a great occasion.

'We've waited a long time for this Sir. Hallo, there's a dirty great hole in your wing and the undercart is nearly shot through! Poor old '*RB*' again! What happened Sir?'

'Afraid one of the bastards got me, but I'm not sure how! Perhaps the Squadron will know when they land. Well Flight, have Maintenance get cracking on '*RB*' right away. I'll want it again soon!'

By this time the Intelligence Officers and ALOs* had arrived. The news spread everywhere. The Wing's first Hun, and the 'Wingco' got it.

As I described the action to the IO the two squadrons roared over and soon the Tempests taxied in one after the other, swung round with a scurry of dust and blown grass, and their motors roared, spluttered and stopped. Alan Dredge climbed down from his cockpit as I walked up.

'Good show Sir, yours burned well. Bob (Moore) got one and damaged another, and Lefty (Witman) got one, I think. No, I'm

* Army Liaison Officers.

176

JN751 *attacks locomotives and a Ju 188 in May 1944* (Author's Collection).

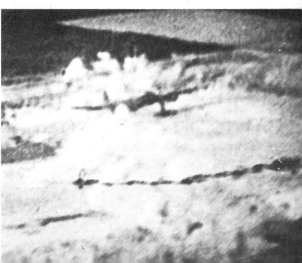

Left *A Newchurch Tempest pursues a V1 over Kent in 1944* ('Tee EM').

Below *A V1 flying bomb explodes under Tempest cannon fire in June 1944* (Author's collection).

Right *'Digger' Cotes-Preedy, commander of 56 Squadron in 122 Tempest Wing at Volkel, Holland, September 1944* (IWM).

Below right *The author at Brussels (Grimberghen) in September 1944, just after leading three squadrons of Tempests out from UK to join 2nd TAF* (IWM).

Tempest Vs: the fastest propeller-driven fighters below 20,000 ft in operational service on either side in 1944 (RAF Museum, Charles Brown Collection).

German ex-guards in the 'cooler' at Luckenwalde in May 1945.

afraid I was too far away myself, but I could see it all. Boy, those 109s burned!'

All the pilots were now gathered into a circle ringed by groundcrew.

'I was on the bastard's tail, shooting the stuffing out of him — the beggar just disintegrated in front of me and nearly took me with him!' These were fragments of the excited conversations which reached me, and then, to me the most interesting of all, Lefty's voice raised above the uproar: 'I was the Wingco's number 2 and I was watching him shooting Hell out of the last poor sucker when suddenly another 109 came streaking down on the Wingco's right, firing all the way. I just gave it one squirt and it blew up!'

Shouts of: 'Where's that line book!'

So that was what hit me. It was lucky that I had had a good number 2.

'OK Spy, when you can get a word in, get the pilots into my office for a post-mortem, the show was a perfect bounce and we can learn quite a lot from it. Yes, I want 486 over. I left them up as cover. They'll be fuming!

Chapter 11

THE FLYING BOMB BATTLE

For 150 Wing the week following D-Day was fully occupied with patrols of the invasion front and deeper fighter sweeps beyond the front towards the Paris area, but then a new diversion occurred.

In the evening of 15 June the Newchurch Tempest squadrons of 150 Wing were warned to come to 'Readiness' before dawn on the following day, after the arrival of a small number of V1s during the previous night. Still no detailed intelligence was available as to what to expect beyond the fact that these were small, pilotless aircraft of unspecified shape, travelling it was thought, at about 400 mph and at heights up to about 5,000 ft.

Soon after dawn on 16 June, a drizzling wet morning, the expected alert warnings came and with Sergeant Bob Cole as my No 2, we led the Wing into an action which was to continue at maximum intensity for the next six weeks, and to destroy over 600 V1s in the process. But now it was all conjecture — what were these pilotless aircraft, and how to destroy them?

Immediately after take-off we were given a heading south-east to a point off Folkestone. There was broken cloud at 2,000 ft and rather poor visibility in showers, and when radar control indicated that our target was closing rapidly ahead and then passing down the port side we had still not seen it, so I pulled around in a tight turn to port and at that moment saw a small dark shape go through a break in the clouds.

Still at full power we dived to increase to absolute maximum (level) speed, about 410 mph indicated at that height, and then suddenly out of the murk to starboard saw what appeared to be a small monoplane with a bulky, glowing jet engine at the back. We crossed in just over Folkestone in heavy rain and rapidly overtook the V1 which was flying at about 370 mph, but it was a very small target and, opening fire from about 400 yards astern, I missed completely with the first burst.

Steadying up at about 300 yards, another short burst hit its port outer wing; and then with all the remaining ammunition a long burst hit it first on the fuselage without immediate effect, and finally on the engine which stopped and it began to go down. The V1 slowed rapidly but remained on an even keel, and as I overtook it on the port side I was able to get a quick look at its slim, pointed fuselage, high mounted ram-jet engine at the back, and short stubby wings. It was painted dull grey overall and the jet pipe at the back was smoke-blackened.

I called in Bob Cole to finish it off, which he did with a well-aimed burst and it rolled over on its back and dived into a field south of Maidstone, exploding with a lot of flame and black smoke and a clear goldfish bowl of blossoming shock-wave which was to become a familiar feature of these activities in the weeks ahead.

While this had been going on the air was full of instructions to other Tempest sections, and a wave of V1s appeared to be coming in. We dived back at full throttle to Newchurch to refuel and re-arm, and found that all the available Tempests were airborne and that approximately fifty V1s had been plotted since we took-off. Reports were coming in of more successes, and Cole and I learnt that our V1 was not the first to be shot down by a fighter; we had been beaten to it by about one hour by a Mosquito night fighter flown by Flight Lieutenant Musgrave.

The remainder of 16 June continued in the pattern of hasty aircraft servicing, a few minutes' 'Readiness' and then scramble again on interception; all pilots and aircraft were in continuous action and at the end of the first morning the Wing score was eleven V1s confirmed destroyed.

At the beginning of this attack there were a number of unknowns which fighter pilots had to evaluate for themselves, such as how to judge range from so small a target: what angles of deflection to attack from to obtain maximum lethality if the shallow astern attack resulted in cannon shells bouncing off the V1's slim fuselage, and assessing the most effective range for opening fire coupled with what would happen if one's cannon shells exploded the warhead of the V1.

All these lessons were learned in the first 24 hours. We found that opening fire at 200 yards was the best range for effectiveness especially when combined with harmonizing the guns specifically for this range, an activity strongly deprecated by No 11 Group headquarters armament branch whose rigid attitude had to be ignored by Newchurch in the immediate urgency of getting the job done — but the question of the danger involved in exploding the V1 war-head was soon revealed.

The first instance of this occurred late on the afternoon of 17 June when a V1 was exploded by cannon fire about 400 yards away from the Tempest concerned. The aircraft went straight through the fireball and returned safely but streaked with smoke and evidence of charring, particularly on the fabric-covered elevators and on the rudder, part of which was burnt off.

On this occasion the pilot came down with burns on his forearm, and this was traced to ingress of flame from the explosion entering the cockpit through the air ventilator, which was naturally open in the hot summer weather and was positioned immediately above the pilot's throttle hand. It was certainly impressive to fly straight through the middle of a 2,000 1b bomb explosion, but not many pilots were hurt doing it and the arm burns problem was solved by keeping the cockpit ventilator closed for V1 operations!

It soon became apparent that the Tempest had just sufficient margin of speed to intercept and overtake the V1s, whereas the Spitfires, Thunderbolts and standard Mustangs which were appearing over Kent in ever increasing numbers, were too slow and were very frequently hindering the faster Tempests in their attacks. This pattern became so plain that after a few more days and a number of instances of damage occurring to the Tempests from wild shooting by free-lancing Thunderbolts, I flew up to Head-quarters 11 Group at Uxbridge on 18 June to report to the SASO, Air Vice Marshal Bouchier, on the progress of the battle, and I recommended certain actions.

Firstly, I suggested that due to the smallness of the V1, additional position indication was needed because, although the radar controlling was adequate to position fighters within half a mile of their target, pilots could often not see these small targets from this range in poor visibility. I suggested that the Observer Corps should be deployed around the coastline from Eastbourne to Folkestone, armed with distress rockets which could be fired in any required direction, and that when any one or two of them saw a V1 approaching the coast they would fire rockets simultaneously which would enable the fighter pilot — already under radar control — to see the probable point of convergence of the rockets as an indication of where to look.

Secondly, I proposed that only the Tempests and other suitable fighters, especially boosted Mustangs and Spitfire 14's, should be concentrated to operate in the main V1 attack area roughly from

Dover to Eastbourne; and that this area should be banned to all other units and free-lance fighter pilots.

These recommendations were accepted and acted on at once, and an immediate rise in interception rate resulted. It now became possible to take off from Newchurch and fly at full throttle under radar control for perhaps twenty or thirty miles, and then be turned in behind a radar-plotted V1 ten miles off the coast, look ahead and see a Coastguard rocket from the coastline and then a second one converging towards the first and there, at or close to the point of convergence, would be the V1.

Sometimes as many as forty or fifty sorties a day were flown by each of the two Tempest squadrons involved, and pilot's individual scores of two or three V1s in a day were becoming frequent.* Losses were relatively low and although we had a number of Tempests damaged by exploding V1s and some resulting forced landings, there were few fatalities. The main loss rate during the first three weeks of the campaign was due to over-exuberance on the part of the anti-aircraft gunners who, whenever in range of a V1, would naturally let go all they had; but without precision radar equipment at that time they invariably tended to under-estimate the lead-angle required, and if their target was being pursued as it so often was by one or two Tempests at approximately two to three hundred yards behind the V1, the fighters collected the majority of the anti-aircraft bursts. Lives were lost because of this, and there was some considerable tension as a result of it both in the squadrons and among the population of Kent who often saw these unfortunate incidents and eventually caused questions in Parliament on the subject; and there was much comment in the Press.

After about four weeks of intensive and successful operations I received notification of a VIP visit for a high level investigation of the Flying Bomb defences; and I was told to provide all facilities and information requested. The visitor turned out to be a Mr Duncan Sandys who had been charged by the Prime Minister with reporting on the success or otherwise of the measures being taken against the V1 attack.

Sandys arrived to the accompaniment of the, by then quite normal in the area, sounds of Tempests diving at full power, cannon fire and exploding V1s. I gave him a general picture of tactics, training standards, details of aircraft performance and aircraft and armament servicing under these intensive operating conditions; and also of the methods employed to coordinate the

* Appendix 3.

181

battle and improve interception and success rates. At this time 150 Wing was approaching its 500th V1 destroyed and the third squadron — No 56 — was just beginning to replace its Spitfire Vs with Tempests, which would shortly increase our capability.

I knew that plans for a crash programme to concentrate the strength of Anti-Aircraft Command along a narrow coastal belt as soon as they could be equipped with new radar direction systems and proximity-fused shells, was nearly complete; but in the meantime the Flying Bomb attack was being contained by the Newchurch Wing plus a few squadrons of other fighters by day, and by the Mosquitos and two squadrons of Tempests from Manston, with some of our own Tempests at night: the widely spaced anti-aircraft defences having been relatively ineffective up to that time and a continuing hazard to our fighters. Individual success rates were also increasing by this time due to the unprecedented amount of target practice resulting in much-improved marksmanship, and most pilots were soon destroying at least one V1 per sortie.

In the light of this situation I felt confident that as Fighter Command in general and 150 Wing in particular were destroying approximately half the daily total of V1s reaching our coast and that as no other effective defence had been forthcoming, we certainly had nothing to be ashamed of; but the other half that were getting through to the suffering population of London were a daily source of bitter frustration and anxiety to us all, and pilots were now sometimes taking the extreme measure of destroying V1s by ramming, after using all their ammunition.

Mr Sandys listened attentively but without noticeable enthusiasm, and after interruptions on some occasions to watch Tempests intercepting V1s overhead (and shooting one down just beyond 56 Squadron's dispersal), he said that he had seen all he needed to and was ready to leave. After a short silence he suddenly went on to say that we were wasting our time in this flying business — in a few years all this sort of thing would be done by rockets.*

Within a few weeks, Anti-Aircraft Command had re-established itself in concentration between our airfield and the coast and from Dover to Hastings: with new radar-sighting accuracy and proximity-fused shells it now produced spectacular results against

* This was a remark which I was to have cause to remember thirteen years later with the publication of the 1957 Sandys White Paper on Defence which apparently banned all future fighter development in this country in favour of totally inflexible missile defence!

the still continuing mass V1 raids. With greatly increased success rate by the guns the fighters were left with much reduced numbers of V1s to deal with, and by early August the Tempest Wing was beginning to return to fighter ground-attack and air superiority operations over Belgium and Holland in support of the advancing armies. On 23 August I shot down my last and thirtieth V1, the 632nd destroyed by the Newchurch Wing;* and on 28 September I led sixty Tempests of 3,486 and 56 Squadrons out to Belgium, where we were to become 122 Wing, 2nd TAF, based for a short time at Brussels-Grimberghen prior to moving right up into the Dutch salient at Volkel within shelling distance of the front line enemy gun positions.

* Appendix 4 and Appendix 5.

Chapter 12

TEMPESTS IN THE 2nd TACTICAL AIR FORCE, AUTUMN 1944

Air Vice Marshal Harry Broadhurst arrived at Grimberghen in the afternoon of 28 September to see his new Wing, and had some characteristically pungent comments to make to the assembled pilots of 486 and 56 Squadrons ending with '... and finally you chaps should remember that over this side your targets will have a habit of shooting back at you!' This reference to the Tempest Wing's enforced preoccupation with V1 flying bombs during the summer over England while the 2nd Tactical Air Force had been fighting its way from Normandy to Holland was shrewdly aimed, and I was delighted when at that very moment the Wing Intelligence Officer handed me a radio message from 'Digger' Cotes-Preedy who was already out leading 3 Squadron on a reconnaissance of the front line in the Arnhem sector — it read '3 Squadron engaged. Three 190s destroyed'.

I passed the message to Broadhurst; he grinned and said nothing.

The Tempests were immediately successful over the battle area and as soon as the Wing moved to Volkel in Holland we were in action daily with FW190 and Me109 formations in the Reichwald Forest area and across the Rhine, and, within weeks, against the new Me262 jet fighter bombers.

On 4 October at Volkel I received in addition, 80 and 274 Squadrons, making 122 Tempest Wing the only five-squadron Wing in 2nd TAF at that time.

I had always felt that Tempests would prove superior to the

FW190 in speed and also in dive capability, and this was clearly established on 2 October when, while leading 3 Squadron, we were bounced by a formation of twelve FW190s which, as we turned into them, tried to dive vertically away from us at about 15,000 ft. I caught one of them in a full throttle dive at about 5,000 ft near Nijmegan while we were both doing more than 500 mph.

Ten days after this event, while engaged in a ground attack on a heavily defended troop train near Arnhem on 12 October, my Tempest suddenly ran out of radiator coolant — whether by enemy fire or not I shall never know — and I had the choice of baling out within sight of some hundreds of German infantry who had just been under heavy fire from the squadron, or to ride the powerless Tempest down to a belly landing. The latter was the natural course under the circumstances, and while peering rather gloomily around for somewhere less hazardous to land on than the woodland which seemed to spread out on all sides, I transmitted to Volkel my position and intention to crash-land and heard them reply, 'Good luck, Corncob leader'.

At the last moment when a crash into the trees seemed inevitable, I caught sight of a small clearing ahead and slightly to the left. With quite violent manoeuvring and using the last few mph of speed in the glide, it proved possible to slide the Tempest quite smoothly on to the ground in a clearing not more than 300 yards across. The aircraft slithered through a fence, over a ditch with a slight jolt, and came to rest against the far fence trailing wires and fencing posts which it had picked up on the way! With the seized engine smelling hot I got out quickly, to find that it was not on fire so I reached back in to the incendiary bomb container which was carried for this purpose; pulled the cap off the bomb and threw it into the cockpit at the junction of the two wing tank fuel pipes and the collector box as the best place to ensure fire.

Throwing my maps back into the cockpit at the same time, I backed off into the edge of the nearby wood and waited for the bomb to go off. After what seemed to be a long time but was probably not more than one minute, the Tempest lit with a satisfying roar and at the same time I saw three of my Tempests circling overhead.

It seemed a rather difficult position to be in. I knew I had landed near Wesel which was a good twenty miles north of the Front, some 45 miles from our Volkel base and on quite the wrong side of the Rhine! It was also an intensely fortified region and I thought that my chances of escaping capture and returning through the area of the ground battle were not very good.

Nevertheless it might be worth hiding during the night in case some rescue operation might be laid on with an escorted light aircraft.*

This was just as well as while casting around in the wood for a hiding place, a young lad in black uniform appeared with a skull and crossbones emblem on his hat. This member of the Hitler Jugend then proceeded to shadow me for the next hour, never getting completely out of range but never too close.

I started to move along a hedgerow down the side of the wood but could not lose the Hitler youth, and finally found myself sandwiched between him and a platoon of very aged soldiers with a younger and aggressive Corporal who seemed rather anxious to see if his Schmeisser automatic would work. While sticking this device somewhat firmly into my middle region he said, 'For you the war is over'. This was perhaps an understatement in the light of the events of the next few months, but I got his point.

In the next few hours one had apparently undergone metamorphosis from the leader of an elite fighter wing at the spearhead of our victorious forces, into a 'Terror Flieger and eater of babies'. It was a formidable contrast, but at no time in my experience during the remaining months of fighting and the collapse and destruction of Germany did our main captors, the Luftwaffe, behave with other than with correctness towards their prisoners. The excesses, and there were many, were meted out by the SS, Gestapo and some elements of the Wehrmacht, and often it seemed that the Luftwaffe were embarrassed but powerless to help on these occasions.

The destruction of a nation seen from behind the wire of a prison cage is an ugly spectacle and there were many bad moments; but the traditional British ability to see the hilarious in any situation was much to the fore. One such occasion occurred at Potsdam in the last weeks of the war at a time of days and nights of continuous air attack by American Fortresses and Thunderbolts and by Lancasters and Mosquitos of Bomber Command. In a lull in the bombing one night a prisoner was talking to an old and infirm guard who looked as if he might collapse at his post at any moment, and when he was asked if this war was worse than World War 1, the soldier replied that he didn't know – he had been too old for that war!

*   *   *

Following my enforced retirement from the operational scene, the

* Such an operation was in fact considered as I discovered after the war, but was finally turned down as impractical.

Tempest Wing continued to achieve great success in 2nd Tactical Air Force and operated in the forefront of the remaining battles until the final victory when they were among the first units to occupy Denmark, flying into Copenhagen Airport before the German forces had capitulated. In this period they achieved fame as one of the most successful units in the Command and, in addition to their ground attack activity, ended up as equal top-scoring Wing against enemy aircraft with a Spitfire Wing which had been on the Continent since soon after D-Day in June (whereas the Tempests had not arrived in 2nd TAF until late September).

The Tempest turned out to be the great fighter which we at Hawkers had predicted*; it was significantly faster at low level than all other allied and opposition fighters except the jets; it was an unusually steady gun platform from which its four 20 mm Hispano cannon could be aimed with effective accuracy at railway engines, road vehicles, barges, gun-sites and similar small targets. Such accuracy also enabled the full weight of fire to be concentrated on the target so that even light tanks and armoured vehicles could also be stopped effectively.

In air combat its speed, manoeuvrability and superior aiming stability, coupled with exceptional combat vision and unobstructed windscreen with the gun-sight directly reflected in it, anticipating the head-up display technology which became fashionable more than twenty years later; all these advantages when added to a rugged airframe with easy and undemanding flying characteristics, had resulted in an aeroplane which created confidence and resulted in high pilot morale, leading inevitably to good operating results.

After the war ended I returned from Germany to the Central Fighter Establishment at Tangmere and in June/July 1945 set about recovering flying practice, flying and assessing thirteen of the latest types of fighter during the month of July 1945, including the Griffon-engined Spitfires, the Merlin-engined Mustang 3, FW 190, Me109G, Ju88 night fighter, and some more time on the Meteor jet which I had first flown at Manston in 1944. After all this I stepped back into a Tempest 5, and while the FW190 and Spitfire 9 remained unexcelled in fighting capability at high altitude and the Mustang at extremely long range, the Tempest was still unquestionably the best all round compromise of fighter characteristics for medium and low altitude.

* The author had been part of the Hawker team of experimental test pilots testing the new Tempest prototypes in the second half of 1943.

Potentially one of the world's great fighters, the Hawker Tempest V came into the war too late to make a major impact other than in the V1 battle, due to lack of numbers; but the quality of the aeroplane and the successes of the few Tempest squadrons will not be forgotten by the men who flew in them, or by those responsible for the defence of London in the summer of 1944.

Chapter 13

PRISONER OF WAR — 1945

As we lay on our bed boards and sacks in Stalag IIIa Luckenwalde in March 1945 in the darkness, comfortably warm and replete after an issue of Red Cross parcels for the first time since January, the excited chatter died away quite suddenly and through the hush came the clear notes of a violin. An Australian Squadron Leader, the pilot of a Lancaster shot down over Berlin two years before, was playing '*Ave Maria*' with such pure tone that the effect was extremely moving, and the spontaneity of the applause which broke out at the final notes left no doubt as to the sincerity of the appreciation of the 'Kriegies'*.

He went on with 'Loch Lomond', 'the Skye Boat Song', 'Jeannie with the Light Brown Hair' and many fine old songs of our country; and with emotions already raised by the great news of the Rhine crossings, aided by the unusual sensation of full bellies, it was not long before he had us all in a sentimental mood. So that it was with no great surprise that I found myself shouting as loudly and enthusiastically as anyone the words of 'We'll hang out the washing on the Siegfried Line', that cheaply popular song which had caused so much derision and finally embarrassment during the first dark months of the war. The incredible complacency and lack of perception shown by the country at that time, and the impudence of that song!

Yet many of us, some only just out of school, had felt in that fateful autumn of 1939 that we were about to take part in a world catastrophe which, if it did not end in the complete military defeat of our country, could only develop into a deadlock of pointless international murder and destruction, lasting many years, and

* Kriegsgefangener — PoW.

189

through which few if any of us newly trained 'cannon fodder' could expect to live.

For my part I remember hurrying from St Athans in Wales through the beautiful Hampshire countryside to spend the one night of my embarkation leave with my family in Sussex before leaving to join my first squadron in France.

It was early November. I had just completed RAF flying training successfully, and was delighted with my posting to a famous fighter squadron flying Hurricanes in France, No. 87. Nevertheless it was not a happy leave. My parents, though inordinately proud of their son and doing their best to pretend belief in my assurances of complete capability of looking after myself, found it hard to disguise their innermost feelings that they were unlikely to see me or in the case of my Mother either of us, again: they had seen war before in 1914–18. So it was in fact a relief to set off on the following morning by train with my father, both of us to join our units in France. I did not feel any great exultation on this momentous day, but rather a mixture of feelings.

A year previously I had left school and now at the age of nineteen when everyday life itself was still a source of frequent embarrassment, I was not only about to join a company of worldly men many years my senior, but I was also leaving home and homeland simultaneously and for the first time, to face the possibility of death or injury at the very moment to which I had looked forward for so many years, the beginning of my own adult life.

Of course one was a little scared of what the future might bring. I could fly as well as could be expected of anyone who had just left flying training school a few weeks before with the impressive total experience of only 115 flying hours, and I enjoyed it enormously. This was a pathetic total, yet I was sufficiently well imbued with the spirit of Colonel Blimp to feel that an Englishman with 100 flying hours was better than a German with 1,000! But inside I knew that experience counted and that experience I distinctly lacked! The end was probably inevitable, but in the meantime I intended to do everything in my limited power to improve my knowledge and capability, make some sort of a mark with the Squadron, enjoy it all, and if the final show came make it a good one.

In those early days of ill-formed and naive opinions one had little idea why all this was necessary. I knew only that England was at war, that I was in the RAF and posted to France and that I would fight as it was my duty to do and probably quite soon at that!

I never doubted the necessity of it all. My home background, the public school system and service training were all having their calculated effect: but at the same time I felt a genuine surge of anger against the German nation which for the second time in the century had thrown the world into war and threatened the existence of my country. In short I had reacted as it was intended that I and my fellow countrymen should react, in their thousands and without question.

In the RAF we had soon begun to realize that our chances were small and many were certain that this was going to be the final curtain for us, though they seldom spoke of it. Then, after the lull of the Phoney War of the winter of 1939–40, it came. One evening in early spring we had returned to our tents in the woods under the stars at Senon in north-east France after a particularly happy party, to be lulled to sleep by a perfect nightingale chorus and then wakened two hours later by the whine, shriek and crash of bombs and the clatter of machine guns.

Spring had merged into summer, summer to autumn, and almost every day had seen greater and greater battles in the air over France, the Channel and finally England. The enemy, flushed with victory, had poured his air armadas over our land, and the villages, fields, woods and streams of my beloved Dorset and Sussex had echoed the ever-increasing roar of engines, the stutter of gunfire and the scream of diving, crashing aircraft as a handful of men and boys vied cheerfully, even joyfully with each other to destroy not one 'Hun' a day, but two, three and more every day — until they themselves died.

My new friends had soon disappeared. Every day we had said 'Good luck, old boy' as we ran out to our Hurricanes, and we meant just that; and every day those on the ground had counted the aircraft as they roared away, and again when they straggled back: the figures seldom tallied. But somehow I had always come back. Perhaps a highly developed instinct for self-preservation had something to do with it, but when in late November 1940 87 Squadron had moved out of the line after a year of continuous operations, with more than one hundred victories to its credit and less than half a dozen of the original pilots, to attempt the defeat of the enemy in his new sphere of attack at night, we all realized that the first chapter was closed.

For some amazing reason some of us had survived and with the knowledge and experience gained in that historic year we had begun to foresee the possibility of continuing to survive and, more amazing still, the strong possibility that after a long and bitter world-wide campaign we would defeat the enemy. It was at about this time that one became conscious of a new and uncomfortable trend of thought in some parts of the country. Increasingly one heard people saying: 'Why are we going on fighting? We shall lose in the end and it will be a good thing for the country. Decadence must give way to the new vitality of Germany, and England will benefit in the end.'

At first we were inclined to laugh outright, feeling that such an attitude was not worthy of the most degenerate savage let alone an Englishman, and we had often pointed out forcibly where the decadence lay. Nevertheless as the months merged into years and the enemy was thrown out of our skies back across the sea and finally deep into the 'Continent of Europe' where even there he was in constant peril, this insidious school of thought continued unabated and was sometimes encountered in social life and even occasionally when, during periods of 'rest' from operations, I flew for factories in the aircraft industry and saw something of the London scene. One never heard a suggestion of these thoughts in the Service or among any men whose war occupations could be said to be 'active', but discussing the point with one of these English 'national socialists' with an address in Chelsea who described his occupation as 'reserved', I was shocked when he said: 'But of course one doesn't expect a fighting man to think. He isn't paid to!' First reactions on these occasions were always the same: 'My God, are we really fighting for these people?' But when a close family connection gave voice to similar pro-Nazi opinions and at the same time to an irrational attack upon the character and policies of Prime Minister Churchill, the man to whom more than any other England owed her salvation, I tried again to understand their point of view. Could our cause after all be a false one?

For my part the situation seemed comparatively lacking in complication. German aggression in Europe had become a direct threat to Great Britain and the Empire, and though unprepared and almost incapable of the task, we had been forced to go to war to defend our national existence. Of this I was convinced and I tended to discredit the floods of references to national honour and duty to smaller countries in the common cause of humanity which poured endlessly from the government information service. This was a fight for survival which was, to my mind, an adequate reason for fighting.

I had gone to war, not buoyed up with empty patriotic fervour although I was and am a patriot, but certain that the lives and ways of life of my family, friends and countrymen were in great danger: that the life which I had hoped to live among those things most dear to me, family, friends, the scent of primroses in a Sussex wood, the splash of rising trout in chalk streams, the piping of redshank on the saltings, and beer, cheese and picked onions at the 'Local', was itself in jeopardy. To preserve all these things was a paramount duty and the risks involved, well worth taking. These were the feelings, the details modified according to individual tastes perhaps (for there were naturally many for whom fish and chips would rank more highly in nostalgic value than primroses) of most of the young men of my generation. Yet were we right? Was it possible that Hitler's Germany had humanitarian motives behind their apparent mania for world domination, and that under Nazi rule not only would this country prosper but the individual retain his freedom?

The roseate statements for radio and press produced by the Ministry of Information under the title 'News' affected few if any of us. We accepted the fact that propaganda was necessary, and that ours was probably no better or worse than that of the enemy. I had not believed in many atrocity stories because I thought that the enemy must be normal people like ourselves with merely an unfortunate tendency to militarism. But despite all this there was still something inexplicably ominous about them. How could the butchers of refugees in Poland, Holland, Belgium and France, and the pilots who attacked and killed ours as they hung defenceless from their parachutes, be regarded as normal humans; and why did our fathers' generation, when approached on this subject, for the most part dismiss it with one word — 'Bastards!'

So, the more I thought about it the more certain I became that, lacking in knowledge of the ways and national character of the enemy though we were, we had been on the right track and that these others were more spineless pacifists than misjudged patriots. Now as I lie on my 'pit' in this dank, evil-smelling darkness of a Luckenwalde PoW barrack, listening to the voices of 200 flyers singing that dreadful song with all the enthusiasm of the knowledge that after five long years our armies have not only reached and broken the Siegfried Line, but have already crossed the Rhine, I realized that we have not been misled.

The nation that stripped Holland of her young men, that forced Russian and Polish women in thousands into labour gangs and beat some of them in our sight; that shot our 50 PoW escapees from Stalag Luft III in cold blood after their recapture; and who have shot, bayonetted or otherwise brutally treated so many of their helpless prisoners between the time of their capture and notification to the Red Cross, the nation which has committed for every one of these crimes in my experience, as many in the experience of nearly every other prisoner of war in Germany, cannot be a nation of fairy godmothers whose only aim in conquering England was the furthering of the nation's prosperity! Our hills and streams, our woodlands and fields, our way of living in our towns and the quiet beauty of our villages; our institutions and heritage would have been lost to us had the enemy conquered.*

But now our armies are marching full tilt into and through the final battle with the Air Force as ever striking at the enemy's heart, and it is nearly over. Our land is safe .... and soon I shall fly again.

Stalag IIIa, Luckenwalde, Potsdam
March 23, 1945

* This passage was written of course with no knowledge of the horrors of the concentration camps which only became revealed after the surrender in May 1945.

Chapter 14

RETROSPECT

In 1988 with the luxury of hindsight one looks back with wonder and gratitude at the time, nearly fifty years past, when our generation became committed to war without argument or discussion. Our country was under threat and we would fight because that was expected of us and our duty. Circumstances and attitudes were vastly different from those of today.

Duty, loyalty, honour — words which can cause a sense of unease and even self-conscious levity in conversation today, were accepted normal values in 1939 throughout the country and not by any means only encountered in the homes of the privileged, and as such they were scarcely discussed. People would do what they had to do, with pride. The fighting, when it began in full ferocity, was borne by the volunteer spirit. All the armed forces were volunteers until 1940 when the call-up became essential.

Then came the disaster of Dunkirk and a defeated army was miraculously saved to fight another day by the extraordinary organization, effort and heroism of a frantically cobbled together evacuation fleet of naval units and civilian small ships. But from that beaten force there was no talk of surrender, only of how and when to get back at the enemy.

The Royal Air Force element of the British Expeditionary Force had fought almost to a standstill over Belgium and Northern France, trying in vain to stem the tide of the enemy advance and finally to protect the Dunkirk bridgehead, and in the process had lost two-thirds of its fighter aircraft before the remainder were finally pulled back to Britain.

Again, the talk at Tangmere, Debden, Church Fenton and all the home stations receiving the battered squadrons, was not of defeat, but only of getting new aircraft and back into action in the violent battle now to be expected over the Channel and, if we could not prevent it, over London itself.

Then it all started again. Battle followed battle, in daylight over London and the South followed by the almost pointless night defence in the Winter Blitz, and night and daylight offensive low-level attacks of 1941. In 1942–43 the fighters took the offensive in sweeps and ground attacks from Normandy to the Dutch Islands. The final air battles for Europe began with the D-Day invasion and, after dealing with the six-week Flying Bomb campaign interlude in mid-summer 1944, swept on through France, driving the enemy back through Belgium and Holland to Germany itself. In all this there was the ever-present warmth of comradeship and mutual respect among those young men who reached their squadrons, trained to 'operational' standard and fought and died in such great numbers, but while they lived, enjoyed their lives and their flying with a lightness of spirit and an underlying strength and pride in their country which are not easy to see today.

At the end of hostilities in 1945 there was, amid widespread scepticism, also a strong sense of new opportunity — now we could rebuild a better life in a finer world. Forty years on, few will deny that much of the nation's energies have been squandered in political in-fighting and diverted by television mind-bending with resultant loss of long-term vision and even the will to be aware of what is happening all around us.

Britons have not lost their qualities of greatness, but we should never be content to be successful only in war. Perhaps now is the time for us to find a new way forward with the spirit of 1940.

Appendix 1

RECORD OF SERVICE IN THE ROYAL AIR FORCE — 1939-46

October 1939	No 11 Group Fighter Pool	St Athan	Hurricanes
November 1939	No 87 Fighter Squadron Air Component/British Expeditionary Force — France	Lille	"
March 1940	" " " "	Amiens	"
April 1940	" " " "	Senon	"
May 1940	" " " "	Lille Marc & Merville	"
June 1940	No 87 Fighter Squadron	Church Fenton	"
July/Sept 1940	" " "	Exeter	"
Sept/October 1940	" " "	Bibury	"
Nov 1940/May 1941	" " "	Charmy Down	"
June/Nov 1941	No 79 Fighter Squadron (Flight Commander)	Fairwood Common	"
Dec 1941/June 1942	Attached for test flying duties to Hawker Aircraft Ltd	Langley	Hurricanes Typhoons
June/July 1942	No 56 Fighter Squadron	Snailwell	Typhoons
July 1942	No 609 WR Fighter Squadron (Flt Comdr)	Duxford	"
Nov 1942/May 1943	" " " (Squadron Commander)	Biggin Hill & Manston	"
June 1943/Jan 1944	Attached to Hawkers Ltd as Experimental Test Pilot		Typhoons & Tempests

February 1944	No 150 Wing (Wing Commander/ Flying) Nos 3, 486 & 56 Squadrons	Castle Camps	Tempest V
April/Sept 1944	” ” ”	Newchurch	”
Sept/October 1944	No 122 Wing 2nd TAF (Wing Commander/Flying) Nos 3, 56, 486, 80 & 274 Squadrons	Grimberghen/ Brussels & Volkel/Holland	”
October 12th 1944	PoW — Stalag Luft 3	Sagan, Silesia	
January/May 1945	” — Stalag 3a	Luckenwalde, Potsdam	
June 1945	Central Fighter Establishment	Tangmere	
August 1945	OATS Course	Cranwell	
Sept/October 1945	Tempest 2 Wing (Wing Commander/Flying)	Chilbolton	Tempest II
Nov 1945/Jan 1946	Air Fighting Development Squadron. Central Fighter Establishment (Commanding)	West Raynham	
January 16th 1946	Released onto Reserve		
1948–1950	611 Squadron R Aux A F (Commanding)	Woodvale	Spitfire 21

APPENDIX 2

EVENING NEWS 6/3/43

TIP-AND-RUN RAIDERS HATE THE TYPHOON

From Our Air Correspondent

Although performance details of the 2,400-h.p. Typhoon, Britain's latest fighter, remain on the secret list there is no doubt what pilots think about it.

"The F.W.190 fighter pilot does not like us," was a typical comment I heard at the West Riding of Yorkshire Auxiliary Squadron, one of the first to be equipped with Typhoons.

This squadron has taken part in hundreds of sweeps since Fighter Command turned to the offensive. It has 172 "kills" to its credit, a large number of trains and locomotives.

The West Riding Squadron has shot down 16 tip-and-run raiders in the last three months. It claimed five of the 13 planes shot down in the daylight raid on London on January 20.

Leading Scorer

Leading scorer in the squadron is the commander Squadron-Leader R. P. Beamont, D.F.C., and bar, of Chichester. He has destroyed five, got two "probables," and damaged 11. He is also building up a reputation as a "night intruder specialist," with particular attention to train-busting. His score of locomotives runs into double figures.

DAILY SKETCH, THURSDAY, MARCH 25, 1943

TYPHOONS WIN 5-0 VICTORY

Typhoons, Britain's new high-speed fighters, shot down five of the 14 enemy aircraft destroyed on Wednesday without loss.

The Air Ministry News Service, disclosing this last night, said that the pilots who took part in the successes belong to the West Riding of York-shire Squadron, commanded by Squadron Leader R. P. Beamont.

Better armoured and with a longer range than either the Hurricane of Spitfire, the Typhoon is a single-seater, single-engined plane with a speed of over 400 m.p.h.

Squadrons equipped with Typhoons between them destroyed 11 sneak raiders in nine days between December 15 and 24 last.

Sir Archibald Sinclair (right), Air Secretary, visiting the West Riding of Yorkshire Typhoon Squadron, which has had great success against "sneak raiders". With him are (left to right) Wing-Cmdr. Desmond Sheen, D.F.C. and Bar (station commander), Group-Capt. Sir Louis Greig, and Squadron-Leader R.P. Beamont, D.F.C. and Bar, 22-year-old leader of the squadron, who has destroyed five aircraft.

Letter from Lord Balfour, Secretary of State for Air

'Air Ministry
King Charles Street,
Whitehall W.1.'
8th February, 1943.

Dear Beamont,

I must send you this line to tell you with what wonder and admiration all of us watched your take-off and flying of the Typhoon yesterday, when you left for Manston. Not only did it impress those like myself, who have not got the knowledge of others, but I wish you could have heard the comments of the Spitfire experts. They said they did not realise the Typhoon could be handled like that.

It was a great pleasure to meet you and have an opportunity of saying how much I admire the particular work on which you and your Squadron are engaged.

I look forward to seeing you at Manston in the not distant future.

Yours sincerely

Squadron Leader R.P. Beamont, D.F.C.,
Royal Air Force Station,
Manston,
Kent.

200

**Letter from A.V.M. Hugh Saunders, Air Officer Commanding
No. 11 Group Fighter Command**

PERSONAL

Headquarters, No. 11. Group,
Royal Air Force,
UXBRIDGE,
Middlesex.

DO/HWLS

14th May, 1943.

Dear *Beamont-*

I should like to congratulate you on your very well deserved D.S.O. Your work with No. 609 Squadron was outstanding and has done much to develop Typhoon technique.

I hope you will have an enjoyable rest with Hawkers, and I look forward to your return to No. 11. Group in due course.

Yours *Sincerely*

W Saunders

Squadron Leader R.P. Beamont, D.S.O., D.F.C.,
Whin Cottage,
Sandheath Road,
HINDHEAD,
Surrey.

THE DAILY SKETCH, MONDAY, MAY 24, 1943

'Master Of Typhoon' Wins D.S.O

Squadron-Leader R. P. Beamont, D.F.C., has put 25 locomotives and many lorries out of action. He is known in the R.A.F. as "the master pilot of the Typhoons."

Now this "outstanding leader" has been awarded the D.S.O.

He was lent to the Hawker Aircraft Company when the Typhoon was being developed, and is now in command of the West Riding Squadron which has destroyed many "sneak" raiders and shot up more than 100 locomotives.

Letter from Air Marshal Sir Trafford Leigh Mallory,
C in C Fighter Command

TLM/30.   21st May, 1943.

Dear *Beaumont*

My very hearty congratulations to you on being awarded a very well earned
D.S.O.

2.   No. 609 Squadron has had a most successful career under your leadership,
and I attribute their success very largely to your own personal efforts.

3.   Good luck to you in the future!

                          Yours *very sincerely*

                          Trafford · Leigh · Mallory

Squadron Leader R.P. Beamont,
        D.S.O., D.F.C.,
No. 609 Squadron,
R.A.F. Station,
MANSTON.

Letter from Lord Balfour

                                              Air Ministry,
                                              King Charles Street,
                                              Whitehall, W.1.

Dear Beaumont   24th May, 1943.

I send you this line of most hearty congratulations on your D.S.O. Directly
I saw you, your Squadron, the Typhoons and the work they were doing, I
knew that it was inevitable.
I do hope your face is none the worse for meeting the instrument panel,
because the last I heard of you you were in Deal hospital.
I hope to come and see your Unit as soon as possible.

                          Yours sincerely,

                          Harold Balfour

Squadron Leader R.P. Beamont,
        D.F.C., D.S.O.,
Royal Air Force Station,
    H.Q. No. 11 Group,
        Uxbridge, Middlesex

APPENDIX 3

LONDON EVENING STANDARD. JUNE 21st 1944
Big Percentage of Fly Bombs Killed

From JAMES STUART, Evening Standard Air Reporter
A KENTISH FIGHTER STATION, Wednesday

The man chiefly responsible for beating the Nazis' flying-bomb in the daytime is 25-year-old Wing Commander R. P. Beamont, D.S.O., D.F.C. and Bar.

"Bob," boyish-looking fighter ace and test pilot, commands a station from which the Tempest, Britain's latest fighter airplane and the fastest in the world, is helping to take much of the sting out of Hitler's no-longer-secret weapon.

Since the enemy launched the winged bomb attacks last Thursday, Beamont's station has provided the most successful counter.

Before I was up for breakfast to-day two of Beamont's boys, out on early morning patrol, had shot down three.

They fell to Flight-sergeant R. Cole, of Norwich (two) and Flight – Lieutenant A. R. Moore, of Reading.

Many of the station's victims have fallen to the Tempests of an R.A.F. squadron led by Squadron Leader Alan Dredge, D.F.C., and others to the pilots of a Royal New Zealand Air Force unit under Squadron Leader John Iremonger.

When the flying bomb attack began, the method of dealing with them in daylight was left to Wing Commander Beamont and his pilots. They have proved more than a match for Hitler's terror weapon.

Optimistic

So successful have their tactics been that Wing Commander Beamont was able to tell me to-day, "We reckon to knock down a large number of all the pilotless aircraft we sight."

That of course, does not mean we have scored a complete victory, for these fighters alone canot hope to sight them all. But Wing Commander Beamont was optimistic that the defences will be able to destroy many. I think his optimism is justified.

On the way here, after dark last night, I heard one of the flying bombs going over. Tracer shells poured up to meet it, and suddenly, some miles away, there was a brilliant orange flash as it crashed earthwards and exploded.

"Then You Duck"

Wing Commander Beamont said: "You can see the cannon-strikes on the bombs and a few flashes. Then, suddenly the whole sky goes black and red and you duck. Everyone who has blown up a winged bomb at short range finds himself on his back when he comes out the other side, probably because the pilot goes through an area of complete vacuum which turns his airplane upside down.

"When you have shot one down and it explodes on the ground you can see a ring of blast. The explosion seems more violent if it hits the deck below you, than it is when you blow it up at 100 yards range.

"Sometimes in attacking them we have had aircraft slightly damaged, but we have had lots of men go right through the blast of the bomb without feeling it very badly."

Wing Commander Beamont, who has destroyed three and shared in the shooting down of two others, disclosed that there are two types of flying bombs, one with square wings and one, slightly bigger, with swept-back, rounded wings.

He told me that at low level he thought the flying bomb, when in full flight, is faster than any German fighter, but they were very vulnerable. Some had been chased from the coast almost up to London before being destroyed.

NWH V BIG GPK 1/30 OP
T NEWCHURCH

[TELEX] FROM A.O.C. NO. 11 GROUP
TO NEWCHURCH FOR W/CDR BEAMONT
INFO ADGB BIGGIN HILL
QQX BT

A206 29 JUNE
PLEASE ACCEPT FOR YOURSELF AND CONVEY TO OFFICERS
COMMANDING NO3. 486 AND 56
    SQUADRONS AND ALL PILOTS OF THE NEWCHURCH WING
THE HEARTIEST CONGRATULATIONS OF ALL MEMBERS OF
MY STAFF AND MYSELF UPON THE DESTRUCTION BY THEM
OF THEIR 200TH PILOTLESS AIRCRAFT. SPECIAL
CONGRATULATIONS ALSO TO NO3 SQUADRON ON GETTING
THEIR FIRST HUNDRED BY THEMSELVES. WE FOLLOW EACH
DAY WITH ADMIRATION THE TRULY SPLENDID WORK YOU
ARE DOING WITH SUCH SKILL AND UNTIRING
DETERMINATION

————BOUCHIER————

BT2355B
IS AR K

APPENDIX 4

Daily Express Sept 9

THEY WERE BIG-PART PLAYERS IN THE DRAMA OF THE EIGHTY DAYS

Wing-Commander R. F. G: Lea, Corporal Eyers, Wing-Commander Roland Beamont and Wing-Commander E. D. Crew were there.

Lea, Deputy Commandant of the Royal Observer Corps, told how the first flying bomb was reported to be heading for England.

Beamont was largely responsible for working out the attack tactics used in the early stages of the battle. He has himself shot down 23 flying bombs.

Crew leads a Mosquito squadron that has been one of the most successful anti-flying bomb units. His own score: 21½.

THE DAILY MAIL, Tuesday, July 25, 1944.

BEAMONT -1st FLY- BOMB ACE
Wins Fourth Medal

By Daily Mail Reporter

Britain's first ace flying-bomb killer has won another award, it is announced to-day.

He is Acting Wing Commander Roland Prosper Beamont, and he wins a Bar to his D.S.O. He also holds the D.F.C. and Bar.

Although the citation makes no mention of his successes against flying bombs, it is known that Wing Commander Beamont, in recent weeks, has shot many of the bombs down into the sea.

Wing Commander Beamont is a

former test pilot, and at 25, commands a station from which the Tempest, fastest aeroplane in the world, operates.

He comes from Chichester, and is known as Britain's ace loco-buster.

Permanent Duty

He is more or less on permanent duty against the flying bomb. I was told last night. He is never far from his fighter and volunteers to go up as soon as his station plotters locate the bomb.

He is now in command of the top scoring pilots who attack the flying bombs.

"We have plenty of good marksmen here, hence our success," he told me.

"And we have developed a technique of attack of our own.

"Some of us have had queer experiences with the flying bombs. We've come back spattered with black oil all over our machines, with fuselage singed, and even with rudders burnt off.

"We do all sorts of things to them—blow their wings off, shoot their engines away, fire their fuel, which sets their bombs off. During one period we knocked down four out of five."

From: Air Commodore C.A. Bouchier, C.B.E., D.F.C.

HEADQUARTERS NO.11 GROUP
ROYAL AIR FORCE
UXBRIDGE.
9th September, 1944.

Reference:
CAB/D.O.

Dear Beamont.

Air Marshal Sir Roderic Hill, K.C.B., M.C., A.F.C., has received a letter from Sir Ernest Gowers, K.C.3., K.B.E., London Regional Defence Commissioner, of which the following is an extract:-

"At a recent meeting of my Standing Committee of Town Clerks of the London Region a spontaneous and unanimous request was made to me that I should convey to you, on behalf of the Local Authorities in the Region, their deep sense of obligation to the Pilots under your Command whose skill and devotion are doing so much to mitigate London's present ordeal. I gladly do this. We are filled with admiration of their magnificent achievements, and I hope you will find it possible to convey this tribute to them so that they may know how fully and gratefully London realises its debt to them."

I feel the foregoing should be brought to the notice of all Wing Leaders, Squadron Commanders and Pilots concerned, not forgetting the splendid work also done by Control Staffs both at Sector and G.C.I. Stations.

Yours sincerely.

C. Bouchier

APPENDIX 5

Daily Telegraph & Morning Post, Thursday, May 30, 1946

British Airman Wins U.S. D.F.C.—Wing Cmdr. Roland P. Beaumont, D.S.O. and bar and D.F.C. and bar, one of the first airmen to attack flying bombs, has received the United States D.F.C.

Chichester Observer
June 8th 1946

PROUD RECORD HONOURED

U.S.A. AWARD FOR CHICHESTER FLYER

The proud flying record of Wing-Commander Roland P. Beaumont, D.S.O and Bar, D.F.C. and Bar, has been added to by his award of the U.S.A. Distinguished Flying Cross.

The citation states: "For extraordinary achievement in aerial flight against the enemy. During his tours of duty Wing-Commander Beamont distinguished himself by outstanding aerial skill and exceptional courage. He was responsible for the development of successful tactics against the flying bombs and destroyed over 30. His unfailing devotion to duty and determination reflect great credit upon himself and the Royal Air Force."

Wing-Commander Beamont is the son of Lieut.-Col. and Mrs. E. C. Beamont, of Downslands Cottage, Summersdale, Chichester.

Wing-Commander Beamont started his flying training at the beginning of 1939 and was commissioned in the R.A.F. at the outbreak of war. Incidentally, Lieut.-Col. Beamont and his son left Chichester together on the same train for war service.

Wing-Commander Beamont served in the Battle of France and Battle of Britain. When commanding the famous 609 (W.R.) Squadron he became known as "Train Buster Beamont." Later, he commanded a Tempest Wing. It was with this command that Wing-Commander Beamont was made responsible for preparing the tactics to be used against the Flying Bombs when they arrived. He was put in the South East and his Wing destroyed 670 Flying Bombs, of which the Wing-Commander's personal bag was 30.

RESTRICTED

HEADQUARTERS
UNITED STATES AIR FORCES IN EUROPE

APO 633, US Army,
GENERAL ORDERS)   4 April 1946

NO ...... 87)

SECTION

AWARDS OF THE DISTINGUISHED FLYING CROSS I
AWARD OF THE BRONZE STAR MEDAL II

I. Under the provisions of Army Regulations 600–45, 22 September 1943, as amended, and Circular #28, Hq, US Forces, European Theater, US Army, 6 March 1946, the DISTINGUISHED FLYING CROSS is awarded to the following named Officers:

WING COMMANDER ROLAND PROSPER BEAMONT, D.S.O., D.F.C., (41819), Central Fighter Establishment, Royal Air Force. For extraordinary achievement in aerial flight against the enemy. During his tours of duty Wing Commander Beamont distinguished himself by outstanding aerial skill and exceptional courage. He was responsible for the development of successful tactics against the flying bombs and destroyed over thirty. His unfailing devotion to duty and determination reflect great credit upon himself and the Royal Air Force.